The life of HENRY WADSWORTH LONG-FELLOW (1807–1882) was a mixture of triumph and tragedy, fulfillment and disappointment. His youthful ambitions were all literary, but to please his father he became a teacher. During the eight years he taught modern languages at Bowdoin College and the eighteen years at Harvard, however, his pen was not idle: thirteen of his books were published, including *Evangeline* (1847), the polemic *Poems on Slavery* (1842), and *The Golden Legend* (1851). In 1855, the year after Longfellow gave up teaching in order to devote his full efforts to writing, his friend Nathaniel Hawthorne wrote him, "No other poet has anything like your vogue." Public triumphs were sometimes overshadowed by private grief. Longfellow was married twice: in 1836 his wife of five years died in childbirth. Seven years later, after a long, sometimes painful courtship, he married Elizabeth Appleton and settled in historic Craigie House, Cambridge. In a tragic accident she was burned to death in 1861, leaving the poet with six children to raise. Longfellow overcame his sorrow and continued his work, which was acclaimed throughout America and Europe. In 1881, the year before his death, his birthday was celebrated in schools all over America. Three years later a bust of Longfellow was unveiled in the Poet's Corner, Westminster Abbey. The drawing above is taken from a steel engraving of the young Longfellow.

# *Evangeline*

## AND SELECTED TALES AND POEMS

### HENRY WADSWORTH LONGFELLOW

SELECTED AND WITH AN INTRODUCTION BY
### HORACE GREGORY

A SIGNET CLASSIC

THIS EDITION OF LONGFELLOW IS
INSCRIBED TO THE MEMORY OF MY MOTHER
ANNA CATHERINE GREGORY,
WHOSE READINGS OF HIS <u>VOICES OF THE NIGHT</u>
ARE AMONG THE CHARMS OF MY EARLIEST MEMORIES.

SIGNET CLASSIC
Published by the Penguin Group
Penguin Books USA Inc., 375 Hudson Street,
New York, New York 10014, U.S.A.
Penguin Books Ltd, 27 Wrights Lane,
London W8 5TZ, England
Penguin Books Australia Ltd, Ringwood
Victoria, Australia
Penguin Books Canada Ltd, 10 Alcorn Avenue,
Toronto, Ontario, Canada M4V 3B2
Penguin Books (N.Z.) Ltd, 182–190 Wairau Road,
Auckland 10, New Zealand

Penguin Books Ltd, Registered Offices:
Harmondsworth, Middlesex, England

Published by Signet Classic, an imprint of Dutton Signet,
a division of Penguin Books USA Inc.

First Printing, September, 1964
21  20  19  18  17

Introduction copyright © 1964 by New American Library, a division of
Penguin Books USA Inc.
Bibliography copyright © New American Library a division of Penguin Books
USA Inc., 1990

# CONTENTS

# INTRODUCTION

## I

HENRY WADSWORTH LONGFELLOW (1807-1882) was the most fashionable American poet of his day. His day was a long one, for it began in the mid-1840's and shone beyond his death into the twilight of the 1890's. Several of his poems had become popular schoolbook favorites, and it was an ignorant child indeed who had not learned by heart the resounding stanzas of "The Village Blacksmith." By 1900 his poems had yet to pay the full price for being so popular for over fifty years. They were admired by the new and extremely fashionable author of *Barrack-Room Ballads,* the Anglo-East Indian Rudyard Kipling. Suddenly in 1912 his verse was read as "old" poetry, while the poems freshly printed in Harriet Monroe's little magazine, *Poetry* (Chicago), represented the "new." At that moment, now over fifty years ago, a book of Longfellow's poems was clearly associated with an *un*fashionable American past: the book seemed not unlike the sight of nineteenth-century bonnets, shawls, frock coats, and age-yellowed wedding dresses hanging in the attic. In the present midcentury, if any dusty attic storerooms still exist (rooms of a kind where one discovers a gilt-edged *Longfellow's Poems* wrapped in a Spanish shawl), they are very rare.

Today, another aspect of Longfellow's poetry is in the making. This is because it is neither in nor out of fashion. At its best—and sometimes at its worst—its music retains the power to command the ear. Often enough its imagery holds the charms of recollected childhoods in the sun. In contrast to these scenes one also glimpses the rush of flowing waters in moonlight. However one reads it, it shows an American delight in the brilliance and facility of its technical achievements: the unrhymed trochees of "Hiawatha," the hexameters of "Evangeline," the clever use of Drayton's "Battle of Agincourt" stanzas—also echoed in Tennyson's "Charge of the Light Brigade"—in the writing of "The Skeleton in Armor." One of the signs of Longfellow's genius was his brilliance in writing the skilled tour de force—an American skill carried forward by active phrasing in which one thinks of his "Let us then be up and doing." This kind of brightness has been characteristic of American verse from Longfellow's youth to the present day.

But before we continue to discuss Longfellow's place in the tradition of American poetry, it is best to look briefly at the list of charges that have been brought against his name. The contra-Longfellow charges came as early as 1840, when an anonymous reviewer of his *Voices of the Night* accused him of plagiarism. This was reiterated five years later by Edgar Allan Poe, who, in reviewing Longfellow's anthology *The Waif,* wrote, "Somebody's a thief." With an air of kindly dignity, Longfellow refused to be drawn into a public quarrel, first of all because his so-called "plagiarisms" were no more than distant echoes of their sources, and secondly, because the very nature (so often misunderstood) of his poetic gifts was transforming, and frequently translating, feelings, observations, and perceptions from one environment—or language—to another. To adverse critics, his withdrawals from direct controversy may well have seemed a sign of snobbery, effeminacy, or dandyism—or an unattractive combination of all three. Behind his well-bred manners and gaily colored waistcoats, he was far more eccentric, more candid, more naïve, more "the real thing" than he seemed—but more of this later. Through the 1840's, he was the highly valued contributor of verse to the *Knickerbocker Magazine,* which was to its many readers what the *New Yorker* is to the American public of today.

In these distant subcurrents of critical disfavor one can now see the beginnings of uneasiness, annoyance, or ridicule that greeted the mention of Longfellow's name fifty years ago. The charges of plagiarism were, of course, long since washed away, but in their stead, something, ever so remotely like them, came in view. From childhood onward his writing of poems demanded a literary precedent. With his mother, the romantic and handsome Zilpah Wadsworth, at the piano, he learned to sing the songs of Sir Walter Scott, Thomas Campbell, and the Anglo-Irish poet, Tom Moore. In America generally, Moore was easily the favorite of these three. Moore's singing of his "Irish Melodies" was edged by sighs and whispers that hinted of melancholy smiles; Moore's visit to the United States had been a great success. He sang his way through one fashionable drawing room to the next. The very language of Moore's melodies was soon accepted as a criterion of poetic diction in America, and it was this criterion that provided a *precedent* for the language and musical ingenuity of nine-tenths of the verse that Longfellow was to write.

During the period (the Napoleonic Wars) out of which Moore's melodies grew, the English language was at its weakest, invaded, as it were, by the hastily scrawled beginnings of popular journalism, words written at "a penny-a-line." The formal distinction and the sharp-edged vigor of Doctor Johnsonian rhetoric were falling away—nor had the richer phrasing and imagery of the romantics had time to establish themselves. The language of the period was not a good precedent to follow: it was feeble in wit, weak in expressing its sentiments—and therefore sentimental. All too frequently readers were asked to share scenes of "human interest" in which middle-class domestic woes and tears were plentiful. "Little Nell," Charles Dickens' try at pathos at his worst, was of this unhappy origin. The language of Moore's melodies, and later, Longfellow's tales, translations, and lyrics, was a refinement of a fashionable poetic speech and sentiment that quickly crossed and recrossed the Atlantic.

Illustrating a refinement of the weakness Longfellow was to make his own are these lines from "Maidenhood":

> Oh, thou child of many prayers!
> Life hath quicksands,—Life hath snares!
> Care and age come unawares!

Longfellow's habit of writing all-too-easily worded sermons into verse came from sources that were also pre-Victorian.

One was in the Protestant ardors of his charming mother, but the others were literary. Longfellow's moralizings were readily accepted both in England and America by a generation whose fathers eagerly bought and read books of sermons—and the fact that sermons then (1790-1845) seemed to overflow into verse only served to make the verse that contained them more popular. The present century's discontent with Longfellow's homilies is that they sound sententious, platitudinous, superficial. They seem tacked on to or artificially built in to the poems in which they appear. Certainly they add nothing to the pictorial perspective and lyrical charm of his verse. It was not so much that Longfellow was insincere—he probably felt that what he preached was true—but that his everyday thinking was of a conservative cast—and consistent with his need to follow literary precedents.

No less annoying to contemporary readers of Longfellow's verse is the spirit—which often threatens to become a little bit too cozy—of domesticity that hovers over many of his lines. It was Thomas Bailly Aldrich who suggested that Longfellow write one of his "fireside poems," "The Hanging of the Crane," which contains the facile picture of:

> A little angel unaware,
> With face as round as is the moon,
> A royal guest with flaxen hair,
> Who, throned upon his lofty chair,
> Drums on the table with his spoon, . . .

Longfellow's "easy writing" never made "hard reading," but the passage of time made some of it look indecently respectable and coy. Longfellow's failings were never petty flaws, but were commensurate with his large intentions and the enduring total of his accomplishments—which were not small. With a few of the twentieth-century contra-Longfellow prejudices out of the way, we can then advance toward the strange, less-well-known aspects of his life and writings.

## II

The best of Longfellow as well as his worst may be

traced back to his adolescence and early manhood. Intimations of the kind of poet he was to become have their sources in the Wadsworth-Longfellow heritage. In 1807 in Portland, Maine, a brisk, colorful seaport town, he was born into the upper gentry of two New England families: his Wadsworth grandfather was a general; his Longfellow grandfather, a judge. His father had been educated at Harvard and practiced law with so much gravity, caution, and skill that he became, if not rich, remarkably prosperous. The conservative cast of Longfellow's mind probably came from examples set before him by his father's behavior and its successful results. His more adventurous affinities and imaginings came from his mother and the Wadsworths. General Peleg Wadsworth, Zilpah's father, dressed from cocked hat to buckled shoes in the high fashion of the mideighteenth century, was a vigorous eccentric, a pioneer, a soldier, a storekeeper, a congressman, a gentleman-farmer. In his childhood reveries, and later in his trips through and across the European continent, it is little wonder that the General's grandson, Henry, delighted in frequent changes of scene and acquired touches of dandyism in his dress. Until he was over forty, Longfellow had exotic lapses from his handsome—he was always good-looking—and habitual air of decorum. Outwardly, he was the normally active and obedient son of a well-to-do lawyer; yet suddenly, and with extreme lassitude, he would make the most of minor illnesses, indulge in "dreams," as he would call them, and secretly send off bits of verse signed "Henry" to the local newspaper. At sixteen, while a sophomore at Bowdoin College, his exotic adventures were expanded by his taking the role of an Indian chieftain in a dramatized debate in which another boy took the less spectacular part of an "English Emigrant."

Longfellow's lapses from cheerfully accepting the world as he found it were, so far as his writings were concerned, significant. They signified his need for remoteness from the everyday prospects of becoming a respectable provincial lawyer like his father. They spurred his desires to know foreign languages, people, and places; they led him into the extremes of wearing fashionable dress in London—an American extreme—which was probably why, when he presented in person his letter of introduction to Bulwer-Lytton (who was a dandy of the British mode) he was so cruelly snubbed. These lapses are also shown by his florid courtship of his second wife, Frances Appleton, in the pages of his novel, *Hyperion*—who, after reading his effusions in the published book, held him off from marrying her for seven years. The lapses were never shocking in a vulgar sense—for even the subconscious Longfellow was of grained and weathered New England gentry—yet they were embarrassing. It was all too apparent that he had his nearly mindless moments, when his desires, if anything, were all too clear, and therefore seemed nakedly naïve. For us, his sudden, instinctive departures from the conventions of his own life and the lives of those around him illuminate his poetry. Behind the facade of his minor illnesses was hidden his fixed determination not to study law, but to be a poet. Throughout his life, the illnesses he enjoyed were never serious, but were severe enough to ensure privacy as well as a release from the pressures of professional discipline. On these occasions he was also free of intellectual duties—and since he was not an intellectual poet, he made use of his freedom as though he were one who walks into a trance with his mind lost and his eyes wide open. He was then living in a "dream."

On leaving Bowdoin, Longfellow's responsibilities were tangible enough. He had persuaded his father that since his abilities were unfitted for law, he would earn his living by becoming a teacher (preferably a college lecturer) of foreign literatures. Both father and son accepted the compromise: the father was assured that his son was not so wild as to hope to earn a living by writing poetry, and the son was relieved from his duty of studying law. Yet the younger Longfellow cordially hated the very thought of academic routines. His father agreed to finance a three-year tour of Europe so as to prepare him for the acceptance of a professorship in modern languages at Bowdoin. Longfellow's compromise was unevenly resolved. Though he could be and was a popular teacher and lecturer at Bowdoin and later as the Smith Professor of Modern Languages at Harvard, he never completely filled the image of the extraverted American college professor.

Fortunately for us, the Longfellow revealed through his lyrics and tales was not the conventional Longfellow who wrote the concluding stanza of "A Psalm of Life," whose philosophy so closely approximates the credo of Emerson's "The American Scholar" as well as that of the nineteenth-century American businessman (and there is also an interesting echo of Byron's "Here's a heart for every fate" concealed within it):

> Let us, then, be up and doing,
> With a heart for any fate;
> Still achieving, still pursuing,
> Learn to labor and to wait.

Longfellow said of the poem that it was "a voice from my inmost heart"—and we can say it came from that side of his heart which strenuously opposed the "dreaming" half of it. The conflict here—which should not be taken with too much psychological literalness—was a conflict of ideals: the ideal man of action, mirrored in his father, the lawyer, and his own role as professor of modern languages, at war with the ideal poet. In other ways the conflict gave color and action to the best of his poetry. The life of action is sounded in the galloping metrics of "Paul Revere's Ride"—yet the story itself makes no pretense at being literal truth: it is a romance, a legend, re-created with extraordinary vividness. Longfellow wrote as though he gazed through a telescope at the ride. In a different fashion the same gaze transforms "The Birds of Killingworth" into a kind of magical light verse. Beneath the surface of an obvious moral, the story is kept in air by undercurrents of humorous, childlike observations and echoes of laughter.

Throughout the great number of pages Longfellow wrote, the words "childhood" and "children" are repeated many times. The images they evoked were in the back chambers as well as in the forefront of his imagination. Although it would be possible to quote the tear-streaked lines of his popular "The Village Blacksmith" as Longfellow at his worst, midway in the poem there is a stanza that shows him very nearly at his best. It is at a moment in the poem that places it in juxtaposition to the sanctimonious moralizings which follow it:

> And children coming home from school
> Look in at the open door;
> They love to see the flaming forge,

> And hear the bellows roar,
> And catch the burning sparks that fly
> Like chaff from a threshing-floor.

The rural-suburban imagery of the last two lines could
not be better; moreover, it is the kind of imagery that re-
mains alive within the charmed circle of childhood mem-
ories. The stanza is also an example of unforced, skillfully
drawn genre painting in verse, and because it is, one can
understand one of the reasons why the poem on its publi-
cation in the *Knickerbocker Magazine* became as popular
in London and Edinburgh as in New York: during the
1840's, genre painting was at the height of its career in
Scotland and England.

But the superlative poem (written almost twenty years
later) of Longfellow's memory of childhood is "My Lost
Youth." There are no moralizings here, no attempted
flights toward portentous meanings, no tears, no melo-
drama. Although its environment, imagery, and feeling
may be called "American," it transcends its national
character as well as the century in which it was written.
On its chosen theme it belongs in the company of the best
romantic poems in English, a small list that would in-
clude Wordsworth's "Tintern Abbey" and Dylan Thomas's
"Fern Hill." Of the poem Longfellow wrote: "March 29:
A day of pain; cowering over the fire. At night, as I lie
in bed, a poem comes into my mind—a memory of Port-
land—my native town, the city by the sea." Next day the
poem was written. Surely this visitation of one of his
minor illnesses revealed the presence of his demon or
genius:

> I remember the black wharves and the slips,
>     And the sea-tides tossing free;
> And Spanish sailors with bearded lips,
> And the beauty and mystery of the ships.
>     And the magic of the sea.
>         And the voice of that wayward song
>         Is singing and saying still:
>         "A boy's will is the wind's will,
> And the thoughts of youth are long, long thoughts."

It is almost unnecessary to add that the music of "My
Lost Youth," like that of the remembered Lapland song

quoted within it, haunts the ear. Whenever Longfellow's demon served him best, one sign of its presence was in the compulsive rhythm, in the very music of the poem's phrasing. Nor did it make much difference from where the music came. So far as the subject of the tale or lyric was concerned, it was Longfellow's gift to make its music seem—if only for the moment—inevitable. He was, consciously or not, the concertmaster, and if not always the originator, the supreme adaptor of musical forms into English verse. In his arrangements and scoring of the hexameter in "Evangeline," not even Tennyson, his British contemporary and a great virtuoso in his own right, could excel him.

It is at the extremes of Longfellow's ingenuities that his verse excels: it may carry the soft intonations of his early "Hymn to Night," or the unrhymed metrics of "Tegnér's Drapa," or the ghostlike echoes of "The Old Clock on the Stairs," or the ringing accents of the last lyric he wrote, "The Bells of San Blas." In the writing of his many sonnets and the blank verse of his plays, one can assume that his musical demon was indifferent. In these the playing is smooth and, of course, correct, but the arrangement is mediocre.

### III

The way to approach the longer poems of Longfellow is to regard them as exotic, at times fantastic, visionary tales. In his youth he greatly admired and attempted to emulate Washington Irving. The prose of Longfellow's early book of European travel sketches, *Outre-Mer*, had for its model Irving's *The Sketch Book*. The refinements of Irving's half-sentimental, half-humorous, swiftly acquired Gothic Muse—the perfect Muse for one of the first of our great American travelers—inspired and for the moment completely charmed the Longfellow who was preparing to teach European languages at Bowdoin. The Muse was as kind to him as to her earlier friend, the graceful Washington Irving. It was she who kept the sensitive, wavering pointer of Longfellow's compass directed toward Northern Europe, and aside from her choice of the Finnish Kalevala for the music of "The Song of Hiawatha," she contributed her share of tears, pathos,

and melodrama to his stanzas on "The Wreck of the
Hesperus" and was probably active in the composition of
the powerful accents overheard in "The Saga of King
Olaf." A deeper colored and fearful aspect of the Gothic
Muse had shown itself to Edgar Allan Poe, and though
he remained adversely critical of Longfellow, his affini-
ties to her guided his praise of Longfellow's song "The
Day Is Done." Irving's influence, however, kept Long-
fellow's tales in verse on the side of comedy—the pathos
or storm of melodrama followed by a happy ending.

In Longfellow's tales one must not look for deep psy-
chological insights. His Evangeline is a patient Griselda of
French-Canadian bucolic origins following the trail of her
betrothed through the wilderness; she is a paragon of
faithfulness. All of Longfellow's women are like figures
seen in a parable or fable; they exist at several removes
from life itself. His heroes are for the most part stalwart
examples of strong, silent meekness like "The Village
Blacksmith," or of somewhat noisy defiance like King Olaf.
These are idealized types, made to prove a sermon or
point a moral. The tales are tales of action, legendary
incident, atmosphere, and feeling. The reasons why
"Evangeline" still retains its power to enchant the reader
are not difficult to rediscover. Longfellow's vision of
Acadie in Nova Scotia was of a pastoral, North Atlantic
Eden, "reflecting an image of heaven." His young lovers
were also the reflected images of Adam and Eve sent
out to wander the North American continent. In this
light the story takes on meaning and resonance and
Longfellow's imagined landscapes endow it with touches
of beauty and mystery rising from the sight of rivers
and plains, prairies and forests. It is significant that Long-
fellow speaks of the Druids in the opening lines of
"Evangeline," for a kind of nature-worship runs its
course throughout the poem.

"Evangeline" presents a curiously mottled picture of
Longfellow's religious associations; he was neither a "free-
thinker" nor a Pantheist, nor a deeply religious poet. Fol-
lowing in the general lead of Emerson, he was a Unitarian,
which, in Longfellow's case, resulted in a Christian "broad-
church" toleration of all faiths on earth with special lean-
ings in "Evangeline" toward nature-worship in the beauty

of its descriptive passages, and toward the Roman
Catholic Church in the sympathetic portrayal of the priest
who guides the poem's heroine. The breadth of Long-
fellow's feelings is important because he has taken a step
that led him in the direction of anthropology and the
composition of "The Song of Hiawatha."

No amount of European travel had weakened Long-
fellow's early interest in the fate of the North American
Indian. His early poem "Burial of the Minnisink" showed
how strong that interest was; its inspiration had pro-
duced one of the best of his youthful poems in which the
last lines were:

> ... One piercing neigh
> Arose, and, on the dead man's plain,
> The rider grasps his steed again.

This is fine and it is in the tradition of an earlier Amer-
ican poem—Philip Freneau's "The Indian Burying
Ground" with the well-remembered lines:

> The hunter still the deer pursues,
> The hunter and the deer a shade!

It would seem that his travels in Europe had actually
intensified Longfellow's delight in the exotic aspects of the
vanishing American Indian. It is even probable that the
impressionable young professor Longfellow had learned to
look at the Indian with the curiosity-and-wonder-inspired
eye of the European. In any case, Longfellow's image
of "The Noble Savage" was not likely to lose its dignity,
for preceding it on the trail marked out ahead were the
footprints of James Fenimore Cooper's *The Last of the
Mohicans*. On the evidence of his "The Skeleton in Ar-
mor," Longfellow brilliantly anticipated twentieth-century
interests in archeology and anthropology, particularly in
their application to folklore and myths. He was less con-
cerned with their realistic historical significance than with
their importance in the imaginative-mythological scheme
of being. Though in his day, except in France, the word
"symbolism" was rarely used, and certainly the conserv-
ative Longfellow was not the man to use it, the tend-
ency in his poetry was in the direction of symbolic

meaning. His great patriotic poem, "The Building of the Ship," was a step in that direction; in "The Song of Hiawatha" the actions of its hero, the beau ideal of "The Noble Savage," are symbolic actions, sustained by the mythology of his people.

Longfellow's preparation for the writing of "Hiawatha," a process that was both subconscious and instinctively deliberate, dated from boyhood to 1854. His published sources were in the works of two pioneer anthropologists, Heckewelder and Schoolcraft. He also cultivated the friendship of an Ojibway chieftain so as to catch the flavor of oral tradition in Indian mythology. The results of Longfellow's research here, as in the best of his adaptations from European literature, created an effect that held few traces of scholarly procedure—it was that of a thorough-going re-creation. As re-created, "The Song of Hiawatha," in twenty-two panoramic episodes, is the transfiguration of an Indian brave into a demigod. His progress from birth through the rites of marriage and through various magical trials to deification, his departure into the sunset, symbolizes the rise and decline of his people and his gods. It is just as well that Longfellow made no attempt to give his "Noble Savage" tragic depth and significance. His dramatic experiments in a tragic vein, his New England Tragedies, are failures, their significance lost in a welter of misplaced sentiment, melodramatic incident, and mediocre blank verse. "Hiawatha" is much happier in its resolution. Hiawatha's goodness is of harmony with nature; he is a child of the Sun and of Indian Summer, and indeed in his good looks and magical powers he has a minor deity resemblance to Apollo. He is what his mythmaking poet and author intended him to be—"my Hiawatha"—the hero of Longfellow's nature-worship, raised to the nth degree, and placed, as if within a shrine, within a poem. Hiawatha's departure is the apotheosis:

> And the evening sun descending
> Set the clouds on fire with redness,
> Burned the broad sky, like a prairie,
> Left upon the level water
> One long track and trail of splendor,
> Down whose stream, as down a river,
> Westward, westward Hiawatha

Sailed into the fiery sunset,
Sailed into the purple vapors,
        *       *       *
To the Islands of the Blessed,
To the Kingdom of Ponemah,
To the Land of the Hereafter!

The flaws in the long work are obvious enough. Caught up in the rhythm he adapted for the poem, Longfellow fell victim to echoing redundancies and banal repetitions. It was the price he had to pay for his facility in playing by ear. Parts of "The Song of Hiawatha" are better than the whole: marvelous passages are to be found in the episodes of "The Four Winds," "Picture-Writing," "The Ghosts," and "Hiawatha's Departure"—certainly, American literature would be far less rich without them. Yet the overall design of the poem should not be as far underrated as it has been; it was more daring in its breaking away from the usual forms of narrative verse than many of its critics have suspected. It was not until T. S. Eliot wrote "The Waste Land" nearly seventy years later that readings in anthropology played so decisive a part in the making of a major poem. This is not to say that "Hiawatha" and "The Waste Land" are alike in any other feature; of course they are not; they are very different poems. While Longfellow in "Hiawatha" did not abandon entirely his storytelling technique, his drifting away into episodes of symbolic action was a turn toward the future of American poetry.

## IV

From the writing of "Hiawatha" onward, we make our approach toward "The White Longfellow," the familiar image of a tall, highly courteous, gracefully white-bearded man of letters who displayed flashes of boyishness in his manner. There was no affectation here. It is wrong to think of him as being "genteel" through any desire to be so. He was a gentleman and knew it and could not act or express his opinions in any other way. He had a good word for everyone, even bad poets. "If I didn't have a good word for them," he said, "who would?" This was unanswerable.

He loved well-appointed, tastefully austere, impressive houses. On his arrival in Cambridge as the young Smith Professor at Harvard he chose for his lodgings rooms in The Craigie House in Brattle Street, a mansion with a historic past. It was a little like living in a museum—and there he stayed for the rest of his life. On his marriage to his second wife, her father, an immensely wealthy man, bought the house and gave it to them. Certainly it provided shelter for himself, his wife, Frances, their three daughters and two sons.

Longfellow's domestic life was less idyllic than a brief glance at it may make it seem. It contained two frightening scenes of death. The first was the death (while they toured Northern Europe) of his young wife, Mary, on a wintry November day in Rotterdam, 1835. A veiled reflection of the scene and the winter day as well is reenacted in the death of Hiawatha's wife. Twenty-six years later the violent death of Frances (the light summer dress she was wearing had caught fire and she was enveloped by flames) was no less shocking. In his attempts to save her, Longfellow was so badly burned that the scars left on his face made it necessary for him to grow a beard—and from this came the figure of "The White Longfellow." For us it is even more important that eighteen years afterward, Frances' death inspired the best, the most moving of his sonnets, "The Cross of Snow." The clarity, the simplicity of the sonnet's language, the austerity of the "cross of snow" as an image, purge the poem of all suggestion of domestic sentimentality. The poem does, however, suggest the atmosphere—and this with restraint, insight, and depth of feeling—of Frances Longfellow's personality. Whatever we know of her holding him at arm's length before their marriage and of her disapproval of his making his personal feelings public in his novels, *Hyperion* and *Kavanaugh,* shows a cool-minded, yet understanding, intelligence. In memory of her the contrasts of fire and snow were deeply appropriate. The poem, unspectacular as it may seem upon first reading, is still another proof of the authenticity of Longfellow's genius.

The Longfellow of "The Craigie House" had other aspects that were carried over from such poems as "The Old Clock on the Stairs" and his echoing "Voices of the Night."

The museumlike character of the mansion he had made his home probably inspired "Haunted Houses," a poem that anticipates in imagery and feeling the ghostly visitations in the poems of W. B. Yeats's middle years:

> So from the world of spirits there descends
> A bridge of light, connecting it with this,
> O'er whose unsteady floor, that sways and bends,
> Wander our thoughts above the dark abyss.

There is a touch of precariousness in these lines, the hints of terror, showing the kinds of restraint of which Longfellow had become a master. This was an exercise, less of "genteel" habit than of growing subtlety and depth of perception. There is also the same play of opposites, "bridge of light" and "dark abyss" as between "fire" and the "cross of snow." A further reach of Longfellow's subtle poetic intelligence and wit is in "In the Churchyard at Cambridge," a poem that supplies an American tradition for the writing of John Crowe Ransom's "Chills and Fever."

There is but one step from these poems to Longfellow's two magnificent elegies: "The Warden of the Cinque Ports"—who was the Duke of Wellington—and "Hawthorne." In the Hawthorne elegy there is a great deal of self-confessional truth in its deceptively simple lines: in them he describes the trancelike states, the illnesses, in which he wrote some of the best of his own poems. Hawthorne and he had known each other slightly since the days when they met at Bowdoin College; it was a friendship of long-sustained acquaintance, mutual courtesies, and infrequent exchanges of ideas and opinions. It was Hawthorne who had first heard the story that inspired Longfellow to write "Evangeline." He decided that it was suited to Longfellow's gifts, not his, and encouraged him in the writing of it. The strong yet thinly woven thread of friendship is implied in the imagery of

> Dark shadows wove on their aerial looms
> Shot through with golden thread—

an atmospheric touch which so often provides the key to meaning in Longfellow's poetry.

In his middle years Longfellow had undertaken the great

task of translating Dante's *Divine Comedy,* and as
he worked toward its completion, he called on two
friends, James Russell Lowell and Charles Eliot Norton,
to spend Wednesday evenings with him—and all three
discussed, criticized, and read aloud the ambitious manu-
script. The result was a substantially impressive version
of the *Comedy;* if anything, it was too substantial, too
overweighted by the large number of poetic inversions
used at line-endings. It was a scholarly and labored
work. Unfortunately, the signs of its labor were not con-
cealed. From the days of his Grand Tour of Europe
to his latter years, his performance as a translator was
extremely erratic: his excellence is shown in "Tegnér's
Drapa" and in his cameolike adaptation of "Saint
Teresa's Book-Mark"—and his badness is illustrated by
(strangely enough, since his "Voices of the Night" was
indebted to them) his versions of several German poets.
One can only say that there were moments when the com-
bination of his learning with his enthusiasm completely
overwhelmed his poetic instincts.

Even as translator, the value of Longfellow's contribu-
tion as a carrier of European culture to the United
States should not be underrated. The translations served
as evidence for his enthusiasms in lecturing on compara-
tive literature at Harvard. His influence was analogous to
the influence exerted by Ezra Pound's importations from
Europe and Asia in the twentieth century. In a cultural
sense he was Pound's predecessor in American poetry—
beyond this of course the likeness of Longfellow to Pound
becomes increasingly tenuous.

Although the greater measure of the popularity Long-
fellow enjoyed at the height of his career cannot be re-
stored, the sentimental trappings of his work can be
swept aside. He now carries less luggage. Fame and mid-
dle-aged friendships brought his name in close association
with James Russell Lowell's, Oliver Wendell Holmes's,
Charles Eliot Norton's, and these, including Longfellow's,
comprised the elite of New England's post-Emersonian cul-
ture. These associations are beginning to drop away. Even
without popular applause, Longfellow's figure is of un-
mistakably larger stature than theirs. A fresh alignment
in which the classic American poets of the nineteenth

century can be seen to complement each other is rising
into view: Whittier (principally because of his "Snow
Bound") and Longfellow are drawn closer to Emily Dick-
inson and Whitman.

In this new perspective Longfellow is seen as sharing
common ground with Whitman in one particular: both
men were national poets whose imaginations contained
vistas of a world beyond the North American continent.
Longfellow's Europe is a living presence in many of his
shorter poems; and in a characteristically different fash-
ion, Whitman evokes a mystical vision of a rounded earth
in "A Passage to India." The likeness is one of being both
international in scope and American in feeling—even to
the flaw of unwearied optimism which too often blurs
distinctions between the good, the bad, and the neither-
bad-nor-good. Both were heirs of the Emersonian Unitar-
ian tradition insofar as they permitted Emerson to do
most of their thinking for them, and both were men of
"goodwill." If Whitman's image was that of a democratic
wanderer of "The Open Road," Longfellow's image was
that of the benevolent, serenely democratic Olympian. In
his early writings, Whitman displayed, and rightly so,
temperamental enthusiasm for Longfellow's verse; and
Longfellow, with the same instinctive sense of rightness,
paid a visit to Whitman at his home in Camden, New
Jersey. Their particular ground in common was large
enough to permit an honest exchange of praise; their
differences were so obvious there could be no rivalry be-
tween them.

As we know, the third figure in the group, Emily Dick-
inson, had no regard for Whitman's writings, nor did
she sit at Longfellow's feet. She was an innovator of an-
other sort than Whitman: her conventions in writing
verse were strictly formed and intense while his were
loosely woven and oracular. Yet she, the transcendental
moralist, aphorist, and wit, drew inspiration from Emer-
son, a source she shared with Longfellow and Whitman.
It is unlikely that the three men, including Whittier, were
more than scarcely aware of her at all, but to us, her
contributions of nearly classical poetic wit, her moments
of sharpness and intensity, are those that her famous
contemporaries could never give us. Her verse, therefore,

is a true complement of theirs; in effect, it completes the picture of a nineteenth-century renaissance in poetry. In his reflections on death in his lines on a Cambridge Churchyard, in his images of haunting angels, it is Longfellow who stands by her side.

After reading the other poets in his American orbit, it is always well to return to Longfellow. His hospitality is greater than theirs: the variety of the forms of verse in which he wrote insures us against confinement in our reading. It is sometimes forgotten that the conversational style of some of *The Tales of a Wayside Inn* is an achievement that is always refreshing. In these Longfellow's dignified, yet lighthearted phrasing is unique; in these his mastery in telling a story and reciting a fable is unequaled in American verse. It is not impossible to regard Longfellow as the perfect host with whom one may witness scenes from his "Hiawatha" and "Evangeline," or if one wishes, one may borrow his romantic telescope to view his lyrical sights of Europe, or on closer yet deeper view, the coast of Maine in a vision of his "lost youth."

HORACE GREGORY

## A Note on the Selections Made in the Editing of This Book

The present selection attempts to reintroduce Longfellow to a new generation of readers. The romantic and lyrical rather than the domesticated and sermon-reciting Longfellow is represented. To show his skill in writing novellas in verse the entire texts of "Evangeline" and "The Courtship of Miles Standish" are included. The passages from "The Song of Hiawatha" are chosen with an eye toward showing the myth-inspired, anthropological character of his famous poem. The Appendix contains a lively example of the young Longfellow's prose—a semi-comic horror tale from his *Outre-Mer*. This is followed by Van Wyck Brooks' vivid sketches of Longfellow at Cambridge and of Schoolcraft's contribution to the Hiawatha myth. To these are added Dr. Norman Holmes Pearson's brilliant commentary on Longfellow's verse in terms of contemporary scholarship and Lewis Carroll's very best of all the many parodies of Hiawatha.

# A Longfellow Chronology

1807: Born February 27, at Portland, Maine, son of Stephen Longfellow and Zilpah Wadsworth Longfellow.

1821: Entered Bowdoin.

1825: Graduated from Bowdoin and invited to become professor of modern languages there.

1826-29: Traveled in Europe, principally in Spain, France, and Germany, to prepare himself for the Bowdoin Professorship of Modern Languages, but the tour was also an excuse to put off as long as possible complete commitment to "the academic life."

1829: Began his duties as professor of modern languages at Bowdoin; found himself a teacher and writer of textbooks rather than a full-fledged lecturing professor.

1831: Married Mary Storer Potter.

1833: Published *Outre-Mer,* prose sketches and tales based on his European tour.

1834-36: Toured Europe.

1835: November 29 at Rotterdam: death of his young wife, Mary, who, according to various legends, resembled Dora, the first wife of Dickens' David Copperfield. Longfellow's memory of her and her death probably helped to make his figure of "The Village Blacksmith" a widower, and almost certainly inspired the death of Hiawatha's wife.

1836: Received Smith Professorship of Modern Languages at Harvard.

1839: Published *Hyperion,* a short novel, and *Voices of the Night,* a book of poems.

1841: Published *Ballads and Other Poems.*

1842: Vacationed at Marienberg on the Rhine, Germany.

1843: Married Frances Appleton.

1847: Completed *"Evangeline"* as well as *Kavenaugh*, a semiautobiographical novel in which he looks back at his teaching experiences at Bowdoin and Harvard and with a charming above-the-battle air satirizes the quarrel between the *Knickerbocker Magazine* faction in New York and the ultra-American nationalists, headed by Cornelius Mathews, a hot and hard-breathing, self-inflated, mediocre novelist. In the novel, Mathews appears as the loud-mouthed "Mr. Churchill." Longfellow was, of course, on the side of the *Knickerbocker,* the magazine that helped to make him famous by publishing the most popular of his early lyrics. Although Longfellow was a staunch patriot, he hated, so far as it was possible for him to hate at all, the professional, antiintellectual American patrioteer.

1854: Retired from Smith Professorship at Harvard.

1855: Completed *"Hiawatha."*

1861: Death of his second wife, Frances.

1863-73: Wrote *Tales of a Wayside Inn.*

1882: Died March 24 at the Craigie House, Cambridge, Mass., which had been George Washington's headquarters during the siege of Boston, and where Longfellow had lived since 1837.

## *HYMN TO THE NIGHT*

I heard the trailing garments of the Night
    Sweep through her marble halls!
I saw her sable skirts all fringed with light
    From the celestial walls!

I felt her presence, by its spell of might,
    Stoop o'er me from above;
The calm, majestic presence of the Night,
    As of the one I love.

I heard the sounds of sorrow and delight,
    The manifold, soft chimes,
That fill the haunted chambers of the Night,
    Like some old poet's rhymes.

From the cool cisterns of the midnight air
    My spirit drank repose;
The fountain of perpetual peace flows there,—
    From those deep cisterns flows.

O holy Night! from thee I learn to bear
    What man has borne before!
Thou layest thy finger on the lips of Care,
    And they complain no more.

Peace! Peace! Orestes-like I breathe this prayer!
    Descend with broad-winged flight,
The welcome, the thrice-prayed for, the most fair,
    The best-beloved Night!

## BURIAL OF THE MINNISINK

On sunny slope and beechen swell,
The shadowed light of evening fell;
And, where the maple's leaf was brown,
With soft and silent lapse came down,
The glory, that the wood receives,
At sunset, in its golden leaves.
Far upward in the mellow light
Rose the blue hills. One cloud of white,
Around a far uplifted cone,
In the warm blush of evening shone;
An image of the silver lakes,
By which the Indian's soul awakes.
But soon a funeral hymn was heard
Where the soft breath of evening stirred
The tall, gray forest; and a band
Of stern in heart, and strong in hand,
Came winding down beside the wave,
To lay the red chief in his grave.
They sang, that by his native bowers
He stood, in the last moon of flowers,
And thirty snows had not yet shed
Their glory on the warrior's head;
But, as the summer fruit decays,
So died he in those naked days.
A dark cloak of the roebuck's skin
Covered the warrior, and within
Its heavy folds the weapons, made
For the hard toils of war, were laid;
The cuirass, woven of plaited reeds,
And the broad belt of shells and beads.
Before, a dark-haired virgin train
Chanted the death dirge of the slain;
Behind, the long procession came
Of hoary men and chiefs of fame,
With heavy hearts, and eyes of grief,
Leading the war-horse of their chief.

Stripped of his proud and martial dress,
Uncurbed, unreined, and riderless,
With darting eye, and nostril spread,
And heavy and impatient tread,
He came; and oft that eye so proud
Asked for his rider in the crowd.
They buried the dark chief; they freed
Beside the grave his battle steed;
And swift an arrow cleaved its way
To his stern heart! One piercing neigh
Arose, and, on the dead man's plain,
The rider grasps his steed again.

## THE SKELETON IN ARMOR

"Speak! speak! thou fearful guest!
Who, with thy hollow breast
Still in rude armor drest,
    Comest to daunt me!
Wrapt not in Eastern balms,
But with thy fleshless palms
Stretched, as if asking alms,
    Why dost thou haunt me?"

Then, from those cavernous eyes
Pale flashes seemed to rise,
As when the Northern skies
    Gleam in December;
And, like the water's flow
Under December's snow,
Came a dull voice of woe
    From the heart's chamber.
"I was a Viking old!
My deeds, though manifold,
No Skald in song has told,
    No Saga taught thee!
Take heed, that in thy verse
Thou dost the tale rehearse,
Else dread a dead man's curse;
    For this I sought thee.

"Far in the Northern Land,
  By the wild Baltic's strand,
  I, with my childish hand,
      Tamed the gerfalcon;
And, with my skates fast-bound,
Skimmed the half-frozen Sound,
That the poor whimpering hound
      Trembled to walk on.

"Oft to his frozen lair
  Tracked I the grisly bear,
  While from my path the hare
      Fled like a shadow;
Oft through the forest dark
Followed the were-wolf's bark,
Until the soaring lark
      Sang from the meadow.

"But when I older grew,
  Joining a corsair's crew,
  O'er the dark sea I flew
      With the marauders.
Wild was the life we led;
Many the souls that sped,
Many the hearts that bled,
      By our stern orders.

"Many a wassail-bout
  Wore the long Winter out;
  Often our midnight shout
      Set the cocks crowing,
As we the Berserk's tale
Measured in cups of ale,
Draining the oaken pail,
      Filled to o'erflowing.

"Once as I told in glee
  Tales of the stormy sea,
  Soft eyes did gaze on me,
      Burning yet tender;
And as the white stars shine
On the dark Norway pine,

On that dark heart of mine
    Fell their soft splendor.

"I wooed the blue-eyed maid,
  Yielding, yet half afraid,
  And in the forest's shade
      Our vows were plighted.
Under its loosened vest
Fluttered her little breast,
Like birds within their nest
      By the hawk frighted.

"Bright in her father's hall
  Shields gleamed upon the wall,
  Loud sang the minstrels all,
      Chanting his glory;
When of old Hildebrand
I asked his daughter's hand,
Mute did the minstrels stand
      To hear my story.

"While the brown ale he quaffed,
  Loud then the champion laughed,
  And as the wind-gusts waft
      The sea-foam brightly,
So the loud laugh of scorn,
Out of those lips unshorn,
From the deep drinking-horn
      Blew the foam lightly.

"She was a Prince's child,
  I but a Viking wild,
  And though she blushed and smiled.
      I was discarded!
Should not the dove so white
Follow the sea-mew's flight,
Why did they leave that night
Her nest unguarded?

"Scarce had I put to sea,
  Bearing the maid with me,
  Fairest of all was she

Among the Norsemen!
When on the white sea-strand.
Waving his armèd hand,
Saw we old Hildebrand,
        With twenty horsemen.

"Then launched they to the blast,
Bent like a reed each mast,
Yet we were gaining fast,
        When the wind failed us;
And with a sudden flaw
Came round the gusty Skaw,
So that our foe we saw
        Laugh as he hailed us.

"And as to catch the gale
Round veered the flapping sail,
'Death!' was the helmsman's hail,
        'Death without quarter!'
Mid-ships with iron keel
Struck we her ribs of steel;
Down her black hulk did reel
        Through the black water!

"As with his wings aslant,
Sails the fierce cormorant,
Seeking some rocky haunt,
        With his prey laden,—
So toward the open main,
Beating to sea again,
Through the wild hurricane,
        Bore I the maiden.

"Three weeks we westward bore,
And when the storm was o'er,
Cloud-like we saw the shore
        Stretching to leeward;
There for my lady's bower
Built I the lofty tower,
Which, to this very hour,
        Stands looking seaward.

"There lived we many years;
Time dried the maiden's tears;

She had forgot her fears,
　　She was a mother;
Death closed her mild blue eyes,
Under that tower she lies;
Ne'er shall the sun arise
　　On such another!

"Still grew my bosom then,
　　Still as a stagnant fen!
Hateful to me were men,
　　The sunlight hateful!
In the vast forest here,
Clad in my warlike gear,
Fell I upon my spear,
　　Oh, death was grateful!

"Thus, seamed with many scars,
Bursting these prison bars,
Up to its native stars
　　My soul ascended!
There from the flowing bowl
Deep drinks the warrior's soul,
*Skoal!* to the Northland! *skoal!*"
　　Thus the tale ended.


## THE WRECK OF THE HESPERUS

It was the schooner Hesperus,
　　That sailed the wintry sea;
And the skipper had taken his little daughter,
　　To bear him company.

Blue were her eyes as the fairy-flax,
　　Her cheeks like the dawn of day,
And her bosom white as the hawthorn buds,
　　That ope in the month of May.

The skipper he stood beside the helm,
　　His pipe was in his mouth,
And he watched how the veering flaw did blow
　　The smoke now West, now South.

Then up and spake an old Sailòr,
 Had sailed to the Spanish Main,
"I pray thee, put into yonder port,
 For I fear a hurricane.

"Last night, the moon had a golden ring,
 And to-night no moon we see!"
The skipper, he blew a whiff from his pipe,
 And a scornful laugh laughed he.

Colder and louder blew the wind,
 A gale from the Northeast,
The snow fell hissing in the brine,
 And the billows frothed like yeast.

Down came the storm, and smote amain
 The vessel in its strength;
She shuddered and paused, like a frighted steed,
 Then leaped her cable's length.

"Come hither! come hither! my little daughtèr,
 And do not tremble so;
For I can weather the roughest gale
 That ever wind did blow."

He wrapped her warm in his seaman's coat
 Against the stinging blast;
He cut a rope from a broken spar,
 And bound her to the mast.

"O father! I hear the church-bells ring,
 Oh say, what may it be?"
" 'Tis a fog-bell on a rock-bound coast!"—
 And he steered for the open sea.

"O father! I hear the sound of guns,
 Oh say, what may it be?"
"Some ship in distress, that cannot live
 In such an angry sea!"

"O father! I see a gleaming light,
 Oh say, what may it be?"
But the father answered never a word,
 A frozen corpse was he.

Lashed to the helm, all stiff and stark,
   With his face turned to the skies,
The lantern gleamed through the gleaming snow
   On his fixed and glassy eyes.

Then the maiden clasped her hands and prayed
   That savèd she might be;
And she thought of Christ, who stilled the wave,
   On the Lake of Galilee.

And fast through the midnight dark and drear,
   Through the whistling sleet and snow,
Like a sheeted ghost, the vessel swept
   Tow'rds the reef of Norman's Woe.

And ever the fitful gusts between
   A sound came from the land;
It was the sound of the trampling surf
   On the rocks and the hard sea-sand.

The breakers were right beneath her bows,
   She drifted a dreary wreck,
And a whooping billow swept the crew
   Like icicles from her deck.

She struck where the white and fleecy waves
   Looked soft as carded wool,
But the cruel rocks, they gored her side
   Like the horns of an angry bull.

Her rattling shrouds, all sheathed in ice,
   With the masts went by the board;
Like a vessel of glass, she stove and sank,
   Ho! ho! the breakers roared!

At daybreak, on the bleak sea-beach,
   A fisherman stood aghast,
To see the form of a maiden fair,
   Lashed close to a drifting mast.

The salt sea was frozen on her breast,
    The salt tears in her eyes;
And he saw her hair, like the brown sea-weed,
    On the billows fall and rise.

Such was the wreck of the Hesperus,
    In the midnight and the snow!
Christ save us all from a death like this,
    On the reef of Norman's Woe!


## THE VILLAGE BLACKSMITH

Under a spreading chestnut-tree
    The village smithy stands;
The smith, a mighty man is he,
    With large and sinewy hands;
And the muscles of his brawny arms
    Are strong as iron bands.

His hair is crisp, and black, and long,
    His face is like the tan;
His brow is wet with honest sweat,
    He earns whate'er he can,
And looks the whole world in the face,
    For he owes not any man.

Week in, week out, from morn till night,
    You can hear his bellows blow;
You can hear him swing his heavy sledge,
    With measured beat and slow,
Like a sexton ringing the village bell,
    When the evening sun is low.

And children coming home from school
    Look in at the open door;
They love to see the flaming forge,
    And hear the bellows roar,
And catch the burning sparks that fly
    Like chaff from a threshing-floor.

He goes on Sunday to the church,
    And sits among his boys;

He hears the parson pray and preach,
    He hears his daughter's voice,
Singing in the village choir,
    And it makes his heart rejoice.

It sounds to him like her mother's voice,
    Singing in Paradise!
He needs must think of her once more,
    How in the grave she lies;
And with his hard, rough hand he wipes
    A tear out of his eyes.

Toiling,—rejoicing,—sorrowing,
    Onward through life he goes;
Each morning sees some task begin,
    Each evening sees it close;
Something attempted, something done,
    Has earned a night's repose.

Thanks, thanks to thee, my worthy friend,
    For the lesson thou hast taught!
Thus at the flaming forge of life
    Our fortunes must be wrought;
Thus on its sounding anvil shaped
    Each burning deed and thought.


## THE WITNESSES


In Ocean's wide domains,
    Half-buried in the sands,
Lie skeletons in chains,
    With shackled feet and hands.

Beyond the fall of dews,
    Deeper than plummet lies,
Float ships, with all their crews,
    No more to sink nor rise.

There the black Slave-ship swims,
    Freighted with human forms,
Whose fettered, fleshless limbs
    Are not the sport of storms.

These are the bones of Slaves;
　　They gleam from the abyss;
They cry, from yawning waves,
　　"We are the Witnesses!"

Within Earth's wide domains
　　Are markets for men's lives;
Their necks are galled with chains,
　　Their wrists are cramped with gyves.

Dead bodies, that the kite
　　In deserts makes its prey;
Murders, that with affright
　　Scare school-boys from their play!

All evil thoughts and deeds;
　　Anger, and lust, and pride;
The foulest, rankest weeds,
　　That choke Life's groaning tide!

These are the woes of Slaves;
　　They glare from the abyss;
They cry, from unknown graves,
　　"We are the Witnesses!"


## THE BELFRY OF BRUGES

In the market-place of Bruges stands the belfry old and
　　brown;
Thrice consumed and thrice rebuilded, still it watches o'er
　　the town.

As the summer morn was breaking, on that lofty tower I
　　stood,
And the world threw off the darkness, like the weeds of
　　widowhood.

Thick with towns and hamlets studded, and with streams
　　and vapors gray,
Like a shield embossed with silver, round and vast the
　　landscape lay.

At my feet the city slumbered. From its chimneys, here
    and there,
Wreaths of snow-white smoke, ascending, vanished, ghost-
    like, into air.

Not a sound rose from the city at that early morning hour,
But I heard a heart of iron beating in the ancient tower.

From their nests beneath the rafters sang the swallows wild
    and high;
And the world, beneath me sleeping, seemed more distant
    than the sky.

Then most musical and solemn, bringing back the olden
    times,
With their strange, unearthly changes rang the melancholy
    chimes,

Like the psalms from some old cloister, when the nuns
    sing in the choir;
And the great bell tolled among them, like the chanting of
    a friar.

Visions of the days departed, shadowy phantoms filled my
    brain;
They who live in history only seemed to walk the earth
    again;

All the Foresters of Flanders,—mighty Baldwin Bras de
    Fer,
Lyderick du Bucq and Cressy, Philip, Guy de Dampierre.

I beheld the pageants splendid that adorned those days
    of old;
Stately dames, like queens attended, knights who bore
    the Fleece of Gold;

Lombard and Venetian merchants with deep-laden
    argosies;
Ministers from twenty nations; more than royal pomp and
    ease.

I beheld proud Maximilian, kneeling humbly on the
    ground;

I beheld the gentle Mary, hunting with her hawk and
  hound;

And her lighted bridal-chamber, where a duke slept with
  the queen,
And the armèd guard around them, and the sword un-
  sheathed between.

I beheld the Flemish weavers, with Namur and Juliers
  bold,
Marching homeward from the bloody battle of the Spurs
  of Gold;

Saw the fight at Minnewater, saw the White Hoods moving
  west,
Saw great Artevelde victorious scale the Golden Dragon's
  nest.

And again the whiskered Spaniard all the land with terror
  smote;
And again the wild alarum sounded from the tocsin's
  throat;

Till the bell of Ghent responded o'er lagoon and dike of
  sand,
"I am Roland! I am Roland! there is victory in the land!"

Then the sound of drums aroused me. The awakened city's
  roar
Chased the phantoms I had summoned back into their
  graves once more.

Hours had passed away like minutes; and, before I was
  aware,
Lo! the shadow of the belfry crossed the sun-illumined
  square.


### THE DAY IS DONE

The day is done, and the darkness
  Falls from the wings of Night,
As a feather is wafted downward
  From an eagle in his flight.

I see the lights of the village
    Gleam through the rain and the mist,
And a feeling of sadness comes o'er me
    That my soul cannot resist:

A feeling of sadness and longing,
    That is not akin to pain,
And resembles sorrow only
    As the mist resembles the rain.

Come, read to me some poem,
    Some simple and heartfelt lay,
That shall soothe this restless feeling,
    And banish the thoughts of day.

Not from the grand old masters,
    Not from the bards sublime,
Whose distant footsteps echo
    Through the corridors of Time.

For, like strains of martial music,
    Their mighty thoughts suggest
Life's endless toil and endeavor;
    And to-night I long for rest.

Read from some humbler poet,
    Whose songs gushed from his heart,
As showers from the clouds of summer,
    Or tears from the eyelids start;

Who, through long days of labor,
    And nights devoid of ease,
Still heard in his soul the music
    Of wonderful melodies.

Such songs have power to quiet
    The restless pulse of care,
And come like the benediction
    That follows after prayer.

Then read from the treasured volume
    The poem of thy choice,
And lend to the rhyme of the poet
    The beauty of thy voice.

And the night shall be filled with music,
    And the cares, that infest the day,
Shall fold their tents, like the Arabs,
    And as silently steal away.


## THE OLD CLOCK ON THE STAIRS

Somewhat back from the village street
Stands the old-fashioned country-seat.
Across its antique portico
Tall poplar-trees their shadows throw;
And from its station in the hall
An ancient timepiece says to all,—

>    "Forever—never!
>        Never—forever!"

Half-way up the stairs it stands,
And points and beckons with its hands
From its case of massive oak,
Like a monk, who, under his cloak,
Crosses himself, and sighs, alas!
With sorrowful voice to all who pass,—

>    "Forever—never!
>        Never—forever!"

By day its voice is low and light;
But in the silent dead of night,
Distinct as a passing footstep's fall,
It echoes along the vacant hall,
Along the ceiling, along the floor,
And seems to say, at each chamber-door,—

>    "Forever—never!
>        Never—forever!"

Through days of sorrow and of mirth,
Through days of death and days of birth,
Throughout every swift vicissitude
Of changeful time, unchanged it has stood,
And as if, like God, it all things saw,
It calmly repeats those words of awe,—

    "Forever—never!
    Never—forever!"

In that mansion used to be
Free-hearted Hospitality;
His great fires up the chimney roared:
The stranger feasted at his board;
But, like the skeleton at the feast,
That warning timepiece never ceased,—

    "Forever—never!
    Never—forever!"

There groups of merry children played,
There youths and maidens dreaming strayed;
O precious hours! O golden prime,
And affluence of love and time!
Even as a miser counts his gold,
Those hours the ancient timepiece told,—

    "Forever—never!
    Never—forever!"

From that chamber, clothed in white,
The bride came forth on her wedding night;
There, in that silent room below,
The dead lay in his shroud of snow;
And in the hush that followed the prayer,
Was heard the old clock on the stair,—

    "Forever—never!
    Never—forever!"

All are scattered now and fled,
Some are married, some are dead;
And when I ask, with throbs of pain,
"Ah! when shall they all meet again?"
As in the days long since gone by,
The ancient timepiece makes reply,—

    "Forever—never!
    Never—forever!"

Never here, forever there,
Where all parting, pain, and care,
And death, and time shall disappear,—
Forever there, but never here!
The horologe of Eternity
Sayeth this incessantly,—


"Forever—never!
Never—forever!"


## EVANGELINE

This is the forest primeval. The murmuring pines and the
    hemlocks,
Bearded with moss, and in garments green, indistinct in
    the twilight,
Stand like Druids of eld, with voices sad and prophetic,
Stand like harpers hoar, with beards that rest on their
    bosoms.
Loud from its rocky caverns, the deep-voiced neighboring
    ocean
Speaks, and in accents disconsolate answers the wail of
    the forest.


This is the forest primeval; but where are the hearts that
    beneath it
Leaped like the roe, when he hears in the woodland the
    voice of the huntsman?
Where is the thatch-roofed village. the home of Acadian
    farmers,—
Men whose lives glided on like rivers that water the wood-
    lands,
Darkened by shadows of earth, but reflecting an image of
    heaven?
Waste are those pleasant farms, and the farmers forever
    departed!
Scattered like dust and leaves, when the mighty blasts
    of October

Seize them, and whirl them aloft, and sprinkle them far
    o'er the ocean.
Naught but tradition remains of the beautiful village of
    Grand-Pré.

Ye who believe in affection that hopes, and endures, and
    is patient,
Ye who believe in the beauty and strength of woman's
    devotion,
List to the mournful tradition, still sung by the pines of
    the forest;
List to a Tale of Love in Acadie, home of the happy.

## PART THE FIRST

### I

In the Acadian land, on the shores of the Basin of Minas,
Distant, secluded, still, the little village of Grand-Pré
Lay in the fruitful valley. Vast meadows stretched to the
    eastward,
Giving the village its name, and pasture to flocks without
    number.
Dikes, that the hands of the farmers had raised with labor
    incessant,
Shut out the turbulent tides; but at stated seasons the
    flood-gates
Opened, and welcomed the sea to wander at will o'er the
    meadows.
West and south there were fields of flax, and orchards and
    cornfields
Spreading afar and unfenced o'er the plain; and away to
    the northward
Blomidon rose, and the forests old, and aloft on the
    mountains
Sea-fogs pitched their tents, and mists from the mighty
    Atlantic
Looked on the happy valley, but ne'er from their station
    descended.
There, in the midst of its farms, reposed the Acadian
    village.

Strongly built were the houses, with frames of oak and
    of hemlock,
Such as the peasants of Normandy built in the reign of
    the Henries.
Thatched were the roofs, with dormer-windows; and gables
    projecting
Over the basement below protected and shaded the door-
    way.
There in the tranquil evenings of summer, when brightly
    the sunset
Lighted the village street, and gilded the vanes on the
    chimneys,
Matrons and maidens sat in snow-white caps and in
    kirtles
Scarlet and blue and green, with distaffs spinning the
    golden
Flax for the gossiping looms, whose noisy shuttles within
    doors
Mingled their sounds with the whir of the wheels and the
    songs of the maidens.
Solemnly down the street came the parish priest, and the
    children
Paused in their play to kiss the hand he extended to bless
    them.
Reverend walked he among them; and up rose matrons and
    maidens,
Hailing his slow approach with words of affectionate wel-
    come.
Then came the laborers home from the field, and serenely
    the sun sank
Down to his rest, and twilight prevailed. Anon from the
    belfry
Softly the Angelus sounded, and over the roofs of the
    village
Columns of pale blue smoke, like clouds of incense
    ascending,
Rose from a hundred hearths, the homes of peace and
    contentment.
Thus dwelt together in love these simple Acadian
    farmers,—
Dwelt in the love of God and of man. Alike were they
    free from

Fear, that reigns with the tyrant, and envy, the vice of
    republics.
Neither locks had they to their doors, nor bars to their
    windows;
But their dwellings were open as day and the hearts of
    the owners;
There the richest was poor, and the poorest lived in
    abundance.

    Somewhat apart from the village, and nearer the Basin
    of Minas,
Benedict Bellefontaine, the wealthiest farmer of Grand-
    Pré,
Dwelt on his goodly acres; and with him, directing his
    household,
Gentle Evangeline lived, his child, and the pride of the
    village.
Stalworth and stately in form was the man of seventy
    winters;
Hearty and hale was he, an oak that is covered with
    snow-flakes;
White as the snow were his locks, and his cheeks as brown
    as the oak-leaves.
Fair was she to behold, that maiden of seventeen
    summers.
Black were her eyes as the berry that grows on the thorn
    by the wayside,
Black, yet how softly they gleamed beneath the brown
    shade of her tresses!
Sweet was her breath as the breath of kine that feed in
    the meadows.
When in the harvest heat she bore to the reapers at
    noontide
Flagons of home-brewed ale, ah! fair in sooth was the
    maiden.
Fairer was she when, on Sunday morn, while the bell
    from its turret
Sprinkled with holy sounds the air, as the priest with his
    hyssop
Sprinkles the congregation, and scatters blessings upon
    them,
Down the long street she passed, with her chaplet of
    beads and her missal,

Wearing her Norman cap, and her kirtle of blue, and the
    ear-rings,
Brought in the olden time from France, and since, as an
    heirloom,
Handed down from mother to child, through long gen-
    erations.
But a celestial brightness—a more ethereal beauty—
Shone on her face and encircled her form, when, after
    confession,
Homeward serenely she walked with God's benediction
    upon her.
When she had passed, it seemed like the ceasing of ex-
    quisite music.

    Firmly built with rafters of oak, the house of the
    farmer
Stood on the side of a hill commanding the sea; and a
    shady
Sycamore grew by the door, with a woodbine wreathing
    around it.
Rudely carved was the porch, with seats beneath; and a
    footpath
Led through an orchard wide, and disappeared in the
    meadow.
Under the sycamore-tree were hives overhung by a pent-
    house,
Such as the traveller sees in regions remote by the road-
    side,
Built o'er a box for the poor, or the blessed image of
    Mary.
Farther down, on the slope of the hill, was the well with
    its moss-grown
Bucket, fastened with iron, and near it a trough for the
    horses.
Shielding the house from storms, on the north, were the
    barns and the farm-yard.
There stood the broad-wheeled wains and the antique
    ploughs and the harrows;
There were the folds for the sheep; and there, in his feath-
    ered seraglio,
Strutted the lordly turkey, and crowed the cock, with the
    selfsame
Voice that in ages of old had startled the penitent Peter.

Bursting with hay were the barns, themselves a village.
In each one
Far o'er the gable projected a roof of thatch; and a
staircase,
Under the sheltering eaves, led up to the odorous corn-
loft.
There too the dove-cot stood, with its meek and innocent
inmates
Murmuring ever of love; while above in the variant
breezes
Numberless noisy weathercocks rattled and sang of muta-
tion.

Thus, at peace with God and the world, the farmer of
Grand-Pré
Lived on his sunny farm, and Evangeline governed his
household.
Many a youth, as he knelt in church and opened his
missal,
Fixed his eyes upon her as the saint of his deepest
devotion;
Happy was he who might touch her hand or the hem of
her garment!
Many a suitor came to her door, by the darkness be-
friended,
And, as he knocked and waited to hear the sound of her
footsteps,
Knew not which beat the louder, his heart or the knocker
of iron;
Or at the joyous feast of the Patron Saint of the village,
Bolder grew, and pressed her hand in the dance as he
whispered
Hurried words of love, that seemed a part of the music.
But, among all who came, young Gabriel only was wel-
come;
Gabriel Lajeunesse, the son of Basil the blacksmith,
Who was a mighty man in the village, and honored of all
men;
For, since the birth of time, throughout all ages and
nations,
Has the craft of the smith been held in repute by the
people.
Basil was Benedict's friend. Their children from earliest
childhood

Grew up together as brother and sister; and Father
　　Felician.
Priest and pedagogue both in the village, had taught them
　　their letters
Out of the selfsame book, with the hymns of the church
　　and the plain-song.
But when the hymn was sung, and the daily lesson com-
　　pleted,
Swiftly they hurried away to the forge of Basil the black-
　　smith.
There at the door they stood, with wondering eyes to be-
　　hold him
Take in his leathern lap the hoof of the horse as a play-
　　thing,
Nailing the shoe in its place; while near him the tire of the
　　cart-wheel
Lay like a fiery snake, coiled round in a circle of cinders.
Oft on autumnal eves, when without in the gathering
　　darkness
Bursting with light seemed the smithy, through every
　　cranny and crevice,
Warm by the forge within they watched the laboring
　　bellows,
And as its panting ceased, and the sparks expired in the
　　ashes,
Merrily laughed, and said they were nuns going into the
　　chapel.
Oft on sledges in winter, as swift as the swoop of the
　　eagle,
Down the hillside bounding, they glided away o'er the
　　meadow.
Oft in the barns they climbed to the populous nests on the
　　rafters,
Seeking with eager eyes that wondrous stone, which the
　　swallow
Brings from the shore of the sea to restore the sight of its
　　fledglings;
Lucky was he who found that stone in the nest of the
　　swallow!
Thus passed a few swift years, and they no longer were
　　children.

He was a valiant youth, and his face, like the face of the
    morning,
Gladdened the earth with its light, and ripened thought
    into action.
She was a woman now, with the heart and hopes of a
    woman.
"Sunshine of Saint Eulalie" was she called; for that was
    the sunshine
Which, as the farmers believed, would load their orchards
    with apples;
She, too, would bring to her husband's house delight and
    abundance,
Filling it with love and the ruddy faces of children.


## II


Now had the season returned, when the nights grow colder
    and longer,
And the retreating sun the sign of the Scorpion enters.
Birds of passage sailed through the leaden air, from the
    ice-bound,
Desolate northern bays to the shores of tropical islands.
Harvests were gathered in; and wild with the winds of
    September
Wrestled the trees of the forest, as Jacob of old with the
    angel.
All the signs foretold a winter long and inclement.
Bees, with prophetic instinct of want, had hoarded their
    honey
Till the hives overflowed; and the Indian hunters asserted
Cold would the winter be, for thick was the fur of the
    foxes.
Such was the advent of autumn. Then followed that beauti-
    ful season,
Called by the pious Acadian peasants the Summer of
    All-Saints!
Filled was the air with a dreamy and magical light; and
    the landscape
Lay as if new-created in all the freshness of childhood.
Peace seemed to reign upon earth, and the restless heart
    of the ocean

Was for a moment consoled. All sounds were in harmony
    blended.
Voices of children at play, the crowing of cocks in the
    farm-yards.
Whir of wings in the drowsy air, and the cooing of pigeons,
All were subdued and low as the murmurs of love, and
    the great sun
Looked with the eye of love through the golden vapors
    around him;
While arrayed in its robes of russet and scarlet and yellow,
Bright with the sheen of the dew, each glittering tree of
    the forest
Flashed like the plane-tree the Persian adorned with man-
    ⁺les and jewels.

  Now recommenced the reign of rest and affection and
    stillness.
Day with its burden and heat had departed, and twilight
    descending
Brought back the evening star to the sky, and the herds to
    the homestead.
Pawing the ground they came, and resting their necks on
    each other,
And with their nostrils distended inhaling the freshness of
    evening.
Foremost, bearing the bell, Evangeline's beautiful heifer,
Proud of her snow-white hide, and the ribbon that waved
    from her collar,
Quietly paced and slow, as if conscious of human affection.
Then came the shepherd back with his bleating flocks from
    the seaside,
Where was their favorite pasture. Behind them followed
    the watch-dog,
Patient, full of importance, and grand in the pride of his
    instinct,
Walking from side to side with a lordly air, and superbly
Waving his busy tail, and urging forward the stragglers;
Regent of flocks was he when the shepherd slept; their
    protector,
When from the forest at night, through the starry silence
    the wolves howled.

Late, with the rising moon, returned the wains from the
    marshes,
Laden with briny hay, that filled the air with its odor.
Cheerily neighed the steeds, with dew on their manes and
    their fetlocks,
While aloft on their shoulders the wooden and ponderous
    saddles,
Painted with brilliant dyes, and adorned with tassels of
    crimson,
Nodded in bright array, like hollyhocks heavy with
    blossoms.
Patiently stood the cows meanwhile, and yielded their
    udders
Unto the milkmaid's hand; whilst loud and in regular
    cadence
Into the sounding pails the foaming streamlets descended.
Lowing of cattle and peals of laughter were heard in the
    farm-yard,
Echoed back by the barns. Anon they sank into stillness;
Heavily closed, with a jarring sound, the valves of the
    barn-doors,
Rattled the wooden bars, and all for a season was silent.

  In-doors, warm by the wide-mouthed fireplace, idly the
    farmer
Sat in his elbow-chair and watched how the flames and the
    smoke-wreaths
Struggled together like foes in a burning city. Behind him,
Nodding and mocking along the wall, with gestures fan-
    tastic,
Darted his own huge shadow, and vanished away into
    darkness.
Faces, clumsily carved in oak, on the back of his arm-
    chair
Laughed in the flickering light; and the pewter plates on
    the dresser
Caught and reflected the flame, as shields of armies the
    sunshine.
Fragments of song the old man sang, and carols of
    Christmas,
Such as at home, in the olden time, his fathers before
    him

Sang in their Norman orchards and bright Burgundian
    vineyards.
Close at her father's side was the gentle Evangeline seated,
Spinning flax for the loom, that stood in the corner be-
    hind her.
Silent awhile were its treadles, at rest was its diligent
    shuttle,
While the monotonous drone of the wheel, like the drone
    of a bagpipe,
Followed the old man's song and united the fragments to-
    gether.
As in a church, when the chant of the choir at intervals
    ceases,
Footfalls are heard in the aisles, or words of the priest at
    the altar,
So, in each pause of the song, with measured motion the
    clock clicked.

Thus as they sat, there were footsteps heard, and, sud-
    denly lifted,
Sounded the wooden latch, and the door swung back on
    its hinges.
Benedict knew by the hob-nailed shoes it was Basil the
    blacksmith,
And by her beating heart Evangeline knew who was with
    him.
"Welcome!" the farmer exclaimed, as their footsteps paused
    on the threshold,
"Welcome, Basil, my friend! Come, take thy place on
    the settle
Close by the chimney-side, which is always empty without
    thee;
Take from the shelf overhead thy pipe and the box of
    tobacco;
Never so much thyself art thou as when through the
    curling
Smoke of the pipe or the forge thy friendly and jovial face
    gleams
Round and red as the harvest moon through the mist of
    the marshes."
Then, with a smile of content, thus answered Basil the
    blacksmith,
Taking with easy air the accustomed seat by the fireside:—

"Benedict Bellefontaine, thou hast ever thy jest and thy
  ballad!
Ever in cheerfullest mood art thou, when others are filled
  with
Gloomy forebodings of ill, and see only ruin before them.
Happy art thou, as if every day thou hadst picked up a
  horseshoe."
Pausing a moment, to take the pipe that Evangeline
  brought him,
And with a coal from the embers had lighted, he slowly
  continued:—
"Four days now are passed since the English ships at their
  anchors
Ride in the Gaspereau's mouth, with their cannon pointed
  against us.
What their design may be is unknown; but all are com-
  manded
On the morrow to meet in the church, where his Maj-
  esty's mandate
Will be proclaimed as law in the land. Alas! in the mean-
  time
Many surmises of evil alarm the hearts of the people."
Then made answer the farmer: "Perhaps some friendlier
  purpose
Brings these ships to our shores. Perhaps the harvests in
  England
By untimely rains or untimelier heat have been blighted,
And from our bursting barns they would feed their cattle
  and children."
"Not so thinketh the folk in the village," said, warmly, the
  blacksmith,
Shaking his head, as in doubt; then, heaving a sigh, he con-
  tinued:—
"Louisburg is not forgotten, nor Beau Séjour, nor Port
  Royal.
Many already have fled to the forest, and lurk on its
  outskirts,
Waiting with anxious hearts the dubious fate of to-
  morrow.
Arms have been taken from us, and war-like weapons of
  all kinds;
Nothing is left but the blacksmith's sledge and the scythe
  of the mower."

Then with a pleasant smile made answer the jovial
    farmer:—
"Safer are we unarmed, in the midst of our flocks and our
    cornfields,
Safer within these peaceful dikes, besieged by the ocean,
Than our fathers in forts, besieged by the enemy's cannon.
Fear no evil, my friend, and to-night may no shadow of
    sorrow
Fall on this house and hearth; for this is the night of the
    contract.
Built are the house and the barn. The merry lads of the
    village
Strongly have built them and well; and, breaking the glebe
    round about them,
Filled the barn with hay, and the house with food for a
    twelvemonth.
René Leblanc will be here anon, with his papers and ink-
    horn.
Shall we not then be glad, and rejoice in the joy of our
    children?"
As apart by the window she stood, with her hand in her
    lover's,
Blushing Evangeline heard the words that her father had
    spoken,
And, as they died on his lips, the worthy notary entered.

### III

Bent like a laboring oar, that toils in the surf of the ocean,
Bent, but not broken, by age was the form of the notary
    public:
Shocks of yellow hair, like the silken floss of the maize,
    hung
Over his shoulders; his forehead was high; and glasses
    with horn bows
Sat astride on his nose, with a look of wisdom supernal.
Father of twenty children was he, and more than a
    hundred
Children's children rode on his knee, and heard his great
    watch tick.
Four long years in the times of the war had he languished
    a captive,
Suffering much in an old French fort as the friend of the
    English.

Now, though warier grown, without all guile or suspicion,
Ripe in wisdom was he, but patient, and simple, and
childlike.
He was beloved by all, and most of all by the children;
For he told them tales of the Loup-garou in the forest,
And of the goblin that came in the night to water the
horses,
And of the white Létiche, the ghost of a child who un-
christened
Died, and was doomed to haunt unseen the chambers of
children;
And how on Christmas eve the oxen talked in the stable,
And how the fever was cured by a spider shut up in a
nutshell,
And of the marvellous powers of four-leaved clover and
horseshoes,
With whatsoever else was writ in the lore of the village.
Then up rose from his seat by the fireside Basil the black-
smith,
Knocked from his pipe the ashes, and slowly extending his
right hand,
"Father Leblanc," he exclaimed, "thou hast heard the talk
in the village,
And, perchance, canst tell us some news of these ships
and their errand."
Then with modest demeanor made answer the notary
public,—
"Gossip enough have I heard, in sooth, yet am never the
wiser;
And what their errand may be I know not better than
others.
Yet am I not of those who imagine some evil intention
Brings them here, for we are at peace; and why then
molest us?"
"God's name!" shouted the hasty and somewhat irascible
blacksmith;
"Must we in all things look for the how, and the why, and
the wherefore?
Daily injustice is done, and might is the right of the
strongest!"
But without heeding his warmth, continued the notary
public,—
"Man is unjust, but God is just; and finally justice

Triumphs; and well I remember a story, that often con-
soled me,
When as a captive I lay in the old French fort at Port
Royal."
This was the old man's favorite tale, and he loved to
repeat it
When his neighbors complained that any injustice was
done them.
"Once in an ancient city, whose name I no longer
remember,
Raised aloft on a column, a brazen statue of Justice
Stood in the public square, upholding the scales in its left
hand,
And in its right a sword, as an emblem that justice pre-
sided
Over the laws of the land, and the hearts and homes of
the people.
Even the birds had built their nests in the scales of the
balance,
Having no fear of the sword that flashed in the sunshine
above them.
But in the course of time the laws of the land were cor-
rupted;
Might took the place of right, and the weak were op-
pressed, and the mighty
Ruled with an iron rod. Then it chanced in a nobleman's
palace
That a necklace of pearls was lost, and erelong a suspicion
Fell on an orphan girl who lived as a maid in the house-
hold.
She, after form of trial condemned to die on the scaffold,
Patiently met her doom at the foot of the statue of
Justice.
As to her Father in heaven her innocent spirit ascended,
Lo! o'er the city a tempest rose; and the bolts of the
thunder
Smote the statue of bronze, and hurled in wrath from its
left hand
Down on the pavement below the clattering scales of the
balance,
And in the hollow thereof was found the nest of a magpie,
Into whose clay-built walls the necklace of pearls was in-
woven."

Silenced, but not convinced, when the story was ended, the
    blacksmith
Stood like a man who fain would speak, but findeth no
    language;
All his thoughts were congealed into lines on his face, as
    the vapors
Freeze in fantastic shapes on the window-panes in the
    winter.

  Then Evangeline lighted the brazen lamp on the table,
Filled, till it overflowed, the pewter tankard with home-
    brewed
Nut-brown ale, that was famed for its strength in the
    village of Grand-Pré;
While from his pocket the notary drew his papers and
    inkhorn,
Wrote with a steady hand the date and the age of the
    parties,
Naming the dower of the bride in flocks of sheep and in
    cattle.
Orderly all things proceeded, and duly and well were com-
    pleted,
And the great seal of the law was set like a sun on the
    margin.
Then from his leathern pouch the farmer threw on the
    table
Three times the old man's fee in solid pieces of silver;
And the notary rising, and blessing the bride and the
    bridegroom,
Lifted aloft the tankard of ale and drank to their welfare.
Wiping the foam from his lip, he solemnly bowed and
    departed,
While in silence the others sat and mused by the fireside,
Till Evangeline brought the draught-board out of its
    corner.
Soon was the game begun. In friendly contention the old
    men
Laughed at each lucky hit, or unsuccessful maneuvre,
Laughed when a man was crowned, or a breach was made
    in the king-row.
Meanwhile apart, in the twilight gloom of a window's
    embrasure,

Sat the lovers, and whispered together, beholding the
    moon rise
Over the pallid sea, and the silvery mists of the meadows.
Silently one by one, in the infinite meadows of heaven,
Blossomed the lovely stars, the forget-me-nots of the
    angels.

    Thus was the evening passed. Anon the bell from the
    belfry
Rang out the hour of nine, the village curfew, and straight-
    way
Rose the guests and departed; and silence reigned in the
    household.
Many a farewell word and sweet good-night on the door-
    step
Lingered long in Evangeline's heart, and filled it with
    gladness.
Carefully then were covered the embers that glowed on
    the hearth-stone,
And on the oaken stairs resounded the tread of the farmer.
Soon with a soundless step the foot of Evangeline followed.
Up the staircase moved a luminous space in the dark-
    ness,
Lighted less by the lamp than the shining face of the
    maiden.
Silent she passed the hall, and entered the door of her
    chamber.
Simple that chamber was, with its curtains of white, and
    its clothes-press
Ample and high, on whose spacious shelves were care-
    fully folded
Linen and woollen stuffs, by the hand of Evangeline
    woven.
This was the precious dower she would bring to her
    husband in marriage,
Better than flocks and herds, being proofs of her skill as
    a housewife.
Soon she extinguished her lamp, for the mellow and radi-
    ant moonlight
Streamed through the windows, and lighted the room, till
    the heart of the maiden

Swelled and obeyed its power, like the tremulous tides of
    the ocean.
Ah! she was fair, exceeding fair to behold, as she stood
    with
Naked snow-white feet on the gleaming floor of her
    chamber!
Little she dreamed that below, among the trees of the
    orchard,
Waited her lover and watched for the gleam of her lamp
    and her shadow.
Yet were her thoughts of him, and at times a feeling of
    sadness
Passed o'er her soul, as the sailing shade of clouds in the
    moonlight
Flitted across the floor and darkened the room for a
    moment.
And, as she gazed from the window, she saw serenely the
    moon pass
Forth from the folds of a cloud, and one star follow her
    footsteps,
As out of Abraham's tent young Ishmael wandered with
    Hagar!

## IV

Pleasantly rose next morn the sun on the village of Grand-
    Pré.
Pleasantly gleamed in the soft, sweet air the Basin of
    Minas,
Where the ships, with their wavering shadows, were rid-
    ing at anchor.
Life had long been astir in the village, and clamorous
    labor
Knocked with its hundred hands at the golden gates of the
    morning.
Now from the country around, from the farms and neigh-
    boring hamlets,
Came in their holiday dresses the blithe Acadian peasants.
Many a glad good-morrow and jocund laugh from the
    young folk
Made the bright air brighter, as up from the numerous
    meadows,

Where no path could be seen but the track of wheels in the
   greensward,
Group after group appeared, and joined, or passed on the
   highway.
Long ere noon, in the village all sounds of labor were
   silenced.
Thronged were the streets with people; and noisy groups
   at the house-doors
Sat in the cheerful sun, and rejoiced and gossiped to-
   gether.
Every house was an inn, where all were welcomed and
   feasted;
For with this simple people, who lived like brothers to-
   gether,
All things were held in common, and what one had was
   another's.
Yet under Benedict's roof hospitality seemed more
   abundant:
For Evangeline stood among the guests of her father;
Bright was her face with smiles, and words of welcome
   and gladness
Fell from her beautiful lips, and blessed the cup as she
   gave it.
   Under the open sky, in the odorous air of the orchard,
Stript of its golden fruit, was spread the feast of betrothal.
There in the shade of the porch were the priest and the
   notary seated;
There good Benedict sat, and sturdy Basil the blacksmith.
Not far withdrawn from these, by the cider-press and the
   beehives,
Michael the fiddler was placed, with the gayest of hearts
   and of waistcoats.
Shadow and light from the leaves alternately played on
   his snow-white
Hair, as it waved in the wind; and the jolly face of the
   fiddler
Glowed like a living coal when the ashes are blown from
   the embers.
Gaily the old man sang to the vibrant sound of his fiddle,
*Tous les Bourgeois de Chartres*, and *Le Carillon de Dun-
   querque*,
And anon with his wooden shoes beat time to the music.
Merrily, merrily whirled the wheels of the dizzying dances

Under the orchard-trees and down the path to the
    meadows;
Old folk and young together, and children mingled among
    them.
Fairest of all the maids was Evangeline, Benedict's
    daughter!
Noblest of all the youths was Gabriel, son of the black-
    smith!

  So passed the morning away. And lo! with a summons
    sonorous
Sounded the bell from its tower, and over the meadows
    a drum beat.
Thronged erelong was the church with men. Without, in
    the churchyard,
Waited the women. They stood by the graves, and hung
    on the headstones
Garlands of autumn-leaves and evergreens fresh from the
    forest.
Then came the guard from the ships, and marching
    proudly among them
Entered the sacred portal. With loud and dissonant clangor
Echoed the sound of their brazen drums from ceiling and
    casement,—
Echoed a moment only, and slowly the ponderous portal
Closed, and in silence the crowd awaited the will of the
    soldiers.
Then uprose their commander, and spake from the steps
    of the altar,
Holding aloft in his hands, with its seals, the royal com-
    mission.
"You are convened this day," he said, "by his Majesty's
    orders.
Clement and kind has he been; but how you have answered
    his kindness,
Let your own hearts reply! To my natural make and my
    temper
Painful the task is I do, which to you I know must be
    grievous.
Yet must I bow and obey, and deliver the will of our
    monarch;
Namely, that all your lands, and dwellings, and cattle of
    all kinds

Forfeited be to the crown; and that you yourselves from
  this province
Be transported to other lands. God grant you may dwell
  there
Ever as faithful subjects, a happy and peaceable people!
Prisoners now I declare you; for such is his Majesty's
  pleasure!"
As, when the air is serene in sultry solstice of summer,
Suddenly gathers a storm, and the deadly sling of the
  hailstones
Beats down the farmer's corn in the field and shatters his
  windows,
Hiding the sun, and strewing the ground with thatch from
  the house-roofs,
Bellowing fly the herds, and seek to break their enclosures;
So on the hearts of the people descended the words of the
  speaker.
Silent a moment they stood in speechless wonder, and then
  rose
Louder and ever louder a wail of sorrow and anger,
And, by one impulse moved, they madly rushed to the
  door-way.
Vain was the hope of escape; and cries and fierce impre-
  cations
Rang through the house of prayer; and high o'er the heads
  of the others
Rose, with his arms uplifted, the figure of Basil the black-
  smith,
As, on a stormy sea, a spar is tossed by the billows.
Flushed was his face and distorted with passion; and wildly
  he shouted,—
"Down with the tyrants of England! we never have sworn
  them allegiance!
Death to these foreign soldiers, who seize on our homes
  and our harvests!"
More he fain would have said, but the merciless hand of
  a soldier
Smote him upon the mouth, and dragged him down to the
  pavement.

In the midst of the strife and tumult of angry contention,
Lo! the door of the chancel opened, and Father Felician
Entered, with serious mien, and ascended the steps of the
  altar.

Raising his reverend hand, with a gesture he awed into
    silence
All that clamorous throng; and thus he spake to his
    people;
Deep were his tones and solemn; in accents measured and
    mournful
Spake he, as, after the tocsin's alarum, distinctly the clock
    strikes.
"What is this that ye do, my children? what madness has
    seized you?
Forty years of my life have I labored among you, and
    taught you,
Not in word alone, but in deed, to love one another!
Is this the fruit of my toils, of my vigils and prayers and
    privations?
Have you so soon forgotten all lessons of love and forgive-
    ness?
This is the house of the Prince of Peace, and would you
    profane it
Thus with violent deeds and hearts overflowing with
    hatred?
Lo! where the crucified Christ from his cross is gazing
    upon you!
See! in those sorrowful eyes what meekness and holy
    compassion!
Hark! how those lips still repeat the prayer, 'O Father,
    forgive them!'
Let us repeat that prayer in the hour when the wicked
    assail us,
Let us repeat it now, and say, 'O Father, forgive them!' "
Few were his words of rebuke, but deep in the hearts of
    his people
Sank they, and sobs of contrition succeeded the passionate
    outbreak,
While they repeated his prayer, and said, "O Father, for-
    give them!"

    Then came the evening service. The tapers gleamed
    from the altar.
Fervent and deep was the voice of the priest, and the
    people responded,
Not with their lips alone, but their hearts; and the Ave
    Maria

Sang they, and fell on their knees, and their souls, with
　　devotion translated,
Rose on the ardor of prayer, like Elijah ascending to
　　heaven.

　Meanwhile had spread in the village the tidings of ill,
　　and on all sides
Wandered, wailing, from house to house the women and
　　children.
Long at her father's door Evangeline stood, with her right
　　hand
Shielding her eyes from the level rays of the sun, that,
　　descending,
Lighted the village street with mysterious splendor, and
　　roofed each
Peasant's cottage with golden thatch, and emblazoned its
　　windows.
Long within had been spread the snow-white cloth on the
　　table;
There stood the wheaten loaf, and the honey fragrant with
　　wild-flowers;
There stood the tankard of ale, and the cheese fresh
　　brought from the dairy,
And, at the head of the board, the great arm-chair of the
　　farmer.
Thus did Evangeline wait at her father's door, as the
　　sunset
Threw the long shadows of trees o'er the broad ambrosial
　　meadows.
Ah! on her spirit within a deeper shadow had fallen,
And from the fields of her soul a fragrance celestial
　　ascended,—
Charity, meekness, love, and hope, and forgiveness, and
　　patience!
Then, all-forgetful of self, she wandered into the village,
Cheering with looks and words the mournful hearts of
　　the women,
As o'er the darkening fields with lingering steps they
　　departed,
Urged by their household cares, and the weary feet of
　　their children.
Down sank the great red sun, and in golden, glimmering
　　vapors

Veiled the light of his face, like the Prophet descending
    from Sinai.
Sweetly over the village the bell of the Angelus sounded.


  Meanwhile, amid the gloom, by the church Evangeline
    lingered.
All was silent within; and in vain at the door and the
    windows
Stood she, and listened and looked, till, overcome by
    emotion,
"Gabriel!" cried she aloud with tremulous voice; but no
    answer
Came from the graves of the dead, nor the gloomier grave
    of the living.
Slowly at length she returned to the tenantless house of
    her father.
Smouldered the fire on the hearth, on the board was the
    supper untasted,
Empty and drear was each room, and haunted with phan-
    toms of terror.
Sadly echoed her step on the stair and the floor of her
    chamber.
In the dead of the night she heard the disconsolate rain
    fall
Loud on the withered leaves of the sycamore-tree by the
    window.
Keenly the lightning flashed; and the voice of the echoing
    thunder
Told her that God was in heaven, and governed the world
    he created!
Then she remembered the tale she had heard of the justice
    of Heaven;
Soothed was her troubled soul, and she peacefully slum-
    bered till morning.


## V


Four times the sun had risen and set; and now on the
    fifth day
Cheerily called the cock to the sleeping maids of the farm-
    house.

Soon o'er the yellow fields, in silent and mournful procession,
Came from the neighboring hamlets and farms the Acadian women,
Driving in ponderous wains their household goods to the seashore,
Pausing and looking back to gaze once more on their dwellings,
Ere they were shut from sight by the winding road and the woodland.
Close at their sides their children ran, and urged on the oxen.
While in their little hands they clasped some fragments of playthings.

Thus to the Gaspereau's mouth they hurried; and there on the sea-beach
Piled in confusion lay the household goods of the peasants.
All day long between the shore and the ships did the boats ply;
All day long the wains came laboring down from the village.
Late in the afternoon, when the sun was near to his setting,
Echoed far o'er the fields came the roll of drums from the churchyard.
Thither the women and children thronged. On a sudden the church-doors
Opened, and forth came the guard, and marching in gloomy procession
Followed the long-imprisoned, but patient, Acadian farmers.
Even as pilgrims, who journey afar from their homes and their country,
Sing as they go, and in singing forget they are weary and wayworn,
So with songs on their lips the Acadian peasants descended
Down from the church to the shore, amid their wives and their daughters.
Foremost the young men came: and, raising together their voices,
Sang with tremulous lips a chant of the Catholic Missions:—

"Sacred heart of the Saviour! O inexhaustible fountain!
Fill our hearts this day with strength and submission and
    patience!"
Then the old men, as they marched, and the women that
    stood by the way-side
Joined in the sacred psalm, and the birds in the sunshine
    above them
Mingled their notes therewith, like voices of spirits de-
    parted.

Half-way down to the shore Evangeline waited in
    silence,
Not overcome with grief, but strong in the hour of
    affliction,—
Calmly and sadly she waited, until the procession ap-
    proached her,
And she beheld the face of Gabriel pale with emotion.
Tears then filled her eyes, and, eagerly running to meet him,
Clasped she his hands, and laid her head on his shoulder,
    and whispered,—
"Gabriel! be of good cheer! for if we love one another
Nothing, in truth, can harm us, whatever mischances may
    happen!"
Smiling she spake these words; then suddenly paused, for
    her father
Saw she slowly advancing. Alas! how changed was his
    aspect!
Gone was the glow from his cheek, and the fire from his
    eye, and his footstep
Heavier seemed with the weight of the heavy heart in his
    bosom.
But with a smile and a sigh, she clasped his neck and
    embraced him,
Speaking words of endearment where words of comfort
    availed not.
Thus to the Gaspereau's mouth moved on that mournful
    procession.

There disorder prevailed, and the tumult and stir of
    embarking.
Busily plied the freighted boats; and in the confusion
Wives were torn from their husbands, and mothers, too
    late, saw their children

Left on the land, extending their arms, with wildest
    entreaties.
So unto separate ships were Basil and Gabriel carried,
While in despair on the shore Evangeline stood with her
    father.
Half the task was not done when the sun went down, and
    the twilight
Deepened and darkened around; and in haste the refluent
    ocean
Fled away from the shore, and left the line of the sand-
    beach
Covered with waifs of the tide, with kelp and the slippery
    sea-weed.
Farther back in the midst of the household goods and the
    wagons,
Like to a gypsy camp, or a leaguer after a battle,
All escape cut off by the sea, and the sentinels near
    them,
Lay encamped for the night the houseless Acadian farmers.
Back to its nethermost caves retreated the bellowing
    ocean,
Dragging adown the beach the rattling pebbles, and
    leaving
Inland and far up the shore the stranded boats of the
    sailors.
Then, as the night descended, the herds returned from
    their pastures;
Sweet was the moist still air with the odor of milk from
    their udders;
Lowing they waited, and long, at the well-known bars of
    the farm-yard,—
Waited and looked in vain for the voice and the hand
    of the milk-maid.
Silence reigned in the streets; from the church no Angelus
    sounded,
Rose no smoke from the roofs, and gleamed no lights from
    the windows.

But on the shores meanwhile the evening fires had been
    kindled,
Built of the drift-wood thrown on the sands from wrecks
    in the tempest.
Round them shapes of gloom and sorrowful faces were
    gathered,

Voices of women were heard, and of men, and the crying
 of children.
Onward from fire to fire, as from hearth to hearth in his
 parish,
Wandered the faithful priest, consoling and blessing and
 cheering,
Like unto shipwrecked Paul on Melita's desolate sea-shore.
Thus he approached the place where Evangeline sat with
 her father,
And in the flickering light beheld the face of the old
 man,
Haggard and hollow and wan, and without either thought
 or emotion,
E'en as the face of a clock from which the hands have
 been taken.
Vainly Evangeline strove with words and caresses to cheer
 him,
Vainly offered him food; yet he moved not, he looked
 not, he spake not,
But, with a vacant stare, ever gazed at the flickering fire-
 light.
"*Benedicite!*" murmured the priest, in tones of compas-
 sion.
More he fain would have said, but his heart was full, and
 his accents
Faltered and paused on his lips, as the feet of a child on
 a threshold,
Hushed by the scene he beholds, and the awful presence
 of sorrow.
Silently, therefore, he laid his hand on the head of the
 maiden,
Raising his tearful eyes to the silent stars that above them
Moved on the way, unperturbed by the wrongs and sor-
 rows of mortals.
Then sat he down at her side, and they wept together in
 silence.

 Suddenly rose from the south a light, as in autumn the
 blood-red
Moon climbs the crystal walls of heaven, and o'er the
 horizon
Titan-like stretches its hundred hands upon the mountain
 and meadow,

Seizing the rocks and the rivers and piling huge shadows
    together.
Broader and ever broader it gleamed on the roofs of the
    village,
Gleamed on the sky and sea, and the ships that lay in the
    roadstead.
Columns of shining smoke uprose, and flashes of flame
    were
Thrust through their folds and withdrawn, like the quiver-
    ing hands of a martyr.
Then as the wind seized the gleeds and the burning thatch,
    and, uplifting,
Whirled them aloft through the air, at once from a hun-
    dred house-tops
Started the sheeted smoke with flashes of flame inter-
    mingled.

  These things beheld in dismay the crowd on the shore
    and on shipboard.
Speechless at first they stood, then cried aloud in their
    anguish,
"We shall behold no more our homes in the village of
    Grand-Pré!"
Loud on a sudden the cocks began to crow in the farm-
    yards,
Thinking the day had dawned; and anon the lowing of
    cattle
Came on the evening breeze, by the barking of dogs
    interrupted.
Then rose a sound of dread, such as startles the sleeping
    encampments
Far in the western prairies or forests that skirt the
    Nebraska,
When the wild horses affrighted sweep by with the speed
    of the whirlwind,
Or the loud bellowing herds of buffaloes rush to the
    river.
Such was the sound that arose on the night, as the herds
    and the horses
Broke through their folds and fences, and madly rushed
    o'er the meadows.

  Overwhelmed with the sight, yet speechless, the priest
    and the maiden

Gazed on the scene of terror that reddened and widened
    before them:
And as they turned at length to speak to their silent
    companion,
Lo! from his seat he had fallen, and stretched abroad on
    the sea-shore
Motionless lay his form, from which the soul had departed.
Slowly the priest uplifted the lifeless head, and the maiden
Knelt at her father's side, and wailed aloud in her terror.
Then in a swoon she sank, and lay with her head on his
    bosom.
Through the long night she lay in deep, oblivious slumber;
And when she awoke from the trance, she beheld a
    multitude near her.
Faces of friends she beheld, that were mournfully gazing
    upon her,
Pallid, with tearful eyes, and looks of saddest compassion.
Still the blaze of the burning village illumined the land-
    scape,
Reddened the sky overhead, and gleamed on the faces
    around her,
And like the day of doom it seemed to her wavering
    senses.
Then a familiar voice she heard, as it said to the people,—
"Let us bury him here by the sea. When a happier season
Brings us again to our homes from the unknown land of
    our exile,
Then shall his sacred dust be piously laid in the church-
    yard."
Such were the words of the priest. And there in haste by
    the sea-side,
Having the glare of the burning village for funeral torches,
But without bell or book, they buried the farmer of
    Grand-Pré.
And as the voice of the priest repeated the service of
    sorrow,
Lo! with a mournful sound, like the voice of a vast con-
    gregation,
Solemnly answered the sea, and mingled its roar with
    the dirges.
'Twas the returning tide, that afar from the waste of the
    ocean,

With the first dawn of the day, came heaving and hurry-
    ing landward.
Then recommenced once more the stir and noise of em-
    barking;
And with the ebb of the tide the ships sailed out of the
    harbor,
Leaving behind them the dead on the shore, and the
    village in ruins.

## PART THE SECOND

### I

Many a weary year had passed since the burning of
    Grand-Pré,
When on the falling tide the freighted vessels departed,
Bearing a nation, with all its household gods, into exile,
Exile without an end, and without an example in story.
Far asunder, on separate coasts, the Acadians landed;
Scattered were they, like flakes of snow, when the wind
    from the northeast
Strikes aslant through the fogs that darken the Banks of
    Newfoundland.
Friendless, homeless, hopeless, they wandered from city
    to city,
From the cold lakes of the North to sultry Southern
    savannas,—
From the bleak shores of the sea to the lands where the
    Father of Waters
Seizes the hills in his hands, and drags them down to the
    ocean,
Deep in their sands to bury the scattered bones of the
    mammoth.
Friends they sought and homes; and many, despairing,
    heart-broken,
Asked of the earth but a grave, and no longer a friend
    nor a fireside.
Written their history stands on tablets of stone in the
    churchyards.
Long among them was seen a maiden who waited and
    wandered,

Lowly and meek in spirit, and patiently suffering all
   things.
Fair was she and young: but, alas! before her extended,
Dreary and vast and silent, the desert of life, with its
   pathway
Marked by the graves of those who had sorrowed and
   suffered before her,
Passions long extinguished, and hopes long dead and
   abandoned,
As the emigrant's way o'er the Western desert is marked
   by
Camp-fires long consumed, and bones that bleach in the
   sunshine.
Something there was in her life incomplete, imperfect,
   unfinished;
As if a morning of June, with all its music and sunshine
Suddenly paused in the sky, and, fading, slowly descended
Into the east again, from whence it late had arisen.
Sometimes she lingered in towns, till, urged by the fever
   within her,
Urged by a restless longing, the hunger and thirst of the
   spirit,
She would commence again her endless search and en-
   deavor;
Sometimes in churchyards strayed, and gazed on the
   crosses and tombstones,
Sat by some nameless grave, and thought that perhaps in
   its bosom
He was already at rest, and she longed to slumber beside
   him.
Sometimes a rumor, a hearsay, an inarticulate whisper,
Came with its airy hand to point and beckon her forward.
Sometimes she spake with those who had seen her beloved
   and known him,
But it was long ago, in some far-off place or forgotten.
"Gabriel Lajeunesse!" they said; "Oh yes! we have seen
   him.
He was with Basil the blacksmith, and both have gone to
   the prairies;
Coureurs-des-Bois are they, and famous hunters and
   trappers."
"Gabriel Lajeunesse!" said others; "Oh yes! we have seen
   him.

He is a Voyageur in the lowlands of Louisiana."
Then would they say, "Dear child! why dream and wait
     for him longer?
Are there not other youths as fair as Gabriel? others
Who have hearts as tender and true, and spirits as loyal?
Here is Baptiste Leblanc, the notary's son, who has loved
     thee
Many a tedious year; come, give him thy hand and be
     happy!
Thou art too fair to be left to braid St. Catherine's tresses."
Then would Evangeline answer, serenely but sadly, "I
     cannot!
Whither my heart has gone, there follows my hand, and
     not elsewhere.
For when the heart goes before, like a lamp, and illumines
     the pathway,
Many things are made clear, that else lie hidden in
     darkness."
Thereupon the priest, her friend and father-confessor,
Said, with a smile, "O daughter! thy God thus speaketh
     within thee!
Talk not of wasted affection, affection never was wasted;
If it enrich not the heart of another, its waters, returning
Back to their springs, like the rain, shall fill them full of
     refreshment;
That which the fountain sends forth returns again to the
     fountain.
Patience; accomplish thy labor; accomplish thy work of
     affection!
Sorrow and silence are strong, and patient endurance is
     godlike,
Therefore accomplish thy labor of love, till the heart is
     made godlike,
Purified, strengthened, perfected, and rendered more
     worthy of heaven!"
Cheered by the good man's words, Evangeline labored
     and waited.
Still in her heart she heard the funeral dirge of the ocean,
But with its sound there was mingled a voice that whis-
     pered, "Despair not!"
Thus did that poor soul wander in want and cheerless
     discomfort,

Bleeding, barefooted, over the shards and thorns of
    existence.
Let me essay, O Muse! to follow the wanderer's foot-
    steps;—
Not through each devious path, each changeful year of
    existence,
But as a traveller follows a streamlet's course through the
    valley:
Far from its margin at times, and seeing the gleam of its
    water
Here and there, in some open space, and at intervals only;
Then drawing nearer its banks, through sylvan glooms that
    conceal it,
Though he behold it not, he can hear its continuous
    murmur;
Happy, at length, if he find the spot where it reaches an
    outlet.

## II

It was the month of May. Far down the Beautiful River,
Past the Ohio shore and past the mouth of the Wabash,
Into the golden stream of the broad and swift Mississippi,
Floated a cumbrous boat, that was rowed by Acadian
    boatmen.
It was a band of exiles: a raft, as it were, from the ship-
    wrecked
Nation, scattered along the coast, now floating together,
Bound by the bonds of a common belief and a common
    misfortune;
Men and women and children, who, guided by hope or by
    hearsay,
Sought for their kith and their kin among the few-acred
    farmers
On the Acadian coast, and in the prairies of fair Opelousas.
With them Evangeline went, and her guide, the Father
    Felician.
Onward o'er sunken sands, through a wilderness sombre
    with forests,
Day after day they glided adown the turbulent river;
Night after night, by their blazing fires, encamped on its
    borders.

Now through rushing chutes, among green islands, where
 plumelike
Cotton-trees nodded their shadowy crests, they swept with
 the current,
Then emerged into broad lagoons, where silvery sand-bars
Lay in the stream, and along the wimpling waves of their
 margin,
Shining with snow-white plumes, large flocks of pelicans
 waded.
Level the landscape grew, and along the shores of the
 river,
Shaded by china-trees, in the midst of luxuriant gardens,
Stood the houses of planters, with negro-cabins and dove-
 cots.
They were approaching the region where reigns perpetual
 summer,
Where through the Golden Coast, and groves of orange
 and citron,
Sweeps with majestic curve the river away to the eastward.
They, too, swerved from their course; and entering the
 Bayou of Plaquemine,
Soon were lost in a maze of sluggish and devious waters,
Which, like a network of steel, extended in every direction.
Over their heads the towering and tenebrous boughs of the
 cypress
Met in a dusky arch, and trailing mosses in mid-air
Waved like banners that hang on the walls of ancient
 cathedrals.
Deathlike the silence seemed, and unbroken, save by the
 herons
Home to their roosts in the cedar-trees returning at sunset,
Or by the owl, as he greeted the moon with demoniac
 laughter.
Lovely the moonlight was as it glanced and gleamed on
 the water,
Gleamed on the columns of cypress and cedar sustaining
 the arches,
Down through whose broken vaults it fell as through
 chinks in a ruin.
Dreamlike, and indistinct, and strange were all things
 around them;
And o'er their spirits there came a feeling of wonder and
 sadness,—

Strange forebodings of ill, unseen and that cannot be
   compassed.
As, at the tramp of a horse's hoof on the turf of the
   prairies,
Far in advance are closed the leaves of the shrinking
   mimosa,
So, at the hoof-beats of fate, with sad forebodings of
   evil,
Shrinks and closes the heart, ere the stroke of doom has
   attained it.
But Evangeline's heart was sustained by a vision, that
   faintly
Floated before her eyes, and beckoned her on through
   the moonlight.
It was the thought of her brain that assumed the shape
   of a phantom.
Through those shadowy aisles had Gabriel wandered be-
   fore her,
And every stroke of the oar now brought him nearer and
   nearer.

   Then in his place, at the prow of the boat, rose one of
   the oarsmen,
And, as a signal sound, if others like them peradventure
Sailed on those gloomy and midnight streams, blew a blast
   on his bugle.
Wild through the dark colonnades and corridors leafy the
   blast rang,
Breaking the seal of silence, and giving tongues to the
   forest.
Soundless above them the banners of moss just stirred to
   the music.
Multitudinous echoes awoke and died in the distance,
Over the watery floor, and beneath the reverberant
   branches;
But not a voice replied; no answer came from the dark-
   ness;
And, when the echoes had ceased, like a sense of pain was
   the silence.
Then Evangeline slept; but the boatmen rowed through
   the midnight,
Silent at times, then singing familiar Canadian boat-songs,
Such as they sang of old on their own Acadian rivers,

While through the night were heard the mysterious sounds
    of the desert,
Far off,—indistinct,—as of wave or wind in the forest,
Mixed with the whoop of the crane and the roar of the
    grim alligator.

  Thus ere another noon they emerged from the shades;
    and before them
Lay, in the golden sun, the lakes of the Atchafalaya.
Water-lilies in myriads rocked on the slight undulations
Made by the passing oars, and, resplendent in beauty, the
    lotus
Lifted her golden crown above the heads of the boatmen.
Faint was the air with the odorous breath of magnolia
    blossoms,
And with the heat of noon; and numberless sylvan islands,
Fragrant and thickly embowered with blossoming hedges
    of roses,
Near to whose shores they glided along, invited to slumber.
Soon by the fairest of these their weary oars were sus-
    pended.
Under the boughs of Wachita willows, that grew by the
    margin,
Safely their boat was moored; and scattered about on the
    greensward,
Tired with their midnight toil, the weary travellers slum-
    bered.
Over them vast and high extended the cope of a cedar.
Swinging from its great arms, the trumpet-flower and the
    grapevine
Hung their ladder of ropes aloft like the ladder of Jacob,
On whose pendulous stairs the angels ascending, descend-
    ing,
Were the swift humming-birds, that flitted from blossom
    to blossom.
Such was the vision Evangeline saw as she slumbered
    beneath it.
Filled was her heart with love, and the dawn of an open-
    ing heaven
Lighted her soul in sleep with the glory of regions
    celestial.

  Nearer, and ever nearer, among the numberless islands,
Darted a light, swift boat, that sped away o'er the water,

Urged on its course by the sinewy arms of hunters and
  trappers.
Northward its prow was turned, to the land of the bison
  and beaver.
At the helm sat a youth, with countenance thoughtful
  and careworn.
Dark and neglected locks overshadowed his brow, and a
  sadness
Somewhat beyond his years on his face was legibly written.
Gabriel was it, who, weary with waiting, unhappy and
  restless,
Sought in the Western wilds oblivion of self and of
  sorrow.
Swiftly they glided along, close under the lee of the island,
But by the opposite bank, and behind a screen of pal-
  mettos,
So that they saw not the boat, where it lay concealed in
  the willows;
All undisturbed by the dash of their oars, and unseen,
  were the sleepers.
Angel of God was there none to awaken the slumbering
  maiden.
Swiftly they glided away, like the shade of a cloud on
  the prairie.
After the sound of their oars on the tholes had died in
  the distance,
As from a magic trance the sleepers awoke, and the
  maiden
Said with a sigh to the friendly priest, "O Father Felician!
Something says in my heart that near me Gabriel wanders.
Is it a foolish dream, an idle and vague superstition?
Or has an angel passed, and revealed the truth to my
  spirit?"
Then, with a blush, she added, "Alas for my credulous
  fancy!
Unto ears like thine such words as these have no mean-
  ing."
But made answer the reverend man, and he smiled as he
  answered,—
"Daughter, thy words are not idle; nor are they to me
  without meaning.
Feeling is deep and still; and the word that floats on the
  surface

Is as the tossing buoy, that betrays where the anchor
    is hidden.
Therefore trust to thy heart, and to what the world calls
    illusions.
Gabriel truly is near thee; for not far away to the south-
    ward,
On the banks of the Têche, are the towns of St. Maur and
    St. Martin.
There the long-wandering bride shall be given again to
    her bridegroom,
There the long-absent pastor regain his flock and his
    sheepfold.
Beautiful is the land, with its prairies and forests of fruit-
    trees;
Under the feet a garden of flowers, and the bluest of
    heavens
Bending above, and resting its dome on the walls of the
    forest.
They who dwell there have named it the Eden of
    Louisiana!"

  With these words of cheer they arose and continued
    their journey.
Softly the evening came. The sun from the western
    horizon
Like a magician extended his golden wand o'er the land-
    scape;
Twinkling vapors arose; and sky and water and forest
Seemed all on fire at the touch, and melted and mingled
    together.
Hanging between two skies, a cloud with edges of silver,
Floated the boat, with its dripping oars, on the motion-
    less water.
Filled was Evangeline's heart with inexpressible sweetness.
Touched by the magic spell, the sacred fountains of feel-
    ing
Glowed with the light of love, as the skies and waters
    around her.
Then from a neighboring thicket the mocking-bird, wildest
    of singers,
Swinging aloft on a willow spray that hung o'er the water,
Shook from his little throat such floods of delirious music,
That the whole air and the woods and the waves seemed
    silent to listen.

Plaintive at first were the tones and sad: then soaring to
    madness
Seemed they to follow or guide the revel of frenzied
    Bacchantes.
Single notes were then heard, in sorrowful, low lamenta-
    tion;
Till, having gathered them all, he flung them abroad in
    derision,
As when, after a storm, a gust of wind through the tree-
    tops
Shakes down the rattling rain in a crystal shower on the
    branches.
With such a prelude as this, and hearts that throbbed
    with emotion,
Slowly they entered the Têche, where it flows through
    the Opelousas,
And, through the amber air, above the crest of the wood-
    land,
Saw the column of smoke that arose from a neighboring
    dwelling;—
Sounds of a horn they heard, and the distant lowing of
    cattle.

## III

Near to the bank of the river, o'ershadowed by oaks,
    from whose branches
Garlands of Spanish moss and of mystic mistletoe flaunted,
Such as the Druids cut down with golden hatchets at
    Yule-tide,
Stood, secluded and still, the house of the herdsman. A
    garden
Girded it round about with a belt of luxuriant blossoms,
Filling the air with fragrance. The house itself was of
    timbers
Hewn from the cypress-tree, and carefully fitted together.
Large and low was the roof; and on slender columns sup-
    ported,
Rose-wreathed, vine-encircled, a broad and spacious
    veranda,
Haunt of the humming-bird and the bee, extended around
    it.

At each end of the house, amid the flowers of the garden,
Stationed the dove-cots were, as love's perpetual symbol,
Scenes of endless wooing, and endless contentions of
rivals.
Silence reigned o'er the place. The line of shadow and
sunshine
Ran near the tops of the trees; but the house itself was in
shadow,
And from its chimney-top, ascending and slowly expand-
ing
Into the evening air, a thin blue column of smoke rose.
In the rear of the house, from the garden gate, ran a
pathway
Through the great groves of oak to the skirts of the limit-
less prairie,
Into whose sea of flowers the sun was slowly descending.
Full in his track of light, like ships with shadowy canvas
Hanging loose from their spars in a motionless calm in the
tropics,
Stood a cluster of trees, with tangled cordage of grape-
vines.

Just where the woodlands met the flowery surf of the
prairie,
Mounted upon his horse, with Spanish saddle and stirrups,
Sat a herdsman, arrayed in gaiters and doublet of deer-
skin.
Broad and brown was the face that from under the Spanish
sombrero
Gazed on the peaceful scene, with the lordly look of its
master.
Round about him were numberless herds of kine, that
were grazing
Quietly in the meadows, and breathing the vapory fresh
ness
That uprose from the river, and spread itself over the
landscape.
Slowly lifting the horn that hung at his side, and ex-
panding
Fully his broad, deep chest, he blew a blast, that re-
sounded
Wildly and sweet and far, through the still damp air of
the evening.

Suddenly out of the grass the long white horns of the
    cattle
Rose like flakes of foam on the adverse currents of ocean.
Silent a moment they gazed, then bellowing rushed o'er
    the prairie,
And the whole mass became a cloud, a shade in the
    distance.
Then, as the herdsman turned to the house, through the
    gate of the garden
Saw he the forms of the priest and the maiden advancing
    to meet him.
Suddenly down from his horse he sprang in amazement,
    and forward
Rushed with extended arms and exclamations of wonder;
When they beheld his face, they recognized Basil the
    blacksmith.
Hearty his welcome was, as he led his guests to the
    garden.
There in an arbor of roses with endless question and
    answer
Gave they vent to their hearts, and renewed their friendly
    embraces,
Laughing and weeping by turns, or sitting silent and
    thoughtful.
Thoughtful, for Gabriel came not; and now dark doubts
    and misgivings
Stole o'er the maiden's heart; and Basil, somewhat em-
    barrassed,
Broke the silence and said, "If you came by the Atcha-
    falaya,
How have you nowhere encountered my Gabriel's boat
    on the bayous?"
Over Evangeline's face at the words of Basil a shade
    passed.
Tears came into her eyes, and she said, with a tremulous
    accent,
"Gone? is Gabriel gone?" and, concealing her face on his
    shoulder,
All her o'erburdened heart gave way, and she wept and
    lamented.
Then the good Basil said,—and his voice grew blithe as he
    said it,—

"Be of good cheer, my child; it is only to-day he departed.
Foolish boy! he has left me alone with my herds and my
    horses.
Moody and restless grown, and tired and troubled, his
    spirit
Could no longer endure the calm of this quiet existence,
Thinking ever of thee, uncertain and sorrowful ever,
Ever silent, or speaking only of thee and his troubles,
He at length had become so tedious to men and to
    maidens,
Tedious even to me, that at length I be-thought me, and
    sent him
Unto the town of Adayes to trade for mules with the
    Spaniards.
Thence he will follow the Indian trails to the Ozark Moun-
    tains,
Hunting for furs in the forests, on rivers trapping the
    beaver.
Therefore be of good cheer; we will follow the fugitive
    lover;
He is not far on his way, and the Fates and the streams
    are against him.
Up and away to-morrow, and through the red dew of the
    morning
We will follow him fast, and bring him back to his prison."

    Then glad voices were heard, and up from the banks of
    the river,
Borne aloft on his comrades' arms, came Michael the
    fiddler.
Long under Basil's roof had he lived like a god on Olym-
    pus,
Having no other care than dispensing music to mortals.
Far renowned was he for his silver locks and his fiddle.
"Long live Michael," they cried. "our brave Acadian
    minstrel!"
As they bore him aloft in triumphal procession; and
    straightway
Father Felician advanced with Evangeline, greeting the
    old man
Kindly and oft, and recalling the past, while Basil, en-
    raptured,

Hailed with hilarious joy his old companions and gossips,
Laughing loud and long, and embracing mothers and
daughters.
Much they marvelled to see the wealth of the ci-devant
blacksmith,
All his domains and his herds, and his patriarchal de-
meanor;
Much they marvelled to hear his tales of the soil and the
climate,
And of the prairies, whose numberless herds were his who
would take them;
Each one thought in his heart, that he, too, would go and
do likewise.
Thus they ascended the steps, and crossing the breezy
veranda,
Entered the hall of the house, where already the supper
of Basil
Waited his late return; and they rested and feasted together.

Over the joyous feast the sudden darkness descended.
All was silent without, and, illuming the landscape witn
silver,
Fair rose the dewy moon and the myriad stars; but within
doors,
Brighter than these, shone the faces of friends in the glim-
mering lamplight.
Then from his station aloft, at the head of the table, the
herdsman
Poured forth his heart and his wine together in endless
profusion.
Lighting his pipe, that was filled with sweet Natchitoches
tobacco,
Thus he spake to his guests, who listened, and smiled as
they listened:—
"Welcome once more, my friends, who long have been
friendless and homeless,
Welcome once more to a home, that is better perchance
than the old one!
Here no hungry winter congeals our blood like the rivers;
Here no stony ground provokes the wrath of the farmer.
Smoothly the ploughshare runs through the soil, as a keel
through the water.

All the year round the orange-groves are in blossom; and grass grows
More in a single night than a whole Canadian summer.
Here, too, numberless herds run wild and unclaimed in the prairies;
Here, too, lands may be had for the asking, and forests of timber
With a few blows of the axe are hewn and framed into houses.
After your houses are built, and your fields are yellow with harvests,
No King George of England shall drive you away from your homesteads,
Burning your dwellings and barns, and stealing your farms and your cattle."
Speaking these words, he blew a wrathful cloud from his nostrils,
While his huge, brown hand came thundering down on the table
So that the guests all started; and Father Felician, astounded,
Suddenly paused, with a pinch of snuff halfway to his nostrils.
But the brave Basil resumed, and his words were milder and gayer:—
"Only beware of the fever, my friends, beware of the fever!
For it is not like that of our cold Acadian climate,
Cured by wearing a spider hung round one's neck in a nutshell!"
Then there were voices heard at the door, and footsteps approaching
Sounded upon the stairs and the floor of the breezy veranda.
It was the neighboring Creoles and small Acadian planters,
Who had been summoned all to the house of Basil the Herdsman.
Merry the meeting was of ancient comrades and neighbors:
Friend clasped friend in his arms; and they who before were as strangers,
Meeting in exile, became straightway as friends to each other,

Drawn by the gentle bond of a common country together.
But in the neighboring hall a strain of music, proceeding
From the accordant strings of Michael's melodious fiddle,
Broke up all further speech. Away, like children delighted,
All things forgotten beside, they gave themselves to the
    maddening
Whirl of the giddy dance, as it swept and swayed to the
    music,
Dreamlike, with beaming eyes and the rush of fluttering
    garments.

  Meanwhile, apart, at the head of the hall, the priest and
    the herdsman
Sat, conversing together of past and present and future;
While Evangeline stood like one entranced, for within her
Olden memories rose, and loud in the midst of the music
Heard she the sound of the sea, and an irrepressible
    sadness
Came o'er her heart, and unseen she stole forth into the
    garden.
Beautiful was the night. Behind the black wall of the forest,
Tipping its summit with silver, arose the moon. On the
    river
Fell here and there through the branches a tremulous
    gleam of the moonlight,
Like the sweet thoughts of love on a darkened and devious
    spirit.
Nearer and round about her, the manifold flowers of the
    garden
Poured out their souls in odors, that were their prayers and
    confessions
Unto the night, as it went its way, like a silent Carthusian.
Fuller of fragrance than they, and as heavy with shadows
    and night-dews,·
Hung the heart of the maiden. The calm and the magical
    moonlight
Seemed to inundate her soul with indefinable longings,
As, through the garden-gate, and beneath the shade of the
    oak-trees,
Passed she along the path to the edge of the measureless
    prairie.
Silent it lay, with a silvery haze upon it, and fire-flies
Gleamed and floated away in mingled and infinite numbers.

Over her head the stars, the thoughts of God in the
    heavens,
Shone on the eyes of man, who had ceased to marvel and
    worship,
Save when a blazing comet was seen on the walls of that
    temple,
As if a hand had appeared and written upon them, "Up-
    harsin."
And the soul of the maiden, between the stars and the fire-
    flies,
Wandered alone, and she cried, "O Gabriel! O my be-
    loved!
Art thou so near unto me, and yet I cannot behold thee?
Art thou so near unto me, and yet thy voice does not
    reach me?
Ah! how often thy feet have trod this path to the prairie!
Ah, how often thine eyes have looked on the woodlands
    around me!
Ah! how often beneath this oak, returning from labor,
Thou hast lain down to rest, and to dream of me in thy
    slumbers!
When shall these eyes behold, these arms be folded about
    thee?"
Loud and sudden and near the notes of a whippoorwill
    sounded
Like a flute in the woods; and anon, through the neighbor-
    ing thickets,
Farther and farther away it floated and dropped into
    silence.
"Patience!" whispered the oaks from oracular caverns of
    darkness:
And, from the moonlit meadow, a sigh responded, "To-
    morrow!"

  Bright rose the sun next day; and all the flowers of the
    garden
Bathed his shining feet with their tears, and anointed his
    tresses
With the delicious balm that they bore in their vases of
    crystal.
"Farewell!" said the priest, as he stood at the shadowy
    threshold;

"See that you bring us the Prodigal Son from his fasting
    and famine,
And, too, the Foolish Virgin, who slept when the bride-
    groom was coming."
"Farewell!" answered the maiden, and, smiling, with Basil
    descended
Down to the river's brink, where the boat-men already
    were waiting.
Thus beginning their journey with morning, and sunshine,
    and gladness,
Swiftly they followed the flight of him who was speeding
    before them,
Blown by the blast of fate like a dead leaf over the desert.
Not that day, nor the next, nor yet the day that succeeded,
Found they the trace of his course, in lake or forest or
    river,
Nor, after many days, had they found him; but vague and
    uncertain
Rumors alone were their guides through a wild and deso-
    late country;
Till, at the little inn of the Spanish town of Adayes,
Weary and worn, they alighted, and learned from the gar-
    rulous landlord,
That on the day before, with horses and guides and com-
    panions,
Gabriel left the village, and took the road of the prairies.

## IV

Far in the West there lies a desert land, where the moun-
    tains
Lift, through perpetual snows, their lofty and luminous
    summits.
Down from their jagged, deep ravines, where the gorge,
    like a gateway,
Opens a passage rude to the wheels of the emigrant's
    wagon,
Westward the Oregon flows and the Walleway and
    Owyhee.
Eastward, with devious course, among the Wind-river
    Mountains,

Through the Sweet-water Valley precipitate leaps the Ne-
braska;
And to the south, from Fontaine-qui-bout and the Spanish
sierras,
Fretted with sands and rocks, and swept by the winds of the
desert,
Numberless torrents, with ceaseless sound, descend to the
ocean,
Like the great chords of a harp, in loud and solemn vi-
brations.
Spreading between these streams are the wondrous, beau-
tiful prairies;
Billowy bays of grass ever rolling in shadow and sunshine,
Bright with luxuriant clusters of roses and purple amor-
phas.
Over them wandered the buffalo herds, and the elk and the
roebuck;
Over them wandered the wolves, and herds of riderless
horses;
Fires that blast and blight, and winds that are weary
with travel;
Over them wander the scattered tribes of Ishmael's chil-
dren,
Staining the desert with blood; and above their terrible
war-trials
Circles and sails aloft, on pinions majestic, the vulture,
Like the implacable soul of a chieftain slaughtered in
battle,
By invisible stairs ascending and scaling the heavens.
Here and there rise smokes from the camps of these savage
marauders;
Here and there rise groves from the margins of swift-run-
ning rivers;
And the grim, taciturn bear, the anchorite monk of the
desert,
Climbs down their dark ravines to dig for roots by the
brook-side,
And over all is the sky, the clear and crystalline heaven,
Like the protecting hand of God inverted above them.

Into this wonderful land, at the base of the Ozark Moun-
tains,
Gabriel far had entered, with hunters and trappers behind
him.

Day after day, with their Indian guides, the maiden and
    Basil
Followed his flying steps, and thought each day to o'ertake
    him.
Sometimes they saw, or thought they saw, the smoke of
    his camp-fire
Rise in the morning air from the distant plain; but at night-
    fall,
When they had reached the place they found only embers
    and ashes.
And, though their hearts were sad at times and their
    bodies were weary,
Hope still guided them on, as the magic Fata Morgana
Showed them her lakes of light, that retreated and vanished
    before them.
  Once, as they sat by their evening fire, there silently
    entered
Into their little camp an Indian woman, whose features
Wore deep traces of sorrow, and patience as great as her
    sorrow.
She was a Shawnee woman returning home to her people,
From the far-off hunting grounds of the cruel Camanches,
Where her Canadian husband, a Coureur-des-Bois, had
    been murdered.
Touched were their hearts at her story, and warmest and
    friendliest welcome
Gave they, with words of cheer, and she sat and feasted
    among them
On the buffalo-meat and the venison cooked on the em-
    bers.
But when their meal was done, and Basil and all his com-
    panions,
Worn with the long day's march and the chase of the deer
    and the bison,
Stretched themselves on the ground, and slept where the
    quivering fire-light
Flashed on their swarthy cheeks, and their forms wrapped
    up in their blankets,
Then at the door of Evangeline's tent she sat and re-
    peated
Slowly, with soft, low voice, and the charm of her Indian
    accent,

All the tale of her love, with its pleasures, and pains, and
   reverses.
Much Evangeline wept at the tale, and to know that an-
   other
Hapless heart like her own had loved and had been dis-
   appointed.
Moved to the depths of her soul by pity and woman's com-
   passion,
Yet in her sorrow pleased that one who had suffered was
   near her,
She in turn related her love and all its disasters.
Mute with wonder the Shawnee sat, and when she had
   ended
Still was mute; but at length, as if a mysterious horror
Passed through her brain, she spake, and repeated the
   tale of the Mowis;
Mowis, the bridegroom of snow, who won and wedded a
   maiden,
But, when the morning came, arose and passed from the
   wigwam,
Fading and melting away and dissolving into the sunshine,
Till she beheld him no more, though she followed far into
   the forest.
Then, in those sweet, low tones, that seemed like a weird
   incantation,
Told she the tale of the fair Lilinau, who was wooed by a
   phantom,
That through the pines o'er her father's lodge, in the hush
   of the twilight,
Breathed like the evening wind, and whispered love to the
   maiden,
Till she followed his green and waving plume through the
   forest,
And nevermore returned, nor was seen again by her
   people.
Silent with wonder and strange surprise, Evangeline lis-
   tened
To the soft flow of her magical words, till the region around
   her
Seemed like enchanted ground, and her swarthy guest the
   enchantress.
Slowly over the tops of the Ozark Mountains the moon
   rose,

Lighting the little tent, and with a mysterious splendor
Touching the sombre leaves, and embracing and filling
    the woodland.
With a delicious sound the brook rushed by, and the
    branches
Swayed and sighed overhead in scarcely audible whispers.
Filled with the thoughts of love was Evangeline's heart,
    but a secret,
Subtile sense crept in of pain and indefinite terror,
As the cold, poisonous snake creeps into the nest of the
    swallow.
It was no earthly fear. A breath from the region of spirits
Seemed to float in the air of night; and she felt for a mo-
    ment
That, like the Indian maid, she, too, was pursuing a phan-
    tom.
With this thought she slept, and the fear and the phantom
    had vanished.


    Early upon the morrow the march was resumed; and the
    Shawnee
Said, as they journeyed along, "On the western slope of
    these mountains
Dwells in his little village the Black Robe chief of the
    Mission.
Much he teaches the people, and tells them of Mary and
    Jesus.
Loud laugh their hearts with joy, and weep with pain,
    as they hear him."
Then, with a sudden and secret emotion, Evangeline an-
    swered,
"Let us go to the Mission, for there good tidings await us!"
Thither they turned their steeds; and behind a spur of the
    mountains,
Just as the sun went down, they heard a murmur of voices,
And in a meadow green and broad, by the bank of a river,
Saw the tents of the Christians, the tents of the Jesuit Mis-
    sion.
Under the towering oak, that stood in the midst of the
    village,
Knelt the Black Robe chief with his children. A crucifix
    fastened

High on the trunk of the tree, and over-shadowed by
    grapevines,
Looked with its agonized face on the multitude kneeling
    beneath it.
This was their rural chapel. Aloft, through the intricate
    arches
Of its aerial roof, arose the chant of their vespers,
Mingling its notes with the soft susurrus and sighs of the
    branches.
Silent, with heads uncovered, the travellers, nearer ap-
    proaching,
Knelt on the swarded floor, and joined in the evening de-
    votions.
But when the service was done, and the benediction had
    fallen
Forth from the hands of the priest, like seed from the
    hands of the sower,
Slowly the reverend man advanced to the strangers, and
    bade them
Welcome; and when they replied, he smiled with benignant
    expression,
Hearing the homelike sounds of his mother-tongue in the
    forest,
And, with words of kindness, conducted them into his
    wigwam.
There upon mats and skins they reposed, and on cakes
    of the maize-ear
Feasted, and slaked their thirst from the water gourd of the
    teacher.
Soon was their story told; and the priest with solemnity
    answered:—
"Not six guns have risen and set since Gabriel, seated
On this mat by my side, where now the maiden reposes,
Told me this same sad tale; then arose and continued his
    journey!"
Soft was the voice of the priest, and he spake with an ac-
    cent of kindness;
But on Evangeline's heart fell his words as in winter the
    snow-flakes
Fall into some lone nest from which the birds have de-
    parted.
"Far to the north he has gone," continued the priest; "but
    in autumn,

When the chase is done, will return again to the Mission."
Then Evangeline said, and her voice was meek and sub-
    missive,
"Let me remain with thee, for my soul is sad and afflicted."
So seemed it wise and well unto all; and betimes on the
    morrow,
Mounting his Mexican steed, with his Indian guides and
    companions,
Homeward Basil returned, and Evangeline stayed at the
    Mission.

  Slowly, slowly, slowly the days succeeded each other,—
Days and weeks and months; and the fields of maize that
    were springing
Green from the ground when a stranger she came, now
    waving above her,
Lifted their slender shafts, with leaves interlacing, and
    forming
Cloisters for mendicant crows and granaries pillaged by
    the squirrels.
Then in the golden weather the maize was husked, and the
    maidens
Blushed at each blood-red ear, for that betokened a lover,
But at the crooked laughed, and called it a thief in the
    corn-field.
Even the blood-red ear to Evangeline brought not her
    lover.
"Patience!" the priest would say; "have faith, and thy
    prayer will be answered!
Look at this vigorous plant that lifts its head from the
    meadow,
See how its leaves are turned to the north, as true as the
    magnet;
This is the compass-flower, that the finger of God has
    planted
Here in the houseless wild, to direct the traveller's journey
Over the sea-like, pathless, limitless waste of the desert.
Such in the soul of man is faith. The blossoms of passion,
Gay and luxuriant flowers, are brighter and fuller of fra-
    grance,
But they beguile us, and lead us astray, and their odor is
    deadly.

Only this humble plant can guide us here, and hereafter
Crown us with asphodel flowers, that are wet with the dews
    of nepenthe."


  So came the autumn, and passed, and the winter,—yet
    Gabriel came not;
Blossomed the opening spring and the notes of the robin
    and bluebird
Sounded sweet upon wold and in wood, yet Gabriel came
    not.
But on the breath of the summer winds a rumor was wafted
Sweeter than song of bird, or hue or odor of blossom.
Far to the north and east, it said, in the Michigan forests,
Gabriel had his lodge by the banks of the Saginaw River.
And, with returning guides, that sought the lakes of St.
    Lawrence,
Saying a sad farewell, Evangeline went from the Mission.
When over weary ways, by long and perilous marches,
She had attained at length the depths of the Michigan
    forests,
Found she the hunter's lodge deserted and fallen to ruin!


  Thus did the long sad years glide on, and in seasons
    and places
Divers and distant far was seen the wandering maiden;—
Now in the Tents of Grace of the meek Moravian Missions,
Now in the noisy camps and the battle-fields of the army,
Now in secluded hamlets, in towns and populous cities.
Like a phantom she came, and passed away unremem-
    bered.
Fair was she and young, when in hope began the long
    journey;
Faded was she and old, when in disappointment it ended.
Each succeeding year stole something away from her
    beauty,
Leaving behind it, broader and deeper, the gloom and
    the shadow.
Then there appeared and spread faint streaks of gray o'er
    her forehead,
Dawn of another life, that broke o'er her earthly horizon,
As in the eastern sky the first faint streaks of the
    morning.

## V

In that delightful land which is washed by the Delaware
waters,
Guarding in sylvan shades the name of Penn the apostle,
Stands on the banks of its beautiful stream the city he
founded.
There all the air is balm, and the peach is the emblem of
beauty,
And the streets still reëcho the names of the trees of the
forest,
As if they fain would appease the Dryads whose haunts
they molested.
There from the troubled sea had Evangeline landed, an
exile,
Finding among the children of Penn a home and a country.
There old René Leblanc had died; and when he departed,
Saw at his side only one of all his hundred descendants.
Something at least there was in the friendly streets of the
city,
Something that spake to her heart, and made her no longer
a stranger;
And her ear was pleased with the Thee and Thou of the
Quakers,
For it recalled the past, the old Acadian country,
Where all men were equal, and all were brothers and sisters.
So, when the fruitless search, the disappointed endeavor,
Ended, to recommence no more upon earth, uncomplain-
ing,
Thither, as leaves to the light, were turned her thoughts
and her footsteps.
As from the mountain's top the rainy mists of the morning
Roll away, and afar we behold the landscape below us,
Sun-illumined, with shining rivers and cities and hamlets,
So fell the mists from her mind, and she saw the world far
below her,
Dark no longer, but all illumined with love; and the path-
way
Which she had climbed so far, lying smooth and fair in the
distance.
Gabriel was not forgotten. Within her heart was his image,

Clothed in the beauty of love and youth, as last she beheld
  him,
Only more beautiful made by his death-like silence and
  absence.
Into her thoughts of him time entered not, for it was not.
Over him years had no power; he was not changed, but
  transfigured;
He had become to her heart as one who is dead, and not
  absent;
Patience and abnegation of self, and devotion to others,
This was the lesson a life of trial and sorrow had taught
  her.
So was her love diffused, but, like to some odorous spices,
Suffered no waste nor loss, though filling the air with
  aroma.
Other hope had she none, nor wish in life, but to follow
Meekly, with reverent steps, the sacred feet of her Saviour.
Thus many years she lived as a Sister of Mercy; frequent-
  ing
Lonely and wretched roofs in the crowded lanes of the
  city,
Where distress and want concealed themselves from the
  sunlight,
Where disease and sorrow in garrets languished neglected.
Night after night, when the world was asleep, as the watch-
  man repeated
Loud, through the gusty streets, that all was well in the
  city,
High at some lonely window he saw the light of her taper.
Day after day, in the gray of the dawn, as slow through the
  suburbs
Plodded the German farmer, with flowers and fruits for
  the market,
Met he that meek, pale face, returning home from its
  watchings.

  Then it came to pass that a pestilence fell on the city,
Presaged by wondrous signs, and mostly by flocks of wild
  pigeons,
Darkening the sun in their flight, with naught in their craws
  but an acorn.
And, as the tides of the sea arise in the month of Sep-
  tember,

Flooding some silver stream, till it spreads to a lake in the
    meadow,
So death flooded life, and, o'erflowing its natural margin,
Spread to a brackish lake, the silver stream of existence.
Wealth had no power to bribe, nor beauty to charm, the
    oppressor;
But all perished alike beneath the scourge of his anger;—
Only, alas! the poor, who had neither friends nor attend-
    ants,
Crept away to die in the almshouse, home of the homeless.
Then in the suburbs it stood, in the midst of meadows and
    woodlands;—
Now the city surrounds it; but still, with its gateway and
    wicket
Meek, in the midst of splendor, its humble walls seemed
    to echo
Softly the words of the Lord: "The poor ye always have
    with you."
Thither, by night and by day, came the Sister of Mercy.
    The dying
Looked up into her face, and thought, indeed, to behold
    there
Gleams of celestial light encircle her forehead with splen-
    dor,
Such as the artist paints o'er the brows of saints and
    apostles,
Or such as hangs by night o'er a city seen at a distance.
Unto their eyes it seemed the lamps of the city celestial,
Into whose shining gates erelong their spirits would enter.

    Thus, on a Sabbath morn, through the streets, deserted
    and silent,
Wending her quiet way, she entered the door of the alms-
    house.
Sweet on the summer air was the odor of flowers in the
    garden;
And she paused on her way to gather the fairest among
    them,
That the dying once more might rejoice in their fragrance
    and beauty.
Then, as she mounted the stairs to the corridors, cooled
    by the east-wind,

Distant and soft on her ear fell the chimes from the belfry
of Christ Church,
While, intermingled with these, across the meadows were
wafted
Sounds of psalms, that were sung by the Swedes in their
church at Wicaco.
Soft as descending wings fell the calm of the hour on her
spirit:
Something within her said, "At length thy trials are ended";
And with light in her looks, she entered the chambers of
sickness.
Noiselessly moved about the assiduous, careful attendants,
Moistening the feverish lip, and the aching brow, and in
silence
Closing the sightless eyes of the dead, and concealing their
faces,
Where on their pallets they lay, like drifts of snow by the
roadside.
Many a languid head, upraised as Evangeline entered,
Turned on its pillow of pain to gaze while she passed, for
her presence
Fell on their hearts like a ray of the sun on the walls of a
prison.
And, as she looked around, she saw how Death, the con-
soler,
Laying his hand upon many a heart, had healed it forever.
Many familiar forms had disappeared in the night time;
Vacant their places were, or filled already by strangers.

Suddenly, as if arrested by fear or a feeling of wonder,
Still she stood, with her colorless lips apart, while a shudder
Ran through her frame, and, forgotten, the flowerets
dropped from her fingers,
And from her eyes and cheeks the light and bloom of the
morning.
Then there escaped from her lips a cry of such terrible
anguish,
That the dying heard it, and started up from their pillows.
On the pallet before her was stretched the form of an old
man.
Long, and thin, and gray were the locks that shaded his
temples;
But, as he lay in the morning light, his face for a moment

Seemed to assume once more the forms of its earlier man-
    hood;
So are wont to be changed the faces of those who are dying.
Hot and red on his lips still burned the flush of the fever,
As if life, like the Hebrew, with blood had besprinkled its
    portals,
That the Angel of Death might see the sign, and pass over.
Motionless, senseless, dying, he lay, and his spirit ex-
    hausted
Seemed to be sinking down through the infinite depths in
    the darkness,
Darkness of slumber and death, forever sinking and sink-
    ing.
Then through those realms of shade, in multiplied rever-
    berations,
Heard he that cry in pain, and through the hush that suc-
    ceeded
Whispered a gentle voice, in accents tender and saint-like,
"Gabriel! O my beloved!" and died away into silence.
Then he beheld, in a dream, once more the home of his
    childhood;
Green Acadian meadows, with sylvan rivers among them,
Village, and mountain, and woodlands; and, walking under
    their shadow,
As in the days of her youth, Evangeline rose in his vision.
Tears came into his eyes; and as slowly he lifted his eyelids,
Vanished the vision away, but Evangeline knelt by his
    bedside.
Vainly he strove to whisper her name, for the accents
    unuttered
Died on his lips, and their motion revealed what his tongue
    would have spoken.
Vainly he strove to rise; and Evangeline, kneeling beside
    him,
Kissed his dying lips, and laid his head on her bosom.
Sweet was the light of his eyes; but suddenly sank into
    darkness,
As when a lamp is blown out by a gust of wind at a case-
    ment.

    All was ended now, the hope, and the fear, and the
    sorrow,

All the aching of heart, the restless, unsatisfied longing,
All the dull, deep pain, and constant anguish of patience!
And, as she pressed once more the lifeless head to her
    bosom,
Meekly she bowed her own, and murmured, "Father, I
    thank thee!"

———————

Still stands the forest primeval; but far away from its
    shadow,
Side by side, in their nameless graves, the lovers are
    sleeping.
Under the humble walls of the little Catholic churchyard,
In the heart of the city, they lie, unknown and unnoticed.
Daily the tides of life go ebbing and flowing beside them,
Thousands of throbbing hearts, where theirs are at rest
    and forever,
Thousands of aching brains, where theirs no longer are
    busy,
Thousands of toiling hands, where theirs have ceased from
    their labors,
Thousands of weary feet, where theirs have completed their
    journey!

Still stands the forest primeval; but under the shade of
    its branches
Dwells another race, with other customs and language.
Only along the shore of the mournful and misty Atlantic
Linger a few Acadian peasants, whose fathers from exile
Wandered back to their native land to die in its bosom.
In the fisherman's cot the wheel and the loom are still
    busy;
Maidens still wear their Norman caps and their kirtles of
    homespun,
And by the evening fire repeat Evangeline's story,
While from its rocky caverns the deep-voiced, neighboring
    ocean
Speaks, and in accents disconsolate answers the wail of
    the forest.

## THE BUILDING OF THE SHIP

"Build me straight, O worthy Master!
  Stanch and strong, a goodly vessel,
That shall laugh at all disaster,
  And with wave and whirlwind wrestle!"

The merchant's word
Delighted the Master heard;
For his heart was in his work, and the heart
Giveth grace unto every Art.
A quiet smile played round his lips,
As the eddies and dimples of the tide
Play round the bows of ships,
That steadily at anchor ride.
And with a voice that was full of glee,
He answered, "Erelong we will launch
A vessel as goodly, and strong, and stanch
As ever weathered a wintry sea!"
And first with nicest skill and art,
Perfect and finished in every part,
A little model the Master wrought,
Which should be to the larger plan
What the child is to the man,
Its counterpart in miniature;
That with a hand more swift and sure
The greater labor might be brought
To answer to his inward thought.
And as he labored, his mind ran o'er
The various ships that were built of yore,
And above them all, and strangest of all
Towered the Great Harry, crank and tall,
Whose picture was hanging on the wall,
With bows and stern raised high in air,
And balconies hanging here and there,
And signal lanterns and flags afloat,
And eight round towers, like those that frown
From some old castle, looking down
Upon the drawbridge and the moat.

And he said with a smile, "Our ship, I wis,
Shall be of another form than this!"
It was of another form, indeed:
Built for freight, and yet for speed,
A beautiful and gallant craft;
Broad in the beam, that the stress of the blast,
Pressing down upon sail and mast,
Might not the sharp bows overwhelm;
Broad in the beam, but sloping aft
With graceful curve and slow degrees,
That she might be docile to the helm,
And that the currents of parted seas,
Closing behind, with mighty force,
Might aid and not impede her course.

In the ship-yard stood the Master,
With the model of the vessel,
That should laugh at all disaster,
And with wave and whirlwind wrestle!

Covering many a rood of ground,
Lay the timber piled around;
Timber of chestnut, and elm, and oak,
And scattered here and there, with these,
The knarred and crooked cedar knees;
Brought from regions far away,
From Pascagoula's sunny bay,
And the banks of the roaring Roanoke!
Ah! what a wondrous thing it is
To note how many wheels of toil
One thought, one word, can set in motion!
There's not a ship that sails the ocean,
But every climate, every soil,
Must bring its tribute, great or small,
And help to build the wooden wall!

The sun was rising o'er the sea,
And long the level shadows lay,
As if they, too, the beams would be
Of some great, airy argosy,
Framed and launched in a single day.
That silent architect, the sun,
Had hewn and laid them every one,

Ere the work of man was yet begun.
Beside the Master, when he spoke,
A youth, against an anchor leaning,
Listened, to catch his slightest meaning.
Only the long waves, as they broke
In ripples on the pebbly beach,
Interrupted the old man's speech.

Beautiful they were, in sooth,
The old man and the fiery youth!
The old man, in whose busy brain
Many a ship that sailed the main
Was modelled o'er and o'er again;—
The fiery youth, who was to be
The heir of his dexterity,
The heir of his house, and his daughter's hand,
When he had built and launched from land
What the elder head had planned.

"Thus," said he, "will we build this ship!
Lay square the blocks upon the slip,
And follow well this plan of mine.
Choose the timbers with greatest care;
Of all that is unsound beware;
For only what is sound and strong
To this vessel shall belong.
Cedar of Maine and Georgia pine
Here together shall combine.
A goodly frame, and a goodly fame,
And the UNION be her name!
For the day that gives her to the sea
Shall give my daughter unto thee!"

The Master's word
Enraptured the young man heard;
And as he turned his face aside,
With a look of joy and a thrill of pride
Standing before
Her father's door,
He saw the form of his promised bride.
The sun shone on her golden hair,
And her cheek was glowing fresh and fair,

With the breath of morn and the soft sea air.
Like a beauteous barge was she,
Still at rest on the sandy beach,
Just beyond the billow's reach:
But he
Was the restless, seething, stormy sea!
Ah, how skilful grows the hand
That obeyeth Love's command!
It is the heart, and not the brain,
That to the highest doth attain,
And he who followeth Love's behest
Far excelleth all the rest!

Thus with the rising of the sun
Was the noble task begun,
And soon throughout the ship-yard's bounds
Were heard the intermingled sounds
Of axes and of mallets, plied
With vigorous arms on every side;
Plied so deftly and so well,
That, ere the shadows of evening fell,
The keel of oak for a noble ship,
Scarfed and bolted, straight and strong,
Was lying ready, and stretched along
The blocks, well placed upon the slip.
Happy, thrice happy, everyone
Who sees his labor well begun,
And not perplexed and multiplied,
By idly waiting for time and tide!

And when the hot, long day was o'er,
The young man at the Master's door
Sat with the maiden calm and still,
And within the porch, a little more
Removed beyond the evening chill,
The father sat, and told them tales
Of wrecks in the great September gales,
Of pirates coasting the Spanish Main,
And ships that never came back again,
The chance and change of a sailor's life,
Want and plenty, rest and strife,
His roving fancy, like the wind,
That nothing can stay and nothing can bind,
And the magic charm of foreign lands,

With shadows of palms, and shining sands,
Where the tumbling surf,
O'er the coral reefs of Madagascar,
Washes the feet of the swarthy Lascar,
As he lies alone and asleep on the turf.
And the trembling maiden held her breath
At the tales of that awful, pitiless sea,
With all its terror and mystery,
The dim, dark sea, so like unto Death,
That divides and yet unites mankind!
And whenever the old man paused, a gleam
From the bowl of his pipe would awhile illume
The silent group in the twilight gloom,
And thoughtful faces, as in a dream;
And for a moment one might mark
What had been hidden by the dark,
That the head of the maiden lay at rest,
Tenderly, on the young man's breast!
Day by day the vessel grew,
With timbers fashioned strong and true,
Stemson and keelson and sternson-knee,
Till, framed with perfect symmetry,
A skeleton ship rose up to view!
And around the bows and along the side
The heavy hammers and mallets plied,
Till after many a week, at length,
Wonderful for form and strength,
Sublime in its enormous bulk,
Loomed aloft the shadowy hulk!
And around it columns of smoke, upwreathing,
Rose from the boiling, bubbling, seething
Caldron, that glowed,
And overflowed
With the black tar, heated for the sheathing.
And amid the clamors
Of clattering hammers,
He who listened heard now and then
The song of the Master and his men:—
"Build me straight, O worthy Master,
    Stanch and strong, a goodly vessel,
That shall laugh at all disaster,
    And with wave and whirlwind wrestle!"

With oaken brace and copper band,
Lay the rudder on the sand,
That, like a thought, should have control
Over the movement of the whole;
And near it the anchor, whose giant hand
Would reach down and grapple with the land,
And immovable and fast
Hold the great ship against the bellowing blast!
And at the bows an image stood,
By a cunning artist carved in wood,
With robes of white, that far behind
Seemed to be fluttering in the wind.
It was not shaped in a classic mould,
Not like a Nymph or Goddess of old,
Or Naiad rising from the water,
But modelled from the Master's daughter!
On many a dreary and misty night,
'Twill be seen by the rays of the signal light,
Speeding along through the rain and the dark,
Like a ghost in its snow-white sark,
The pilot of some phantom bark,
Guiding the vessel, in its flight,
By a path none other knows aright!

Behold, at last,
Each tall and tapering mast
Is swung into its place;
Shrouds and stays
Holding it firm and fast!

Long ago,
In the deer-haunted forests of Maine,
When upon mountain and plain
Lay the snow,
They fell,—those lordly pines!
Those grand, majestic pines!
'Mid shouts and cheers
The jaded steers,
Panting beneath the goad,
Dragged down the weary, winding road
Those captive kings so straight and tall,
To be shorn of their streaming hair,
And naked and bare,

To feel the stress and the strain
Of the wind and the reeling main,
Whose roar
Would remind them forevermore
Of their native forests they should not see again.

And everywhere
The slender, graceful spars
Poise aloft in the air,
And at the mast-head,
White, blue, and red,
A flag unrolls the stripes and stars.
Ah! when the wanderer, lonely, friendless,
In foreign harbors shall behold
That flag unrolled,
'Twill be as a friendly hand
Stretched out from his native land,
Filling his heart with memories sweet and endless!

All is finished! and at length
Has come the bridal day
Of beauty and of strength.
To-day the vessel shall be launched!
With fleecy clouds the sky is blanched,
And o'er the bay,
Slowly, in all his splendors dight,
The great sun rises to behold the sight.
The ocean old,
Centuries old,
Strong as youth, and as uncontrolled,
Paces restless to and fro,
Up and down the sands of gold.
His beating heart is not at rest;
And far and wide,
With ceaseless flow,
His beard of snow
Heaves with the heaving of his breast.
He waits impatient for his bride.
There she stands,
With her foot upon the sands,
Decked with flags and streamers gay,
In honor of her marriage day,
Her snow-white signals fluttering, blending,

Round her like a veil descending,
Ready to be
The bride of the gray old sea.

On the deck another bride
Is standing by her lover's side.
Shadows from the flags and shrouds,
Like the shadows cast by clouds,
Broken by many a sudden fleck,
Fall around them on the deck.

The prayer is said,
The service read,
The joyous bridegroom bows his head;
And in tears the good old Master
Shakes the brown hand of his son,
Kisses his daughter's glowing cheek
In silence, for he cannot speak,
And ever faster
Down his own the tears begin to run.
The worthy pastor—
The shepherd of that wandering flock,
That has the ocean for its wold,
That has the vessel for its fold,
Leaping ever from rock to rock—
Spake, with accents mild and clear,
Words of warning, words of cheer,
But tedious to the bridegroom's ear.
He knew the chart
Of the sailor's heart,
All its pleasures and its griefs,
All its shallows and rocky reefs,
All those secret currents, that flow
With such resistless undertow,
And lift and drift, with terrible force,
The will from its moorings and its course.
Therefore he spake, and thus said he:—

"Like unto ships far off at sea,
Outward or homeward bound, are we.
Before, behind, and all around,
Floats and swings the horizon's bound,
Seems at its distant rim to rise

And climb the crystal wall of the skies,
And then again to turn and sink,
As if we could slide from its outer brink.
Ah! it is not the sea,
It is not the sea that sinks and shelves,
But ourselves
That rock and rise
With endless and uneasy motion,
Now touching the very skies,
Now sinking into the depths of ocean.
Ah! if our souls but poise and swing
Like the compass in its brazen ring,
Ever level and ever true
To the toil and the task we have to do,
We shall sail securely, and safely reach
The Fortunate Isles, on whose shining beach
The sights we see, and the sounds we hear,
Will be those of joy and not of fear!"

Then the Master,
With a gesture of command,
Waved his hand;
And at the word,
Loud and sudden there was heard,
All around them and below,
The sound of hammers, blow on blow,
Knocking away the shores and spurs.
And see! she stirs!
She starts,—she moves,—she seems to feel
The thrill of life along her keel,
And, spurning with her foot the ground,
With one exulting, joyous bound,
She leaps into the ocean's arms!

And lo! from the assembled crowd
There rose a shout, prolonged and loud,
That to the ocean seemed to say,
"Take her, O bridegroom, old and gray,
Take her to thy protecting arms,
With all her youth and all her charms!"

How beautiful she is! How fair
She lies within those arms, that press

Her form with many a soft caress
Of tenderness and watchful care!
Sail forth into the sea, O ship!
Through wind and wave, right onward steer!
The moistened eye, the trembling lip,
Are not the signs of doubt or fear.

Sail forth into the sea of life,
O gentle, loving, trusting wife,
And safe from all adversity
Upon the bosom of that sea
Thy comings and thy goings be!
For gentleness and love and trust
Prevail o'er angry wave and gust;
And in the wreck of noble lives
Something immortal still survives!

Thou, too, sail on, O Ship of State!
Sail on, O UNION, strong and great!
Humanity with all its fears,
With all the hopes of future years,
Is hanging breathless on thy fate!
We know what Master laid thy keel,
What Workmen wrought thy ribs of steel,
Who made each mast, and sail, and rope,
What anvils rang, what hammers beat,
In what a forge and what a heat
Were shaped the anchors of thy hope!
Fear not each sudden sound and shock,
'Tis of the wave and not the rock;
'Tis but the flapping of the sail,
And not a rent made by the gale!
In spite of rock and tempest's roar,
In spite of false lights on the shore,
Sail on, nor fear to breast the sea!
Our hearts, our hopes, are all with thee,
Our hearts, our hopes, our prayers, our tears,
Our faith triumphant o'er our fears,
Are all with thee,—are all with thee!

## TEGNÉR'S DRAPA

I heard a voice, that cried,
"Balder the Beautiful
Is dead, is dead!"
And through the misty air
Passed like the mournful cry
Of sunward sailing cranes.
I saw the pallid corpse
Of the dead sun
Borne through the Northern sky.
Blasts from Niffelheim
Lifted the sheeted mists
Around him as he passed.
And the voice forever cried,
"Balder the Beautiful
Is dead, is dead!"
And died away
Through the dreary night,
In accents of despair.
Balder the Beautiful,
God of the summer sun,
Fairest of all the Gods!
Light from his forehead beamed,
Runes were upon his tongue,
As on the warrior's sword.
All things in earth and air
Bound were by magic spell
Never to do him harm;
Even the plants and stones;
All save the mistletoe,
The sacred mistletoe!
Hœder, the blind old God,
Whose feet are shod with silence,
Pierced through that gentle breast
With his sharp spear, by fraud,

Made of the mistletoe,
The accursed mistletoe!
They laid him in his ship,
With horse and harness,
As on a funeral pyre.
Odin placed
A ring upon his finger,
And whispered in his ear.
They launched the burning ship!
It floated far away
Over the misty sea,
Till like the sun it seemed,
Sinking beneath the waves.
Balder returned no more!
So perish the old Gods!
But out of the sea of Time
Rises a new land of song,
Fairer than the old.
Over its meadows green
Walk the young bards and sing.
Build it again,
O ye bards,
Fairer than before!
Ye fathers of the new race,
Feed upon morning dew,
Sing the new Song of Love!
The law of force is dead!
The law of love prevails!
Thor, the thunderer,
Shall rule the earth no more,
No more, with threats,
Challenge the meek Christ.
Sing no more,
O ye bards of the North,
Of Vikings and of Jarls!
Of the days of Eld
Preserve the freedom only,
Not the deeds of blood!

## *from* THE SONG OF HIAWATHA

### II

### THE FOUR WINDS

"Honor be to Mudjekeewis!"
Cried the warriors, cried the old men
When he came in triumph homeward
With the sacred Belt of Wampum,
From the regions of the North-Wind,
From the kingdom of Wabasso,
From the land of the White Rabbit.

He had stolen the Belt of Wampum
From the neck of Mishe-Mokwa,
From the Great Bear of the mountains,
From the terror of the nations,
As he lay asleep and cumbrous
On the summit of the mountains,
Like a rock with mosses on it,
Spotted brown and gray with mosses.

Silently he stole upon him
Till the red nails of the monster
Almost touched him, almost scared him,
Till the hot breath of his nostrils
Warmed the hands of Mudjekeewis,
As he drew the Belt of Wampum
Over the round ears, that heard not,
Over the small eyes, that saw not,
Over the long nose and nostrils,
The black muffle of the nostrils,
Out of which the heavy breathing
Warmed the hands of Mudjekeewis.

Then he swung aloft his war-club,
Shouted loud and long his war-cry,
Smote the mighty Mishe-Mokwa
In the middle of the forehead,
Right between the eyes he smote him.

With the heavy blow bewildered,
Rose the Great Bear of the mountains;

But his knees beneath him trembled,
And he whimpered like a woman,
As he reeled and staggered forward.
As he sat upon his haunches;
And the mighty Mudjekeewis,
Standing fearlessly before him,
Taunted him in loud derision,
Spake disdainfully in this wise:—

"Hark you, Bear! you are a coward;
And no Brave, as you pretended;
Else you would not cry and whimper
Like a miserable woman!
Bear! you know our tribes are hostile,
Long have been at war together;
Now you find that we are strongest,
You go sneaking in the forest,
You go hiding in the mountains!
Had you conquered me in battle
Not a groan would I have uttered;
But you, Bear! sit here and whimper,
And disgrace your tribe by crying,
Like a wretched Shaugodaya,
Like a cowardly old woman!"

Then again he raised his war-club,
Smote again the Mishe-Mokwa
In the middle of his forehead,
Broke his skull, as ice is broken
When one goes to fish in Winter.
Thus was slain the Mishe-Mokwa,
He the Great Bear of the mountains,
He the terror of the nations.

"Honor be to Mudjekeewis!"
With a shout exclaimed the people,
"Honor be to Mudjekeewis!
Henceforth he shall be the West-Wind,
And hereafter and forever
Shall he hold supreme dominion
Over all the winds of heaven.
Call him no more Mudjekeewis,
Call him Kabeyun, the West-Wind!"

Thus was Mudjekeewis chosen
Father of the Winds of Heaven.
For himself he kept the West-Wind,

Gave the others to his children;
Unto Wabun gave the East-Wind,
Gave the South to Shawondasee,
And the North-Wind, wild and cruel,
To the fierce Kabibonokka.

Young and beautiful was Wabun;
He it was who brought the morning,
He it was whose silver arrows
Chased the dark o'er hill and valley;
He it was whose cheeks were painted
With the brightest streaks of crimson,
And whose voice awoke the village,
Called the deer, and called the hunter.

Lonely in the sky was Wabun;
Though the birds sang gaily to him,
Though the wild-flowers of the meadow
Filled the air with odors for him;
Though the forests and the rivers
Sang and shouted at his coming,
Still his heart was sad within him,
For he was alone in heaven.

But one morning, gazing earthward,
While the village still was sleeping,
And the fog lay on the river,
Like a ghost, that goes at sunrise,
He beheld a maiden walking
All alone upon a meadow,
Gathering water-flags and rushes
By a river in the meadow.

Every morning, gazing earthward,
Still the first thing he beheld there
Was her blue eyes looking at him,
Two blue lakes among the rushes.
And he loved the lonely maiden,
Who thus waited for his coming;
For they both were solitary,
She on earth and he in heaven.

And he wooed her with caresses,
Wooed her with his smile of sunshine,
With his flattering words he wooed her,
With his sighing and his singing,
Gentlest whispers in the branches,
Softest music, sweetest odors,

Till he drew her to his bosom,
Folded in his robes of crimson,
Till into a star he changed her,
Trembling still upon his bosom;
And forever in the heavens
They are seen together walking,
Wabun and the Wabun-Annung,
Wabun and the Star of Morning.

But the fierce Kabibonokka
Had his dwelling among icebergs,
In the everlasting snow-drifts,
In the kingdom of Wabasso,
In the land of the White Rabbit.
He it was whose hand in Autumn
Painted all the trees with scarlet,
Stained the leaves with red and yellow;
He it was who sent the snow-flakes,
Sifting, hissing through the forest,
Froze the ponds, the lakes, the rivers,
Drove the loon and sea-gull southward,
Drove the cormorant and curlew
To their nests of sedge and sea-tang
In the realms of Shawondasee.

Once the fierce Kabibonokka
Issued from his lodge of snow-drifts,
From his home among the icebergs,
And his hair, with snow besprinkled,
Streamed behind him like a river,
Like a black and wintry river,
As he howled and hurried southward,
Over frozen lakes and moorlands.

There among the reeds and rushes
Found he Shingebis, the diver,
Trailing strings of fish behind him,
O'er the frozen fens and moorlands,
Lingering still among the moorlands,
Though his tribe had long departed
To the land of Shawondasee.

Cried the fierce Kabibonokka,
"Who is this that dares to brave me?
Dares to stay in my dominions,
When the Wawa has departed,
When the wild-goose has gone southward,

And the heron, the Shuh-shuh-gah,
Long ago departed southward?
I will go into his wigwam,
I will put his smouldering fire out!"
And at night Kabibonokka
To the lodge came wild and wailing,
Heaped the snow in drifts about it,
Shouted down into the smoke-flue,
Shook the lodge-poles in his fury,
Flapped the curtain of the door-way.
Shingebis, the diver, feared not,
Shingebis, the diver, cared not;
Four great logs had he for firewood,
One for each moon of the winter,
And for food the fishes served him.
By his blazing fire he sat there,
Warm and merry, eating, laughing,
Singing, "O Kabibonokka,
You are but my fellow-mortal!"
Then Kabibonokka entered,
And though Shingebis, the diver,
Felt his presence by the coldness,
Felt his icy breath upon him,
Still he did not cease his singing,
Still he did not leave his laughing,
Only turned the log a little,
Only made the fire burn brighter,
Made the sparks fly up the smoke-flue.
From Kabibonokka's forehead,
From his snow-besprinkled tresses,
Drops of sweat fell fast and heavy,
Making dints upon the ashes,
As along the eaves of lodges,
As from drooping boughs of hemlock,
Drips the melting snow in spring-time,
Making hollows in the snow-drifts.
Till at last he rose defeated,
Could not bear the heat and laughter,
Could not bear the merry singing,
But rushed headlong through the door-way,
Stamped upon the crusted snow-drifts,
Stamped upon the lakes and rivers,
Made the snow upon them harder,

Made the ice upon them thicker,
Challenged Shingebis, the diver,
To come forth and wrestle with him,
To come forth and wrestle naked
On the frozen fens and moorlands.

Forth went Shingebis, the diver,
Wrestled all night with the North-Wind,
Wrestled naked on the moorlands
With the fierce Kabibonokka,
Till his panting breath grew fainter,
Till his frozen grasp grew feebler,
Till he reeled and staggered backward,
And retreated, baffled, beaten,
To the kingdom of the Wabasso,
To the land of the White Rabbit,
Hearing still the gusty laughter,
Hearing Shingebis, the diver,
Singing, "O Kabibonokka,
You are but my fellow-mortal!"

Shawondasee, fat and lazy,
Had his dwelling far to southward,
In the drowsy, dreamy sunshine,
In the never-ending Summer.
He it was who sent the wood-birds,
Sent the robin, the Opechee,
Sent the bluebird, the Owaissa,
Sent the Shawshaw, sent the swallow,
Sent the wild-goose, Wawa, northward,
Sent the melons and tobacco,
And the grapes in purple clusters.

From his pipe the smoke ascending
Filled the sky with haze and vapor,
Filled the air with dreamy softness,
Gave a twinkle to the water,
Touched the rugged hills with smoothness,
Brought the tender Indian Summer
To the melancholy north-land,
In the dreary Moon of Snow-shoes.

Listless, careless Shawondasee!
In his life he had one shadow,
In his heart one sorrow had he.
Once, as he was gazing northward,
Far away upon a prairie

He beheld a maiden standing,
Saw a tall and slender maiden
All alone upon a prairie;
Brightest green were all her garments,
And her hair was like the sunshine.

Day by day he gazed upon her,
Day by day he sighed with passion,
Day by day his heart within him
Grew more hot with love and longing
For the maid with yellow tresses.
But he was too fat and lazy
To bestir himself and woo her.
Yes, too indolent and easy
To pursue her and persuade her;
So he only gazed upon her,
Only sat and sighed with passion
For the maiden of the prairie.

Till one morning, looking northward,
He beheld her yellow tresses
Changed and covered o'er with whiteness,
Covered as with whitest snow-flakes,
"Ah! my brother from the North-land,
From the kingdom of Wabasso,
From the land of the White Rabbit!
You have stolen the maiden from me,
You have laid your hand upon her,
You have wooed and won my maiden,
With your stories of the North-land!"

Thus the wretched Shawondasee
Breathed into the air his sorrow;
And the South-Wind o'er the prairie
Wandered warm with sighs of passion,
With the sighs of Shawondasee,
Till the air seemed full of snow-flakes,
Full of thistle-down the prairie,
And the maid with hair like sunshine
Vanished from his sight forever;
Never more did Shawondasee
See the maid with yellow tresses!

Poor, deluded Shawondasee!
'Twas no woman that you gazed at,
'Twas no maiden that you sighed for,
'Twas the prairie dandelion

That through all the dreamy Summer
You had gazed at with such longing,
You had sighed for with such passion,
And had puffed away forever,
Blown into the air with sighing.
Ah! deluded Shawondasee!

Thus the Four Winds were divided;
Thus the sons of Mudjekeewis
Had their stations in the heavens,
At the corners of the heavens;
For himself the West-Wind only
Kept the mighty Mudjekeewis.

## XI

### HIAWATHA'S WEDDING-FEAST

You shall hear how Pau-Puk-Keewis,
How the handsome Yenadizze
Danced at Hiawatha's wedding;
How the gentle Chibiabos,
He the sweetest of musicians,
Sang his songs of love and longing;
How Iagoo, the great boaster,
He the marvellous story-teller,
Told his tales of strange adventure,
That the feast might be more joyous,
That the time might pass more gaily
And the guests be more contented.

Sumptuous was the feast Nokomis
Made at Hiawatha's wedding;
All the bowls were made of bass-wood,
White and polished very smoothly,
All the spoons of horn of bison,
Black and polished very smoothly.

She had sent through all the village
Messengers with wands of willow,
As a sign of invitation,
As a token of the feasting;
And the wedding guests assembled,
Clad in all their richest raiment,

Robes of fur and belts of wampum,
Splendid with their paint and plumage,
Beautiful with beads and tassels.

First they ate the sturgeon, Nahma,
And the pike, the Maskenozha,
Caught and cooked by old Nokomis;
Then on pemican they feasted,
Pemican and buffalo marrow,
Haunch of deer and hump of bison,
Yellow cakes of the Mondamin,
And the wild rice of the river.

But the gracious Hiawatha,
And the lovely Laughing Water,
And the careful old Nokomis,
Tasted not the food before them,
Only waited on the others,
Only served their guests in silence.

And when all the guests had finished,
Old Nokomis, brisk and busy,
From an ample pouch of otter,
Filled the red-stone pipes for smoking
With tobacco from the South-land,
Mixed with bark of the red willow,
And with herbs and leaves of fragrance.

Then she said, "O Pau-Puk-Keewis,
Dance for us your merry dances,
Dance the Beggar's Dance to please us,
That the feast may be more joyous,
That the time may pass more gaily,
And our guests be more contented!"

Then the handsome Pau-Puk-Keewis,
He the idle Yenadizze,
He the merry mischief-maker,
Whom the people called the Storm-Fool,
Rose among the guests assembled.

Skilled was he in sports and pastimes,
In the merry dance of snow-shoes,
In the play of quoits and ball-play;
Skilled was he in games of hazard,
In all games of skill and hazard,
Pugasaing, the Bowl and Counters,
Kuntassoo, the Game of Plum-stones.
Though the warriors called him Faint-Heart,

Called him Coward, Shaugodaya,
Idler, gambler, Yenadizze,
Little heeded he their jesting,
Little cared he for their insults,
For the women and the maidens,
Loved the handsome Pau-Puk-Keewis.

He was dressed in shirt of doeskin,
White and soft, and fringed with ermine,
All inwrought with beads of wampum;
He was dressed in deer-skin leggings,
Fringed with hedgehog quills and ermine,
And in moccasins of buck-skin,
Thick with quills and beads embroidered.
On his head were plumes of swan's down,
On his heels were tails of foxes,
In one hand a fan of feathers,
And a pipe was in the other.

Barred with streaks of red and yellow,
Streaks of blue and bright vermilion,
Shone the face of Pau-Puk-Keewis.
From his forehead fell his tresses,
Smooth, and parted like a woman's,
Shining bright with oil, and plaited,
Hung with braids of scented grasses,
As among the guests assembled,
To the sound of flutes and singing,
To the sound of drums and voices,
Rose the handsome Pau-Puk-Keewis,
And began his mystic dances.

First he danced a solemn measure,
Very slow in step and gesture,
In and out among the pine-trees,
Through the shadows and the sunshine,
Treading softly like a panther.
Then more swiftly and still swifter,
Whirling, spinning round in circles,
Leaping o'er the guests assembled,
Eddying round and round the wigwam,
Till the leaves went whirling with him,
Till the dust and wind together
Swept in eddies round about him.

Then along the sandy margin
Of the lake, the Big-Sea-Water,

On he sped with frenzied gestures,
Stamped upon the sand, and tossed it
Wildly in the air around him;
Till the wind became a whirlwind,
Till the sand was blown and sifted
Like great snowdrifts o'er the landscape,
Heaping all the shores with Sand Dunes,
Sand Hills of the Nagow Wudjoo!

Thus the merry Pau-Puk-Keewis
Danced his Beggar's Dance to please them,
And, returning, sat down laughing
There among the guests assembled,
Sat and fanned himself serenely
With his fan of turkey-feathers.

Then they said to Chibiabos,
To the friend of Hiawatha,
To the sweetest of all singers,
To the best of all musicians,
"Sing to us, O Chibiabos!
Songs of love and songs of longing,
That the feast may be more joyous,
That the time may pass more gaily,
And our guests be more contented!"

And the gentle Chibiabos
Sang in accents sweet and tender,
Sang in tones of deep emotion,
Songs of love and songs of longing;
Looking still at Hiawatha,
Looking at fair Laughing Water,
Sang he softly, sang in this wise:

"Onaway! Awake, beloved!
Thou the wild-flower of the forest!
Thou the wild-bird of the prairie!
Thou with eyes so soft and fawn-like!

"If thou only lookest at me,
I am happy, I am happy,
As the lilies of the prairie,
When they feel the dew upon them!

"Sweet thy breath is as the fragrance
Of the wild-flowers in the morning,
As their fragrance is at evening,
In the Moon when leaves are falling.

"Does not all the blood within me

Leap to meet thee, leap to meet thee,
As the springs to meet the sunshine,
In the Moon when nights are brightest?
    "Onaway! my heart sings to thee,
Sings with joy when thou art near me.
As the sighing, singing branches
In the pleasant Moon of Strawberries!
    "When thou art not pleased, beloved,
Then my heart is sad and darkened,
As the shining river darkens
When the clouds drop shadows on it!
    "When thou smilest, my beloved,
Then my troubled heart is brightened,
As in sunshine gleam the ripples
That the cold wind makes in rivers.
    "Smiles the earth, and smile the waters,
Smile the cloudless skies above us,
But I lose the way of smiling
When thou art no longer near me!
    "I myself, myself! behold me!
Blood of my beating heart, behold me!
Oh awake, awake, beloved!
Onaway! awake, beloved!"
    Thus the gentle Chibiabos
Sang his song of love and longing;
And Iagoo, the great boaster,
He the marvellous story-teller,
He the friend of old Nokomis,
Jealous of the sweet musician,
Jealous of the applause they gave him,
Saw in all the eyes around him,
Saw in all their looks and gestures,
That the wedding guests assembled
Longed to hear his pleasant stories,
His immeasurable falsehoods.
    Very boastful was Iagoo;
Never heard he an adventure
But himself had met a greater;
Never any deed of daring
But himself had done a bolder;
Never any marvellous story
But himself could tell a stranger.
    Would you listen to his boasting,

Would you only give him credence,
No one ever shot an arrow
Half so far and high as he had;
Ever caught so many fishes,
Ever killed so many reindeer,
Ever trapped so many beaver!

None could run so fast as he could,
None could dive so deep as he could,
None could swim so far as he could;
None had made so many journeys,
None had seen so many wonders,
As this wonderful Iagoo,
As this marvellous story-teller!

Thus his name became a by-word
And a jest among the people;
And whene'er a boastful hunter
Praised his own address too highly,
Or a warrior, home returning,
Talked too much of his achievements,
All his hearers cried, "Iagoo!
Here's Iagoo come among us!"

He it was who carved the cradle
Of the little Hiawatha,
Carved its framework out of linden,
Bound it strong with reindeer sinews;
He it was who taught him later
How to make his bows and arrows,
How to make the bows of ash-tree,
And the arrows of the oak-tree.
So among the guests assembled
At my Hiawatha's wedding
Sat Iagoo, old and ugly,
Sat the marvellous story-teller.

And they said, "O good Iagoo,
Tell us now a tale of wonder,
Tell us of some strange adventure,
That the feast may be more joyous,
That the time may pass more gaily,
And our guests be more contented!"

And Iagoo answered straightway,
"You shall hear a tale of wonder,
You shall hear the strange adventures

Of Osseo, the Magician,
From the Evening Star descended."

## XII

### THE SON OF THE EVENING STAR

Can it be the sun descending
O'er the level plain of water?
Or the Red Swan floating, flying,
Wounded by the magic arrow,
Staining all the waves with crimson,
With the crimson of its life-blood,
Filling all the air with splendor,
With the splendor of its plumage?

Yes; it is the sun descending,
Sinking down into the water;
All the sky is stained with purple,
All the water flushed with crimson!
No; it is the Red Swan floating,
Diving down beneath the water;
To the sky its wings are lifted,
With its blood the waves are reddened!

Over it the Star of Evening
Melts and trembles through the purple,
Hangs suspended in the twilight.
No; it is a bead of wampum
On the robes of the Great Spirit
As he passes through the twilight,
Walks in silence through the heavens.

This with joy beheld Iagoo
And he said in haste: "Behold it!
See the sacred Star of Evening!
You shall hear a tale of wonder,
Hear the story of Osseo,
Son of the Evening Star, Osseo!

"Once, in days no more remembered,
Ages nearer the beginning,
When the heavens were closer to us,
And the Gods were more familiar,
In the North-land lived a hunter,
With ten young and comely daughters,
Tall and lithe as wands of willow;
Only Oweenee, the youngest,

She the wilful and the wayward,
She the silent, dreamy maiden,
Was the fairest of the sisters.

"All these women married warriors,
Married brave and haughty husbands;
Only Oweenee, the youngest,
Laughed and flouted all her lovers,
All her young and handsome suitors,
And then married old Osseo,
Old Osseo, poor and ugly,
Broken with age and weak with coughing,
Always coughing like a squirrel.

"Ah, but beautiful within him
Was the spirit of Osseo,
From the Evening Star descended,
Star of Evening, Star of Woman,
Star of tenderness and passion!
All its fire was in his bosom,
All its beauty in his spirit,
All its mystery in his being,
All its splendor in his language!

"And her lovers, the rejected,
Handsome men with belts of wampum,
Handsome men with paint and feathers,
Pointed at her in derision,
Followed her with jest and laughter.
But she said: 'I care not for you,
Care not for your belts of wampum,
Care not for your paint and feathers,
Care not for your jests and laughter;
I am happy with Osseo!'

"Once to some great feast invited,
Through the damp and dusk of evening,
Walked together the ten sisters,
Walked together with their husbands;
Slowly followed old Osseo,
With fair Oweenee beside him;
All the others chatted gaily,
These two only walked in silence.

"At the western sky Osseo
Gazed intent, as if imploring,
Often stopped and gazed imploring
At the trembling Star of Evening,
At the tender Star of Woman;

And they heard him murmur softly,
'*Ah, showain nemeshin, Nosa!*
Pity, pity me, my father!'
    " 'Listen!' said the eldest sister,
'He is praying to his father!
What a pity that the old man
Does not stumble in the pathway,
Does not break his neck by falling!'
And they laughed till all the forest
Rang with their unseemly laughter.
    "On their pathway through the woodlands
Lay an oak, by storms uprooted,
Lay the great trunk of an oak-tree,
Buried half in leaves and mosses,
Mouldering, crumbling, huge and hollow.
And Osseo, when he saw it,
Gave a shout, a cry of anguish,
Leaped into its yawning cavern,
At one end went in an old man,
Wasted, wrinkled, old, and ugly;
From the other came a young man,
Tall and straight and strong and handsome.
    "Thus Osseo was transfigured,
Thus restored to youth and beauty;
But, alas for good Osseo,
And for Oweenee, the faithful!
Strangely, too, was she transfigured.
Changed into a weak old woman,
With a staff she tottered onward,
Wasted, wrinkled, old, and ugly!
And the sisters and their husbands
Laughed until the echoing forest
Rang with their unseemly laughter.
    "But Osseo turned not from her,
Walked with slower step beside her,
Took her hand, as brown and withered
As an oak-leaf is in Winter,
Called her sweetheart, Nenemoosha,
Soothed her with soft words of kindness,
Till they reached the lodge of feasting,
Till they sat down in the wigwam,
Sacred to the Star of Evening,
To the tender Star of Woman.

"Wrapt in visions, lost in dreaming,
At the banquet sat Osseo;
All were merry, all were happy,
All were joyous but Osseo.
Neither food nor drink he tasted,
Neither did he speak nor listen,
But as one bewildered sat he,
Looking dreamily and sadly,
First at Oweenee, then upward
At the gleaming sky above them.

"Then a voice was heard, a whisper,
Coming from the starry distance,
Coming from the empty vastness,
Low, and musical, and tender;
And the voice said: 'O Osseo!
O my son, my best beloved!
Broken are the spells that bound you,
All the charms of the magicians,
All the magic powers of evil;
Come to me; ascend, Osseo!

" 'Taste the food that stands before you:
It is blessed and enchanted,
It has magic virtues in it,
It will change you to a spirit.
All your bowls and all your kettles
Shall be wood and clay no longer;
But the bowls be changed to wampum,
And the kettles shall be silver;
They shall shine like shells of scarlet,
Like the fire shall gleam and glimmer.

" 'And the women shall no longer
Bear the dreary doom of labor,
But be changed to birds, and glisten
With the beauty of the starlight,
Painted with the dusky splendors
Of the skies and clouds of evening!'

"What Osseo heard as whispers,
What as words he comprehended,
Was but music to the others,
Music as of birds afar off,
Of the whippoorwill afar off,
Of the lonely Wawonaissa
Singing in the darksome forest.

"Then the lodge began to tremble,
Straight began to shake and tremble,
And they felt it rising, rising,
Slowly through the air ascending,
From the darkness of the tree-tops
Forth into the dewy starlight,
Till it passed the topmost branches;
And behold! the wooden dishes
All were changed to shells of scarlet!
And behold! the earthen kettles
All were changed to bowls of silver!
And the roof-poles of the wigwam
Were as glittering rods of silver,
And the roof of bark upon them
As the shining shards of beetles.

"Then Osseo gazed around him,
And he saw the nine fair sisters,
All the sisters and their husbands,
Changed to birds of various plumage.
Some were jays and some were magpies,
Others thrushes, others blackbirds;
And they hopped, and sang, and twittered,
Perked and fluttered all their feathers,
Strutted in their shining plumage,
And their tails like fans unfolded.

"Only Oweenee, the youngest,
Was not changed, but sat in silence,
Wasted, wrinkled, old, and ugly,
Looking sadly at the others;
Till Osseo, gazing upward,
Gave another cry of anguish,
Such a cry as he had uttered
By the oak-tree in the forest.

"Then returned her youth and beauty,
And her soiled and tattered garments
Were transformed to robes of ermine,
And her staff became a feather,
Yes, a shining silver feather!

"And again the wigwam trembled,
Swayed and rushed through airy currents,
Through transparent cloud and vapor,
And amid celestial splendors
On the Evening Star alighted,

As a snow-flake falls on snow-flake,
As a leaf drops on a river,
As the thistle-down on water.
    "Forth with cheerful words of welcome
Came the father of Osseo,
He with radiant locks of silver,
He with eyes serene and tender.
And he said: 'My son, Osseo,
Hang the cage of birds you bring there,
Hang the cage with rods of silver,
And the birds with glistening feathers,
At the doorway of my wigwam.'
    "At the door he hung the bird-cage,
And they entered in and gladly
Listened to Osseo's father,
Ruler of the Star of Evening,
As he said: 'O my Osseo!
I have had compassion on you,
Given you back your youth and beauty,
Into birds of various plumage
Changed your sisters and their husbands;
Changed them thus because they mocked you
In the figure of the old man,
In that aspect sad and wrinkled,
Could not see your heart of passion,
Could not see your youth immortal;
Only Oweenee, the faithful,
Saw your naked heart and loved you.
    " 'In the lodge that glimmers yonder,
In the little star that twinkles
Through the vapors, on the left hand,
Lives the envious Evil Spirit,
The Wabeno, the magician,
Who transformed you to an old man.
Take heed lest his beams fall on you,
For the rays he darts around him
Are the power of his enchantment,
Are the arrows that he uses.'
    "Many years, in peace and quiet,
On the peaceful Star of Evening
Dwelt Osseo with his father;
Many years, in song and flutter,
At the doorway of the wigwam,

Hung the cage with rods of silver,
And fair Oweenee, the faithful,
Bore a son unto Osseo,
With the beauty of his mother,
With the courage of his father.

"And the boy grew up and prospered,
And Osseo, to delight him,
Made him little bows and arrows,
Opened the great cage of silver,
And let loose his aunts and uncles,
All those birds with glossy feathers,
For his little son to shoot at.

"Round and round they wheeled and darted,
Filled the Evening Star with music,
With their songs of joy and freedom;
Filled the Evening Star with splendor,
With the fluttering of their plumage;
Till the boy, the little hunter,
Bent his bow and shot an arrow,
Shot a swift and fatal arrow,
And a bird, with shining feathers,
At his feet fell wounded sorely.

"But, O wondrous transformation!
'Twas no bird he saw before him,
'Twas a beautiful young woman,
With the arrow in her bosom!

"When her blood fell on the planet,
On the sacred Star of Evening,
Broken was the spell of magic,
Powerless was the strange enchantment,
And the youth, the fearless bowman,
Suddenly felt himself descending,
Held by unseen hands, but sinking
Downward through the empty spaces,
Downward through the clouds and vapors,
Till he rested on an island,
On an island, green and grassy,
Yonder in the Big-Sea-Water.

"After him he saw descending
All the birds with shining feathers,
Fluttering, falling, wafted downward,
Like the painted leaves of Autumn;

And the lodge with poles of silver,
With its roof like wings of beetles,
Like the shining shards of beetles,
By the winds of heaven uplifted,
Slowly sank upon the island,
Bringing back the good Osseo,
Bringing Oweenee, the faithful.
  "Then the birds, again transfigured,
Reassumed the shape of mortals,
Took their shape, but not their stature;
They remained as Little People,
Like the pygmies, the Puk-Wudjies,
And on pleasant nights of Summer,
When the Evening Star was shining,
Hand in hand they danced together
On the island's craggy headlands,
On the sand-beach low and level.
  "Still their glittering lodge is seen there,
On the tranquil Summer evenings,
And upon the shore the fisher
Sometimes hears their happy voices,
Sees them dancing in the starlight!"
  When the story was completed,
When the wondrous tale was ended,
Looking round upon his listeners,
Solemnly Iagoo added:
"There are great men, I have known such,
Whom their people understand not,
Whom they even make a jest of,
Scoff and jeer at in derision.
From the story of Osseo
Let us learn the fate of jesters!"
  All the wedding guests delighted
Listened to the marvellous story,
Listened laughing and applauding,
And they whispered to each other:
"Does he mean himself, I wonder?
And are we the aunts and uncles?"
  Then again sang Chibiabos,
Sang a song of love and longing,
In those accents sweet and tender,
In those tones of pensive sadness,

Sang a maiden's lamentation
For her lover, her Algonquin.

"When I think of my beloved,
Ah me! think of my beloved,
When my heart is thinking of him,
O my sweetheart, my Algonquin!

"Ah me! when I parted from him,
Round my neck he hung the wampum,
As a pledge, the snow-white wampum,
O my sweetheart, my Algonquin!

"I will go with you, he whispered,
Ah me! to your native country;
Let me go with you, he whispered,
O my sweetheart, my Algonquin!

"Far away, away, I answered,
Very far away, I answered,
Ah me! is my native country,
O my sweetheart, my Algonquin!

"When I looked back to behold him,
Where we parted, to behold him,
After me he still was gazing,
O my sweetheart, my Algonquin!

"By the tree he still was standing,
By the fallen tree was standing,
That had dropped into the water,
O my sweetheart, my Algonquin!

"When I think of my beloved,
Ah me! think of my beloved,
When my heart is thinking of him,
O my sweetheart, my Algonquin!"

Such was Hiawatha's Wedding,
Such the dance of Pau-Puk-Keewis,
Such the story of Iagoo,
Such the songs of Chibiabos;
Thus the wedding banquet ended,
And the wedding guests departed,
Leaving Hiawatha happy
With the night and Minnehaha.

# XIV

## PICTURE-WRITING

In those days said Hiawatha,
"Lo! how all things fade and perish!
From the memory of the old men
Pass away the great traditions,
The achievements of the warriors,
The adventures of the hunters,
All the wisdom of the Medas,
All the craft of the Wabenos,
All the marvellous dreams and visions
Of the Jossakeeds, the Prophets!

"Great men die and are forgotten,
Wise men speak; their words of wisdom
Perish in the ears that hear them,
Do not reach the generations
That, as yet unborn, are waiting
In the great, mysterious darkness
Of the speechless days that shall be!

"On the grave-posts of our fathers
Are no signs, no figures painted;
Who are in those graves we know not,
Only know they are our fathers.
Of what kith they are and kindred,
From what old, ancestral Totem,
Be it Eagle, Bear, or Beaver,
They descended, this we know not,
Only know they are our fathers.

"Face to face we speak together,
But we cannot speak when absent,
Cannot send our voices from us
To the friends that dwell afar off;
Cannot send a secret message,
But the bearer learns our secret,
May pervert it, may betray it,
May reveal it unto others."

Thus said Hiawatha, walking

In the solitary forest,
Pondering, musing in the forest,
On the welfare of his people.

From his pouch he took his colors,
Took his paints of different colors,
On the smooth bark of a birch-tree
Painted many shapes and figures,
Wonderful and mystic figures,
And each figure had a meaning,
Each some word or thought suggested.

Gitche Manito the Mighty,
He, the Master of Life, was painted
As an egg, with points projecting
To the four winds of the heavens.
Everywhere is the Great Spirit,
Was the meaning of this symbol.

Mitche Manito the Mighty,
He the dreadful Spirit of Evil,
As a serpent was depicted,
As Kenabeek, the great serpent.
Very crafty, very cunning,
Is the creeping Spirit of Evil,
Was the meaning of this symbol.

Life and Death he drew as circles,
Life was white, but Death was darkened;
Sun and moon and stars he painted,
Man and beast, and fish and reptile,
Forests, mountains, lakes, and rivers.

For the earth he drew a straight line,
For the sky a bow above it;
White the space between for daytime,
Filled with little stars for night-time;
On the left a point for sunrise,
On the right a point for sunset,
On the top a point for noontide,
And for rain and cloudy weather
Waving lines descending from it.

Footprints pointing towards a wigwam
Were a sign of invitation,
Were a sign of guests assembling;
Bloody hands with palms uplifted
Were a symbol of destruction,
Were a hostile sign and symbol.

All these things did Hiawatha
Show unto his wondering people,
And interpreted their meaning,
And he said: "Behold, your grave-posts
Have no mark, no sign, nor symbol,
Go and paint them all with figures;
Each one with its household symbol,
With its own ancestral Totem;
So that those who follow after
May distinguish them and know them."

And they painted on the grave-posts
On the graves yet unforgotten,
Each his own ancestral Totem,
Each the symbol of his household;
Figures of the Bear and Reindeer,
Of the Turtle, Crane, and Beaver,
Each inverted as a token
That the owner was departed,
That the chief who bore the symbol
Lay beneath in dust and ashes.

And the Jossakeeds, the Prophets,
The Wabenos, the Magicians,
And the Medicine-men, the Medas,
Painted upon bark and deer-skin
Figures for the songs they chanted,
For each song a separate symbol,
Figures mystical and awful,
Figures strange and brightly colored;
And each figure had its meaning,
Each some magic song suggested.

The Great Spirit, the Creator,
Flashing light through all the heaven;
The Great Serpent, the Kenabeek,
With his bloody crest erected,
Creeping, looking into heaven;
In the sky the sun, that listens,
And the moon eclipsed and dying;
Owl and eagle, crane and hen-hawk,
And the cormorant, bird of magic;
Headless men, that walk the heavens,
Bodies lying pierced with arrows,
Bloody hands of death uplifted,
Flags on graves, and great war-captains

Grasping both the earth and heaven!
Such as these the shapes they painted
On the birch-bark and the deer-skin;
Songs of war and songs of hunting,
Songs of medicine and of magic,
All were written in these figures,
For each figure had its meaning,
Each its separate song recorded.

Nor forgotten was the Love-Song,
The most subtle of all medicines,
The most potent spell of magic,
Dangerous more than war or hunting!
Thus the Love-Song was recorded,
Symbol and interpretation.

First a human figure standing,
Painted in the brightest scarlet;
'Tis the lover, the musician,
And the meaning is, "My painting
Makes me powerful over others."

Then the figure seated, singing,
Playing on a drum of magic,
And the interpretation, "Listen!
'Tis my voice you hear, my singing!'

Then the same red figure seated
In the shelter of a wigwam,
And the meaning of the symbol,
"I will come and sit beside you
In the mystery of my passion!"

Then two figures, man and woman,
Standing hand in hand together
With their hands so clasped together
That they seemed in one united,
And the words thus represented
Are, "I see your heart within you,
And your cheeks are red with blushes!"

Next the maiden on an island,
In the centre of an island;
And the song this shape suggested
Was, "Though you were at a distance,
Were upon some far-off island,
Such the spell I cast upon you,
Such the magic power of passion,
I could straightway draw you to me!"

Then the figure of the maiden
Sleeping, and the lover near her,
Whispering to her in her slumbers,
Saying, "Though you were far from me
In the land of Sleep and Silence,
Still the voice of love would reach you!"
And the last of all the figures
Was a heart within a circle,
Drawn within a magic circle;
And the image had this meaning:
"Naked lies your heart before me,
To your naked heart I whisper!"
Thus it was that Hiawatha,
In his wisdom, taught the people
All the mysteries of painting,
All the art of Picture-Writing,
On the smooth bark of the birch-tree,
On the white skin of the reindeer,
On the grave-posts of the village.

## XIX

### THE GHOSTS

Never stoops the soaring vulture
On his quarry in the desert,
On the sick or wounded bison,
But another vulture, watching
From his high aerial look-out,
Sees the downward plunge, and follows;
And a third pursues the second,
Coming from the invisible ether,
First a speck, and then a vulture,
Till the air is dark with pinions.
So disasters come not singly;
But as if they watched and waited,
Scanning one another's motions,
When the first descends, the others
Follow, follow, gathering flock-wise
Round their victim, sick and wounded,

First a shadow, then a sorrow,
Till the air is dark with anguish.

Now, o'er all the dreary North-land,
Mighty Peboan, the Winter,
Breathing on the lakes and rivers,
Into stone had changed their waters.
From his hair he shook the snow-flakes,
Till the plains were strewn with whiteness,
One uninterrupted level,
As if, stooping, the Creator
With his hand had smoothed them over.

Through the forest, wide and wailing,
Roamed the hunter on his snow-shoes;
In the village worked the women,
Pounded maize, or dressed the deer-skin;
And the young men played together
On the ice the noisy ball-play,
On the plain the dance of snow-shoes.

One dark evening, after sundown,
In her wigwam Laughing Water
Sat with old Nokomis, waiting
For the steps of Hiawatha
Homeward from the hunt returning.

On their faces gleamed the firelight,
Painting them with streaks of crimson,
In the eyes of old Nokomis
Glimmered like the watery moonlight,
In the eyes of Laughing Water
Glistened like the sun in water;
And behind them crouched their shadows
In the corners of the wigwam,
And the smoke in wreaths above them
Climbed and crowded through the smoke-
        flue.

Then the curtain of the doorway
From without was slowly lifted;
Brighter glowed the fire a moment,
And a moment swerved the smoke-wreath,
As two women entered softly,
Passed the doorway uninvited,
Without word of salutation,
Without sign of recognition,

Sat down in the farthest corner,
Crouching low among the shadows.

From their aspect and their garments,
Strangers seemed they in the village;
Very pale and haggard were they,
As they sat there sad and silent,
Trembling, cowering with the shadows.

Was it the wind above the smoke-flue,
Muttering down into the wigwam?
Was it the owl, the Koko-koho,
Hooting from the dismal forest?
Sure a voice said in the silence:
"These are corpses clad in garments,
These are ghosts that come to haunt you,
From the kingdom of Ponemah,
From the land of the Hereafter!"

Homeward now came Hiawatha
From his hunting in the forest,
With the snow upon his tresses,
And the red deer on his shoulders.
At the feet of Laughing Water
Down he threw his lifeless burden;
Nobler, handsomer she thought him,
Than when first he came to woo her,
First threw down the deer before her,
As a token of his wishes,
As a promise of the future.

Then he turned and saw the strangers,
Cowering, crouching with the shadows;
Said within himself, "Who are they?
What strange guests has Minnehaha?"
But he questioned not the strangers,
Only spake to bid them welcome
To his lodge, his food, his fireside.

When the evening meal was ready,
And the deer had been divided,
Both the pallid guests, the strangers,
Springing from among the shadows,
Seized upon the choicest portions,
Seized the white fat of the roebuck,
Set apart for Laughing Water,

For the wife of Hiawatha;
Without asking, without thanking,
Eagerly devoured the morsels,
Flitted back among the shadows
In the corner of the wigwam.

Not a word spake Hiawatha,
Not a motion made Nokomis,
Not a gesture Laughing Water;
Not a change came o'er their features;
Only Minnehaha softly
Whispered, saying, "They are famished;
Let them do what best delights them;
Let them eat, for they are famished."

Many a daylight dawned and darkened,
Many a night shook off the daylight
As the pine shakes off the snow-flakes
From the midnight of its branches;
Day by day the guests unmoving
Sat there silent in the wigwam;
But by night, in storm or starlight,
Forth they went into the forest,
Bringing fire-wood to the wigwam,
Bringing pine-cones for the burning,
Always sad and always silent.

And whenever Hiawatha
Came from fishing or from hunting,
When the evening meal was ready,
And the food had been divided,
Gliding from their darksome corner,
Came the pallid guests, the strangers,
Seized upon the choicest portions
Set aside for Laughing Water,
And without rebuke or question
Flitted back among the shadows.

Never once had Hiawatha
By a word or look reproved them;
Never once had old Nokomis
Made a gesture of impatience;
Never once had Laughing Water
Shown resentment at the outrage.
All had they endured in silence,
That the rights of guest and stranger,

That the virtue of free-giving,
By a look might not be lessened,
By a word might not be broken.

Once at midnight Hiawatha,
Ever wakeful, ever watchful,
In the wigwam, dimly lighted
By the brands that still were burning,
By the glimmering, flickering firelight,
Heard a sighing, oft repeated,
Heard a sobbing, as of sorrow.

From his couch rose Hiawatha,
From his shaggy hides of bison,
Pushed aside the deer-skin curtain,
Saw the pallid guests, the shadows,
Sitting upright on their couches,
Weeping in the silent midnight.

And he said: "O guests! why is it
That your hearts are so afflicted,
That you sob so in the midnight?
Has perchance the old Nokomis,
Has my wife, my Minnehaha,
Wronged or grieved you by unkindness,
Failed in hospitable duties?"

Then the shadows ceased from weeping,
Ceased from sobbing and lamenting,
And they said, with gentle voices:
"We are ghosts of the departed,
Souls of those who once were with you.
From the realms of Chibiabos
Hither have we come to try you,
Hither have we come to warn you.

"Cries of grief and lamentation
Reach us in the Blessed Islands;
Cries of anguish from the living,
Calling back their friends departed,
Sadden us with useless sorrow.
Therefore have we come to try you;
No one knows us, no one heeds us.
We are but a burden to you,
And we see that the departed
Have no place among the living.

"Think of this, O Hiawatha!
Speak of it to all the people,

That henceforward and forever
They no more with lamentations
Sadden the souls of the departed
In the Islands of the Blessed.

"Do not lay such heavy burdens
In the graves of those you bury,
Not such weight of furs and wampum,
Not such weight of pots and kettles,
For the spirits faint beneath them.
Only give them food to carry,
Only give them fire to light them.

"Four days is the spirit's journey
To the land of ghosts and shadows,
Four its lonely night encampments;
Four times must their fires be lighted.
Therefore, when the dead are buried,
Let a fire, as night approaches,
Four times on the grave be kindled,
That the soul upon its journey
May not lack the cheerful firelight,
May not grope about in darkness.

"Farewell, noble Hiawatha!
We have put you to the trial,
To the proof have put your patience,
By the insult of our presence,
By the outrage of our actions.
We have found you great and noble.
Fail not in the greater trial,
Faint not in the harder struggle."

When they ceased, a sudden darkness
Fell and filled the silent wigwam.
Hiawatha heard a rustle
As of garments trailing by him,
Heard the curtain of the doorway
Lifted by a hand he saw not,
Felt the cold breath of the night air,
For a moment saw the starlight;
But he saw the ghosts no longer,
Saw no more the wandering spirits
From the kingdom of Ponemah,
From the land of the Hereafter.

# XXII

## HIAWATHA'S DEPARTURE

By the shore of Gitche Gumee,
By the shining Big-Sea-Water,
At the doorway of his wigwam,
In the pleasant Summer morning,
Hiawatha stood and waited.
All the air was full of freshness,
All the earth was bright and joyous,
And before him, through the sunshine,
Westward toward the neighboring forest
Passed in golden swarms the Ahmo,
Passed the bees, the honey-makers,
Burning, singing in the sunshine.

Bright above him shone the heavens,
Level spread the lake before him;
From its bosom leaped the sturgeon,
Sparkling, flashing in the sunshine;
On its margin the great forest
Stood reflected in the water,
Every tree-top had its shadow,
Motionless beneath the water.

From the brow of Hiawatha
Gone was every trace of sorrow,
As the fog from off the water,
As the mist from off the meadow.
With a smile of joy and triumph,
With a look of exultation,
As of one who in a vision
Sees what is to be, but is not,
Stood and waited Hiawatha.

Toward the sun his hands were lifted,
Both the palms spread out against it,
And between the parted fingers
Fell the sunshine on his features,
Flecked with light his naked shoulders,
As it falls and flecks an oak-tree

149

Through the rifted leaves and branches.
O'er the water floating, flying,
Something in the hazy distance,
Something in the mists of morning,
Loomed and lifted from the water,
Now seemed floating, now seemed flying,
Coming nearer, nearer, nearer.

Was it Shingebis the diver?
Or the pelican, the Shada?
Or the heron, the Shuh-shuh-gah?
Or the white goose, Waw-be-wawa,
With the water dripping, flashing,
From its glossy neck and feathers?

It was neither goose nor diver,
Neither pelican nor heron,
O'er the water floating, flying,
Through the shining mist of morning,
But a birch canoe with paddles,
Rising, sinking on the water,
Dripping, flashing in the sunshine;
And within it came a people
From the distant land of Wabun,
From the farthest realms of morning
Came the Black-Robe chief, the Prophet,
He the Priest of Prayer, the Pale-face,
With his guides and his companions.

And the noble Hiawatha,
With his hands aloft extended,
Held aloft in sign of welcome,
Waited, full of exultation,
Till the birch canoe with paddles
Grated on the shining pebbles,
Stranded on the sandy margin,
Till the Black-Robe chief, the Pale-face,
With the cross upon his bosom,
Landed on the sandy margin.

Then the joyous Hiawatha
Cried aloud and spake in this wise:
"Beautiful is the sun, O strangers,
When you come so far to see us!
All our town in peace awaits you,
All our doors stand open for you;

You shall enter all our wigwams,
For the heart's right hand we give you.

"Never bloomed the earth so gaily,
Never shone the sun so brightly,
As to-day they shine and blossom
When you come so far to see us!
Never was our lake so tranquil,
Nor so free from rocks and sand-bars;
For your birch canoe in passing
Has removed both rock and sand-bar.

"Never before had our tobacco
Such a sweet and pleasant flavor,
Never the broad leaves of our cornfields
Were so beautiful to look on,
As they seem to us this morning,
When you come so far to see us!"

And the Black-Robe chief made answer,
Stammered in his speech a little,
Speaking words yet unfamiliar:
"Peace be with you, Hiawatha,
Peace be with you and your people,
Peace of prayer, and peace of pardon,
Peace of Christ, and joy of Mary!"

Then the generous Hiawatha
Led the strangers to his wigwam,
Seated them on skins of bison,
Seated them on skins of ermine,
And the careful old Nokomis
Brought them food in bowls of basswood,
Water brought in birchen dippers,
And the calumet, the peace-pipe,
Filled and lighted for their smoking.

All the old men of the village,
All the warriors of the nation,
All the Jossakeeds, the Prophets,
The magicians, the Wabenos,
And the Medicine-men, the Medas,
Came to bid the strangers welcome;
"It is well," they said, "O brothers,
That you come so far to see us!"

In a circle round the doorway,
With their pipes they sat in silence,

Waiting to behold the strangers,
Waiting to receive their message;
Till the Black-Robe chief, the Pale-face,
From the wigwam came to greet them,
Stammering in his speech a little,
Speaking words yet unfamiliar;
"It is well," they said, "O brother,
That you come so far to see us!"

Then the Black-Robe chief, the Prophet,
Told his message to the people,
Told the purport of his mission,
Told them of the Virgin Mary,
And her blessed Son, the Saviour,
How in distant lands and ages
He had lived on earth as we do;
How he fasted, prayed, and labored;
How the Jews, the tribe accursed,
Mocked him, scourged him, crucified him;
How he rose from where they laid him,
Walked again with his disciples,
And ascended into heaven.

And the chiefs made answer, saying:
"We have listened to your message,
We have heard your words of wisdom,
We will think on what you tell us.
It is well for us, O brothers,
That you come so far to see us!"

Then they rose up and departed
Each one homeward to his wigwam,
To the young men and the women
Told the story of the strangers
Whom the Master of Life had sent them
From the shining land of Wabun.

Heavy with the heat and silence
Grew the afternoon of Summer;
With a drowsy sound the forest
Whispered round the sultry wigwam,
With a sound of sleep the water
Rippled on the beach below it;
From the cornfields shrill and ceaseless
Sang the grasshopper, Pah-puk-keena;
And the guests of Hiawatha,

Weary with the heat of Summer,
Slumbered in the sultry wigwam.

Slowly o'er the simmering landscape
Fell the evening's dusk and coolness,
And the long and level sunbeams
Shot their spears into the forest,
Breaking through its shields of shadow,
Rushed into each secret ambush,
Searched each thicket, dingle, hollow;
Still the guests of Hiawatha
Slumbered in the silent wigwam.

From his place rose Hiawatha,
Bade farewell to old Nokomis,
Spake in whispers, spake in this wise,
Did not wake the guests, that slumbered

"I am going, O Nokomis,
On a long and distant journey,
To the portals of the Sunset,
To the regions of the home-wind,
Of the Northwest-Wind, Keewaydin.
But these guests I leave behind me,
In your watch and ward I leave them;
See that never harm comes near them,
See that never fear molests them,
Never danger nor suspicion,
Never want of food or shelter,
In the lodge of Hiawatha!"

Forth into the village went he,
Bade farewell to all the warriors,
Bade farewell to all the young men,
Spake persuading, spake in this wise:

"I am going, O my people,
On a long and distant journey;
Many moons and many winters
Will have come, and will have vanished,
Ere I come again to see you.
But my guests I leave behind me;
Listen to their words of wisdom,
Listen to the truth they tell you,
For the Master of Life has sent them
From the land of light and morning!"

On the shore stood Hiawatha,
Turned and waved his hand at parting;

On the clear and luminous water
Launched his birch canoe for sailing,
From the pebbles of the margin
Shoved it forth into the water;
Whispered to it, "Westward! westward!"
And with speed it darted forward.

And the evening sun descending
Set the clouds on fire with redness,
Burned the broad sky, like a prairie,
Left upon the level water
One long track and trail of splendor,
Down whose stream, as down a river,
Westward, westward Hiawatha
Sailed into the fiery sunset,
Sailed into the purple vapors,
Sailed into the dusk of evening.

And the people from the margin
Watched him floating, rising, sinking,
Till the birch canoe seemed lifted
High into that sea of splendor,
Till it sank into the vapors
Like the new moon slowly, slowly
Sinking in the purple distance.

And they said, "Farewell forever!"
Said, "Farewell, O Hiawatha!"
And the forests, dark and lonely,
Moved through all their depths of darkness
Sighed, "Farewell, O Hiawatha!"
And the waves upon the margin
Rising, rippling on the pebbles,
Sobbed, "Farewell, O Hiawatha!"
And the heron, the Shuh-shuh-gah,
From her haunts among the fen-lands,
Screamed, "Farewell, O Hiawatha!"

Thus departed Hiawatha,
Hiawatha the Beloved,
In the glory of the sunset,
In the purple mists of evening,
To the regions of the home-wind,
Of the Northwest-Wind, Keewaydin,
To the Islands of the Blessed,
To the Kingdom of Ponemah,
To the Land of the Hereafter!

# THE CELESTIAL PILOT

One of Longfellow's earliest translations from the Italian, "The Celestial Pilot" was included in his book of poems, *Voices of the Night*. It is a passage from Dante's *Divina Commedia*, Purgatorio II, 13-51.

AND now, behold! as at the approach of morning,
　Through the gross vapors, Mars grows fiery red
　Down in the west upon the ocean floor,
Appeared to me,—may I again behold it!
　A light along the sea, so swiftly coming,
　Its motion by no flight of wing is equalled.
And when therefrom I had withdrawn a little
　Mine eyes, that I might question my conductor,
　Again I saw it brighter grown and larger.
Thereafter, on all sides of it, appeared
　I knew not what of white, and underneath,
　Little by little, there came forth another.
My master yet had uttered not a word.
　While the first whiteness into wings unfolded;
　But, when he clearly recognized the pilot,
He cried aloud: "Quick, quick, and bow the knee!
　Behold the Angel of God! fold up thy hands!
　Henceforward shalt thou see such officers!
See, how he scorns all human arguments,
　So that no oar he wants, nor other sail
　Than his own wings, between so distant shores!
See, how he holds them, pointed straight to heaven,
　Fanning the air with the eternal pinions,
　That do not moult themselves like mortal hair!"
And then, as nearer and more near us came
　The Bird of Heaven, more glorious he appeared,
　So that the eye could not sustain his presence,
But down I cast it; and he came to shore
　With a small vessel, gliding swift and light,
　So that the water swallowed naught thereof.
Upon the stern stood the Celestial Pilot!
　Beatitude seemed written in his face!
　And more than a hundred spirits sat within.
*"In exitu Israel de Ægypto!"*

Thus sang they all together in one voice,
  With whatso in that Psalm is after written.
Then made he sign of holy rood upon them,
  Whereat all cast themselves upon the shore,
  And he departed swiftly as he came.


## THE BELLS OF LYNN

### HEARD AT NAHANT

O CURFEW of the setting sun! O Bells of Lynn!
O requiem of the dying day! O Bells of Lynn!

From the dark belfries of yon cloud-cathedral wafted,
Your sounds aerial seem to float, O Bells of Lynn!

Borne on the evening wind across the crimson twilight,
O'er land and sea they rise and fall, O Bells of Lynn!

The fisherman in his boat, far out beyond the headland,
Listens, and leisurely rows ashore, O Bells of Lynn!

Over the shining sands the wandering cattle homeward
Follow each other at your call, O Bells of Lynn!

The distant lighthouse hears, and with his flaming signal
Answers you, passing the watchword on, O Bells of Lynn!

And down the darkening coast run the tumultuous surges,
And clap their hands, and shout to you, O Bells of Lynn!

Till from the shuddering sea, with your wild incantations,
Ye summon up the spectral moon, O Bells of Lynn!

And startled at the sight, like the weird woman of Endor,
Ye cry aloud, and then are still, O Bells of Lynn!


## SANDALPHON

HAVE you read in the Talmud of old,
In the Legends the Rabbins have told
  Of the limitless realms of the air,

Have you read it,—the marvellous story
Of Sandalphon, the Angel of Glory,
  Sandalphon, the Angel of Prayer?

How, erect, at the outermost gates
Of the City Celestial he waits,
  With his feet on the ladder of light,
That, crowded with angels unnumbered,
By Jacob was seen, as he slumbered
  Alone in the desert at night?

The Angels of Wind and of Fire
Chant only one hymn, and expire
  With the song's irresistible stress;
Expire in their rapture and wonder,
As harp-strings are broken asunder
  By music they throb to express.

But serene in the rapturous throng,
Unmoved by the rush of the song,
  With eyes unimpassioned and slow,
Among the dead angels, the deathless
Sandalphon stands listening breathless
  To sounds that ascend from below;—

From the spirits on earth that adore,
From the souls that entreat and implore
  In the fervor and passion of prayer;
From the hearts that are broken with losses,
And weary with dragging the crosses
  Too heavy for mortals to bear.

And he gathers the prayers as he stands,
And they change into flowers in his hands,
  Into garlands of purple and red;
And beneath the great arch of the portal,
Through the streets of the City Immortal
  Is wafted the fragrance they shed.

It is but a legend, I know,—
A fable, a phantom, a show,

Of the ancient Rabbinical lore;
Yet the old mediæval tradition,
The beautiful, strange superstition,
  But haunts me and holds me the more.

When I look from my window at night,
And the welkin above is all white,
  All throbbing and panting with stars,
Among them majestic is standing
Sandalphon the angel, expanding
  His pinions in nebulous bars.

And the legend, I feel, is a part
Of the hunger and thirst of the heart,
  The frenzy and fire of the brain,
That grasps at the fruitage forbidden,
The golden pomegranates of Eden,
  To quiet its fever and pain.

## VITTORIA COLONNA

ONCE more, once more, Inarimé,
  I see thy purple halls!—once more
I hear the billows of the bay
  Wash the white pebbles on thy shore.

High o'er the sea-surge and the sands,
  Like a great galleon wrecked and cast
Ashore by storms, thy castle stands,
  A mouldering landmark of the Past.

Upon its terrace-walk I see
  A phantom gliding to and fro;
It is Colonna,—it is she
  Who lived and loved so long ago.

Pescara's beautiful young wife
  The type of perfect womanhood,
Whose life was love, the life of life,
  That time and change and death withstood.
For death, that breaks the marriage band

In others, only closer pressed
The wedding ring upon her hand
    And closer locked and barred her breast.

She knew the life-long martyrdom,
    The weariness, the endless pain
Of waiting for some one to come
    Who nevermore would come again.

The shadows of the chestnut trees,
    The odor of the orange blooms,
The song of birds, and, more than these,
    The silence of deserted rooms;
The respiration of the sea,
    The soft caresses of the air,
All things in nature seemed to be
    But ministers of her despair;

Till the o'erburdened heart, so long
    Imprisoned in itself, found vent
And voice in one impassioned song
    Of inconsolable lament.

Then as the sun, though hidden from sight,
    Transmutes to gold the leaden mist,
Her life was interfused with light,
    From realms that, though unseen, exist.

Inarimé! Inarimé!
    Thy castle on the crags above
In dust shall crumble and decay,
    But not the memory of her love.


## HELEN OF TYRE


WHAT phantom is this that appears
Through the purple mists of the years,
    Itself but a mist like these?
A woman of cloud and of fire;
It is she; it is Helen of Tyre,

The town in the midst of the seas.

O Tyre! in thy crowded streets
The phantom appears and retreats,
     And the Israelites that sell
Thy lilies and lions of brass,
Look up as they see her pass,
     And murmur "Jezebel!"

Then another phantom is seen
At her side, in a gray gabardine,
     With beard that floats to his waist;
It is Simon Magus, the Seer;
He speaks, and she pauses to hear
     The words he utters in haste.

He says: "From this evil fame,
From this life of sorrow and shame,
     I will lift thee and make thee mine;
Thou hast been Queen Candace,
And Helen of Troy, and shalt be
     The Intelligence Divine!"

Oh, sweet as the breath of morn,
To the fallen and forlorn
     Are whispered words of praise;
For the famished heart believes
The falsehood that tempts and deceives,
     And the promise that betrays.

So she follows from land to land
The wizard's beckoning hand,
     As a leaf is blown by the gust,
Till she vanishes into night.
O reader, stoop down and write
     With thy finger in the dust.

O town in the midst of the seas,
With thy rafts of cedar trees,
     Thy merchandise and thy ships,
Thou, too, art become as naught,
A phantom, a shadow, a thought,
     A name upon men's lips.

A mist was driving down the British Channel,
 The day was just begun,
And through the window-panes, on floor and panel,
 Streamed the red autumn sun.

It glanced on flowing flag and rippling pennon,
 And the white sails of ships;
And, from the frowning rampart, the black cannon
 Hailed it with feverish lips.

Sandwich and Romney, Hastings, Hithe, and Dover
 Were all alert that day,
To see the French war-steamers speeding over,
 When the fog cleared away.

Sullen and silent, and like couchant lions,
 Their cannon, through the night,
Holding their breath, had watched, in grim defiance,
 The sea-coast opposite.

And now they roared at drum-beat from their stations
 On every citadel;
Each answering each, with morning salutations,
 That all was well.

And down the coast, all taking up the burden,
 Replied the distant forts,
As if to summon from his sleep the Warden
 And Lord of the Cinque Ports.

Him shall no sunshine from the fields of azure,
 No drum-beat from the wall,
No morning gun from the black fort's embrasure,
 Awaken with its call!
No more, surveying with an eye impartial
 The long line of the coast,
Shall the gaunt figure of the old Field Marshal
 Be seen upon his post!

For in the night, unseen, a single warrior,
    In sombre harness mailed,
Dreaded of man, and surnamed the Destroyer,
    The rampart wall had scaled.

He passed into the chamber of the sleeper,
    The dark and silent room,
And as he entered, darker grew, and deeper,
    The silence and the gloom.

He did not pause to parley or dissemble,
    But smote the Warden hoar;
Ah! what a blow! that made all England tremble
    And groan from shore to shore.

Meanwhile, without, the surly cannon waited,
    The sun rose bright o'erhead;
Nothing in Nature's aspect intimated
    That a great man was dead.

## HAUNTED HOUSES

All houses wherein men have lived and died
    Are haunted houses. Through the open doors
The harmless phantoms on their errands glide,
    With feet that make no sound upon the floors.

We meet them at the doorway, on the stair,
    Along the passages they come and go,
Impalpable impressions on the air,
    A sense of something moving to and fro.

There are more guests at table than the hosts
    Invited; the illuminated hall
Is thronged with quiet, inoffensive ghosts,
    As silent as the pictures on the wall.
The stranger at my fireside cannot see
    The forms I see, nor hear the sounds I hear;
He but perceives what is; while unto me
    All that has been is visible and clear.

We have no title-deeds to house or lands;
    Owners and occupants of earlier dates
From graves forgotten stretch their dusty hands,
    And hold in mortmain still their old estates.

The spirit-world around this world of sense
    Floats like an atmosphere, and everywhere
Wafts through these earthly mists and vapors dense
    A vital breath of more ethereal air.

Our little lives are kept in equipoise
    By opposite attractions and desires;
The struggle of the instinct that enjoys,
    And the more noble instinct that aspires.

These perturbations, this perpetual jar
    Of earthly wants and aspirations high,
Come from the influence of an unseen star,
    An undiscovered planet in our sky.

And as the moon from some dark gate of cloud
    Throws o'er the sea a floating bridge of light,
Across whose trembling planks our fancies crowd
    Into the realm of mystery and night,—

So from the world of spirits there descends
    A bridge of light, connecting it with this,
O'er whose unsteady floor, that sways and bends,
    Wander our thoughts above the dark abyss.


### IN THE CHURCHYARD AT CAMBRIDGE

In the village churchyard she lies,
Dust is in her beautiful eyes,
    No more she breathes, nor feels, nor stirs;
At her feet and at her head
Lies a slave to attend the dead,
    But their dust is white as hers.

Was she, a lady of high degree,
So much in love with the vanity
    And foolish pomp of this world of ours?

Or was it Christian charity,
And lowliness and humility,
        The richest and rarest of all dowers?

Who shall tell us? No one speaks;
No color shoots into those cheeks,
        Either of anger or of pride,
At the rude question we have asked;
Nor will the mystery be unmasked
        By those who are sleeping at her side.

Hereafter?—And do you think to look
On the terrible pages of that Book
        To find her failings, faults, and errors?
Ah, you will then have other cares,
In your own shortcomings and despairs,
        In your own secret sins and terrors!

## MY LOST YOUTH

Often I think of the beautiful town
    That is seated by the sea;
Often in thought go up and down
The pleasant streets of that dear old town,
    And my youth comes back to me.
        And a verse of a Lapland song
        Is haunting my memory still:
        "A boy's will is the wind's will,
And the thoughts of youth are long, long thoughts."

I can see the shadowy lines of its trees,
    And catch, in sudden gleams,
The sheen of the far-surrounding seas,
And islands that were the Hesperides
    Of all my boyish dreams.
        And the burden of that old song,
        It murmurs and whispers still:
        "A boy's will is the wind's will,
And the thoughts of youth are long, long thoughts."

I remember the black wharves and the slips,
   And the sea-tides tossing free;
And Spanish sailors with bearded lips,
And the beauty and mystery of the ships,
   And the magic of the sea.
      And the voice of that wayward song
      Is singing and saying still:
      "A boy's will is the wind's will,
And the thoughts of youth are long, long thoughts."

I remember the bulwarks by the shore,
   And the fort upon the hill;
The sunrise gun, with its hollow roar,
The drum-beat repeated o'er and o'er,
   And the bugle wild and shrill.
      And the music of that old song
      Throbs in my memory still:
      "A boy's will is the wind's will,
And the thoughts of youth are long, long thoughts."

I remember the sea-fight far away,
   How it thundered o'er the tide!
And the dead captains, as they lay
In their graves, o'erlooking the tranquil bay
   Where they in battle died.
      And the sound of that mournful song
      Goes through me with a thrill:
      "A boy's will is the wind's will,
And the thoughts of youth are long, long thoughts."

I can see the breezy dome of groves,
   The shadows of Deering's Woods;
And the friendships old and the early loves
Come back with a Sabbath sound, as of doves
   In quiet neighborhoods.
      And the verse of that sweet old song,
      It flutters and murmurs still:
      "A boy's will is the wind's will,
And the thoughts of youth are long, long thoughts."
I remember the gleams and glooms that dart
   Across the school-boy's brain;
The song and the silence in the heart,

That in part are prophecies, and in part
  Are longings wild and vain.
    And the voice of that fitful song
    Sings on, and is never still:
    "A boy's will is the wind's will,
And the thoughts of youth are long, long thoughts."
There are things of which I may not speak;
  There are dreams that cannot die;
There are thoughts that make the strong heart weak,
And bring a pallor into the cheek,
  And a mist before the eye.
    And the words of that fatal song
    Come over me like a chill:
    "A boy's will is the wind's will,
And the thoughts of youth are long, long thoughts."
Strange to me now are the forms I meet
  When I visit the dear old town;
But the native air is pure and sweet
And the trees that o'ershadow each well-known street,
  As they balance up and down,
    Are singing the beautiful song,
    Are sighing and whispering still:
    "A boy's will is the wind's will,
And the thoughts of youth are long, long thoughts."
And Deering's Woods are fresh and fair,
  And with joy that is almost pain
My heart goes back to wander there,
And among the dreams of the days that were,
  I find my lost youth again.
    And the strange and beautiful song,
    The groves are repeating it still:
    "A boy's will is the wind's will,
And the thoughts of youth are long, long thoughts."

## THE CHILDREN'S HOUR

Between the dark and the daylight,
  When the night is beginning to lower,
Comes a pause in the day's occupations,
  That is known as the Children's Hour.

I hear in the chamber above me
  The patter of little feet,
The sound of a door that is opened,
  And voices soft and sweet.

From my study I see in the lamplight,
  Descending the broad hall stair,
Grave Alice, and laughing Allegra,
  And Edith with golden hair.

A whisper, and then a silence:
  Yet I know by their merry eyes
They are plotting and planning together
  To take me by surprise.

A sudden rush from the stairway,
  A sudden raid from the hall!
By three doors left unguarded
  They enter my castle wall!

They climb up into my turret
  O'er the arms and back of my chair;
If I try to escape, they surround me;
  They seem to be everywhere.

They almost devour me with kisses,
  Their arms about me entwine,
Till I think of the Bishop of Bingen
  In his Mouse-Tower on the Rhine!

Do you think, O blue-eyed banditti,
  Because you have scaled the wall,
Such an old mustache as I am
  Is not a match for you all!

I have you fast in my fortress,
  And will not let you depart,
But put you down into the dungeon
  In the round-tower of my heart.

And there will I keep you forever,
  Yes, forever and a day,
Till the walls shall crumble to ruin,
  And moulder in dust away!

## PAUL REVERE'S RIDE

Listen, my children, and you shall hear
Of the midnight ride of Paul Revere,
On the eighteenth of April, in Seventy-five;
Hardly a man is now alive
Who remembers that famous day and year.

He said to his friend, "If the British march
By land or sea from the town to-night,
Hang a lantern aloft in the belfry arch
Of the North Church tower as a signal light,—
One, if by land, and two, if by sea;
And I on the opposite shore will be,
Ready to ride and spread the alarm
Through every Middlesex village and farm,
For the country folk to be up and to arm."

Then he said, "Good night!" and with muffled oar
Silently rowed to the Charlestown shore,
Just as the moon rose over the bay,
Where swinging wide at her moorings lay
The Somerset, British man-of-war;
A phantom ship, with each mast and spar
Across the moon like a prison bar,
And a huge black hulk, that was magnified
By its own reflection in the tide.
Meanwhile, his friend, through alley and street,
Wanders and watches with eager ears,
Till in the silence around him he hears
The muster of men at the barrack door,
The sound of arms, and the tramp of feet,
And the measured tread of the grenadiers,
Marching down to their boats on the shore.

Then he climbed the tower of the Old North Church,
By the wooden stairs, with stealthy tread,
To the belfry-chamber overhead,
And startled the pigeons from their perch
On the sombre rafters, that round him made

Masses and moving shapes of shade,—
By the trembling ladder, steep and tall,
To the highest window in the wall,
Where he paused to listen and look down
A moment on the roofs of the town,
And the moonlight flowing over all.

Beneath, in the churchyard, lay the dead,
In their night-encampment on the hill,
Wrapped in silence so deep and still
That he could hear, like a sentinel's tread,
The watchful night-wind, as it went
Creeping along from tent to tent,
And seeming to whisper, "All is well!"
A moment only he feels the spell
Of the place and the hour, and the secret dread
Of the lonely belfry and the dead;
For suddenly all his thoughts are bent
On a shadowy something far away,
Where the river widens to meet the bay,—
A line of black that bends and floats
On the rising tide, like a bridge of boats.

Meanwhile, impatient to mount and ride,
Booted and spurred, with a heavy stride
On the opposite shore walked Paul Revere.
Now he patted his horse's side,
Now gazed at the landscape far and near,
Then, impetuous, stamped the earth,
And turned and tightened his saddle-girth;
But mostly he watched with eager search
The belfry-tower of the Old North Church,
As it rose above the graves on the hill,
Lonely and spectral and sombre and still.
And lo! as he looks, on the belfry's height
A glimmer, and then a gleam of light!
He springs to the saddle, the bridle he turns,
But lingers and gazes, till full on his sight
A second lamp in the belfry burns!

A hurry of hoofs in a village street,
A shape in the moonlight, a bulk in the dark,

And beneath, from the pebbles, in passing, a spark
Struck out by a steed flying fearless and fleet:
That was all! And yet, through the gloom and the light,
The fate of a nation was riding that night;
And the spark struck out by that steed, in his flight,
Kindled the land into flame with its heat.

He has left the village and mounted the steep,
And beneath him, tranquil and broad and deep,
Is the Mystic, meeting the ocean tides;
And under the alders that skirt its edge,
Now soft on the sand, now loud on the ledge,
Is heard the tramp of his steed as he rides.

It was twelve by the village clock,
When he crossed the bridge into Medford town.
He heard the crowing of the cock,
And the barking of the farmer's dog,
And felt the damp of the river fog,
That rises after the sun goes down.

It was one by the village clock,
When he galloped into Lexington.
He saw the gilded weathercock
Swim in the moonlight as he passed,
And the meeting-house windows, blank and bare,
Gaze at him with a spectral glare,
As if they already stood aghast
At the bloody work they would look upon.

It was two by the village clock,
When he came to the bridge in Concord town.
He heard the bleating of the flock,
And the twitter of birds among the trees,
And felt the breath of the morning breeze
Blowing over the meadows brown.
And one was safe and asleep in his bed
Who at the bridge would be first to fall,
Who that day would be lying dead,
Pierced by a British musket-ball.

You know the rest. In the books you have read,
How the British Regulars fired and fled,—

How the farmers gave them ball for ball,
From behind each fence and farm-yard wall,
Chasing the red-coats down the lane,
Then crossing the fields to emerge again
Under the trees at the turn of the road,
And only pausing to fire and load.

So through the night rode Paul Revere;
And so through the night went his cry of alarm
To every Middlesex village and farm,—
A cry of defiance and not of fear,
A voice in the darkness, a knock at the door,
And a word that shall echo forevermore!
For, borne on the night-wind of the Past,
Through all our history, to the last,
In the hour of darkness and peril and need,
The people will waken and listen to hear
The hurrying hoof-beats of that steed,
And the midnight message of Paul Revere.


## from THE SAGA OF KING OLAF

### I

#### THE CHALLENGE OF THOR

I am the God Thor,
I am the War God,
I am the Thunderer!
Here in my Northland,
My fastness and fortress,
Reign I forever!

Here amid icebergs
Rule I the nations;
This is my hammer,
Miölner the mighty;
Giants and sorcerers
Cannot withstand it!

These are the gauntlets
Wherewith I wield it,
And hurl it afar off;
This is my girdle;
Whenever I brace it,
Strength is redoubled!

The light thou beholdest
Stream through the heavens,
In flashes of crimson,
Is but my red beard
Blown by the night-wind,
Affrighting the nations!

Jove is my brother;
Mine eyes are the lightning;
The wheels of my chariot
Roll in the thunder,
The blows of my hammer
Ring in the earthquake!

Force rules the world still,
Has ruled it, shall rule it;
Meekness is weakness,
Strength is triumphant,
Over the whole earth
Still is it Thor's-Day!

Thou art a God too,
O Galilean!
And thus single-handed
Unto the combat,
Gauntlet or Gospel,
Here I defy thee!

# VI

### THE WRAITH OF ODIN

The guests were loud, the ale was strong,
King Olaf feasted late and long;
The hoary Scalds together sang;
O'erhead the smoky rafters rang.
  Dead rides Sir Morten of Fogelsang.

The door swung wide, with creak and din;
A blast of cold night-air came in,
And on the threshold shivering stood
A one-eyed guest, with cloak and hood.
  Dead rides Sir Morten of Fogelsang.

The King exclaimed, "O graybeard pale!
Come warm thee with this cup of ale."
The foaming draught the old man quaffed,
The noisy guests looked on and laughed.
  Dead rides Sir Morten of Fogelsang.

Then spake the King: "Be not afraid:
Sit here by me." The guest obeyed,
And, seated at the table, told
Tales of the sea, and Sagas old.
  Dead rides Sir Morten of Fogelsang.

And ever, when the tale was o'er,
The King demanded yet one more;
Till Sigurd the Bishop smiling said,
" 'Tis late, O King, and time for bed."
  Dead rides Sir Morten of Fogelsang.

The King retired; the stranger guest
Followed and entered with the rest;
The lights were out, the pages gone,
But still the garrulous guest spake on.
  Dead rides Sir Morten of Fogelsang.

As one who from a volume reads,
He spake of heroes and their deeds,

Of lands and cities he had seen,
And stormy gulfs that tossed between.
  Dead rides Sir Morten of Fogelsang.


Then from his lips in music rolled
The Havamal of Odin old,
With sounds mysterious as the roar
Of billows on a distant shore.
  Dead rides Sir Morten of Fogelsang.


"Do we not learn from runes and rhymes
Made by the gods in elder times,
And do not still the great Scalds teach
That silence better is than speech?"
  Dead rides Sir Morten of Fogelsang.


Smiling at this, the King replied,
"Thy lore is by thy tongue belied;
For never was I so enthralled
Either by Saga-man or Scald."
  Dead rides Sir Morten of Fogelsang.


The Bishop said, "Late hours we keep!
Night wanes, O King! 't is time for sleep!"
Then slept the King, and when he woke
The guest was gone, the morning broke.
  Dead rides Sir Morten of Fogelsang.


They found the doors securely barred,
They found the watch-dog in the yard,
There was no footprint in the grass,
And none had seen the stranger pass.
  Dead rides Sir Morten of Fogelsang.


King Olaf crossed himself and said:
"I know that Odin the Great is dead;
Sure is the triumph of our Faith,
The one-eyed stranger was his wraith."
  Dead rides Sir Morten of Fogelsang.

## THE BIRDS OF KILLINGWORTH

It was the season, when through all the land
　The merle and mavis build, and building sing
Those lovely lyrics, written by His hand,
　Whom Saxon Cædmon calls the Blithe-heart King;
When on the boughs the purple buds expand,
　The banners of the vanguard of the Spring,
And rivulets, rejoicing, rush and leap,
And wave their fluttering signals from the steep.

The robin and the bluebird, piping loud,
　Filled all the blossoming orchards with their glee;
The sparrows chirped as if they still were proud
　Their race in Holy Writ should mentioned be;
And hungry crows, assembled in a crowd,
　Clamored their piteous prayer incessantly,
Knowing who hears the ravens cry, and said:
"Give us, O Lord, this day, our daily bread!"

Across the Sound the birds of passage sailed,
　Speaking some unknown language strange and sweet
Of tropic isle remote, and passing hailed
　The village with the cheers of all their fleet;
Or quarrelling together, laughed and railed
　Like foreign sailors, landed in the street
Of seaport town, and with outlandish noise
Of oaths and gibberish frightening girls and boys.

Thus came the jocund Spring in Killingworth,
　In fabulous days, some hundred years ago;
And thrifty farmers, as they tilled the earth,
　Heard with alarm the cawing of the crow,
That mingled with the universal mirth,
　Cassandra-like, prognosticating woe;
They shook their heads, and doomed with dreadful words
To swift destruction the whole race of birds.

And a town-meeting was convened straight-way
　To set a price upon the guilty heads

Of these marauders, who, in lieu of pay,
   Levied black-mail upon the garden beds
And cornfields, and beheld without dismay
   The awful scarecrow, with his fluttering shreds;
The skeleton that waited at their feast,
Whereby their sinful pleasure was increased.

Then from his house, a temple painted white,
   With fluted columns, and a roof of red,
The Squire came forth, august and splendid sight!
   Slowly descending, with majestic tread,
Three flights of steps, nor looking left nor right,
   Down the long street he walked, as one who said,
"A town that boasts inhabitants like me
Can have no lack of good society!"

The Parson, too, appeared, a man austere,
   The instinct of whose nature was to kill;
The wrath of God he preached from year to year,
   And read, with fervor, Edwards on the Will;
His favorite pastime was to slay the deer
   In Summer on some Adirondac hill;
E'en now, while walking down the rural lane,
He lopped the wayside lilies with his cane.

From the Academy, whose belfry crowned
   The hill of Science with its vane of brass,
Came the Preceptor, gazing idly round,
   Now at the clouds, and now at the green grass,
And all absorbed in reveries profound
   Of fair Almira in the upper class,
Who was, as in a sonnet he had said,
As pure as water, and as good as bread.

And next the Deacon issued from his door,
   In his voluminous neck-cloth, white as snow;
A suit of sable bombazine he wore;
   His form was ponderous, and his step was slow;
There never was so wise a man before;
   He seemed the incarnate "Well, I told you so!"
And to perpetuate his great renown
There was a street named after him in town.

These came together in the new town-hall,
   With sundry farmers from the region round.

The Squire presided, dignified and tall,
  His air impressive and his reasoning sound;
Ill fared it with the birds, both great and small;
  Hardly a friend in all that crowd they found,
But enemies enough, who every one
Charged them with all the crimes beneath the sun.

When they had ended, from his place apart
  Rose the Preceptor, to redress the wrong,
And, trembling like a steed before the start,
  Looked round bewildered on the expectant throng;
Then thought of fair Almira, and took heart
  To speak out what was in him, clear and strong,
Alike regardless of their smile or frown,
And quite determined not to be laughed down.

"Plato, anticipating the Reviewers,
  From his Republic banished without pity
The Poets; in this little town of yours,
  You put to death, by means of a Committee,
The ballad-singers and the Troubadours,
  The street-musicians of the heavenly city,
The birds, who make sweet music for us all
In our dark hours, as David did for Saul.

"The thrush that carols at the dawn of day
  From the green steeples of the piny wood;
The oriole in the elm; the noisy jay,
  Jargoning like a foreigner at his food;
The bluebird balanced on some topmost spray,
  Flooding with melody the neighborhood;
Linnet and meadow-lark, and all the throng
That dwell in nests, and have the gift of song.

"You slay them all! and wherefore? for the gain
  Of a scant handful more or less of wheat,
Or rye, or barley, or some other grain,
  Scratched up at random by industrious feet,
Searching for worm or weevil after rain!
  Or a few cherries, that are not so sweet
As are the songs these uninvited guests
Sing at their feast with comfortable breasts.

"Do you ne'er think what wondrous beings these?
  Do you ne'er think who made them, and who taught

The dialect they speak, where melodies
   Alone are the interpreters of thought?
Whose household words are songs in many keys,
   Sweeter than instrument of man e'er caught!
Whose habitations in the tree-tops even
Are half-way houses on the road to heaven!

"Think, every morning when the sun peeps through
   The dim, leaf-latticed windows of the grove,
How jubilant the happy birds renew
   Their old, melodious madrigals of love!
And when you think of this, remember too
   'T is always morning somewhere, and above
The awakening continents, from shore to shore,
Somewhere the birds are singing evermore.

"Think of your woods and orchards without birds!
   Of empty nests that cling to boughs and beams
As in an idiot's brain remembered words
   Hang empty 'mid the cobwebs of his dreams!
Will bleat of flocks or bellowing of herds
   Make up for the lost music, when your teams
Drag home the stingy harvest, and no more
The feathered gleaners follow to your door?

"What! would you rather see the incessant stir
   Of insects in the windrows of the hay,
And hear the locust and the grasshopper
   Their melancholy hurdy-gurdies play?
Is this more pleasant to you than the whir
   Of meadow-lark, and her sweet roundelay,
Or twitter of little field-fares, as you take
Your nooning in the shade of bush and brake?

"You call them thieves and pillagers; but know,
   They are the wingèd wardens of your farms,
Who from the cornfields drive the insidious foe,
   And from your harvests keep a hundred harms;
Even the blackest of them all, the crow,
   Renders good service as your man-at-arms,
Crushing the beetle in his coat of mail,
And crying havoc on the slug and snail.

"How can I teach your children gentleness,
    And mercy to the weak, and reverence
For Life, which, in its weakness or excess,
    Is still a gleam of God's omnipotence,
Or Death, which, seeming darkness, is no less
    The selfsame light, although averted hence,
When by your laws, your actions, and your speech,
You contradict the very things I teach?"

With this he closed; and through the audience went
    A murmur, like the rustle of dead leaves;
The farmers laughed and nodded, and some bent
    Their yellow heads together like their sheaves;
Men have no faith in fine-spun sentiment
    Who put their trust in bullocks and in beeves.
The birds were doomed; and, as the record shows.
A bounty offered for the heads of crows.

There was another audience out of reach,
    Who had no voice nor vote in making laws,
But in the papers read his little speech,
    And crowned his modest temples with applause;
They made him conscious, each one more than each,
    He still was victor, vanquished in their cause.
Sweetest of all the applause he won from thee,
O fair Almira at the Academy!

And so the dreadful massacre began;
    O'er fields and orchards, and o'er woodland crests,
The ceaseless fusillade of terror ran.
    Dead fell the birds, with blood-stains on their breasts,
Or wounded crept away from sight of man,
    While the young died of famine in their nests;
A slaughter to be told in groans, not words.
The very St. Bartholomew of Birds!

The Summer came, and all the birds were dead,
    The days were like hot coals; the very ground
Was burned to ashes; in the orchards fed
    Myriads of caterpillars, and around
The cultivated fields and garden beds
    Hosts of devouring insects crawled, and found
No foe to check their march, till they had made
The land a desert without leaf or shade.

Devoured by worms, like Herod, was the town,
  Because, like Herod, it had ruthlessly
Slaughtered the Innocents. From the trees spun down
  The canker-worms upon the passers-by,
Upon each woman's bonnet, shawl, and gown,
  Who shook them off with just a little cry;
They were the terror of each favorite walk,
The endless theme of all the village talk.

The farmers grew impatient, but a few
  Confessed their error, and would not complain,
For after all, the best thing one can do
  When it is raining, is to let it rain.
Then they repealed the law, although they knew
  It would not call the dead to life again;
As school-boys, finding their mistake too late,
Draw a wet sponge across the accusing slate.

That year in Killingworth the Autumn came
  Without the light of his majestic look,
The wonder of the falling tongues of flame,
  The illumined pages of his Doom's-Day book.
A few lost leaves blushed crimson with their shame,
  And drowned themselves despairing in the brook,
While the wild wind went moaning everywhere,
Lamenting the dead children of the air!

But the next Spring a stranger sight was seen,
  A sight that never yet by bard was sung,
As great a wonder as it would have been
  If some dumb animal had found a tongue!
A wagon, overarched with evergreen,
  Upon whose boughs were wicker cages hung,
All full of singing birds, came down the street,
Filling the air with music wild and sweet.

From all the country round these birds were brought,
  By order of the town, with anxious quest,
And, loosened from their wicker prisons, sought
  In woods and fields the places they loved best,
Singing loud canticles, which many thought
  Were satires to the authorities addressed,

While others, listening in green lanes, averred
Such lovely music never had been heard!

But blither still and louder carolled they
   Upon the morrow, for they seemed to know
It was the fair Almira's wedding-day,
   And everywhere, around, above, below,
When the Preceptor bore his bride away,
   Their songs burst forth in joyous overflow,
And a new heaven bent over a new earth
Amid the sunny farms of Killingworth.

## THE SPANISH JEW'S TALE

### AZRAEL

King Solomon, before his palace gate
At evening, on the pavement tessellate
Was walking with a stranger from the East,
Arrayed in rich attire as for a feast,
The mighty Runjeet-Sing, a learned man,
And Rajah of the realms of Hindostan.
And as they walked the guest became aware
Of a white figure in the twilight air,
Gazing intent, as one who with surprise
His form and features seemed to recognize;
And in a whisper to the king he said:
"What is yon shape, that, pallid as the dead,
Is watching me, as if he sought to trace
In the dim light the features of my face?"

The king looked, and replied: "I know him well;
It is the Angel men call Azrael,
'T is the Death Angel; what hast thou to fear?"
And the guest answered: "Lest he should come near.
And speak to me, and take away my breath!
Save me from Azrael, save me from death!
O king, that hast dominion o'er the wind.
Bid it arise and bear me hence to Ind."

The king gazed upward at the cloudless sky,

Whispered a word, and raised his hand on high,
And lo! the signet-ring of chrysoprase
On his uplifted finger seemed to blaze
With hidden fire, and rushing from the west
There came a mighty wind, and seized the guest
And lifted him from earth, and on they passed,
His shining garments streaming in the blast,
A silken banner o'er the walls upreared,
A purple cloud, that gleamed and disappeared.
Then said the Angel, smiling: "If this man
Be Rajah Runjeet-Sing of Hindostan,
Thou hast done well in listening to his prayer;
I was upon my way to seek him there."


## CHARLEMAGNE

Olger the Dane and Desiderio,
King of the Lombards, on a lofty tower
Stood gazing northward o'er the rolling plains,
League after league of harvests, to the foot
Of the snow-crested Alps, and saw approach
A mighty army, thronging all the roads
That led into the city. And the King
Said unto Olger, who had passed his youth
As hostage at the court of France, and knew
The Emperor's form and face: "Is Charlemagne
Among that host?" And Olger answered: "No."

And still the innumerable multitude
Flowed onward and increased, until the King
Cried in amazement: "Surely Charlemagne
Is coming in the midst of all these knights!"
And Olger answered slowly: "No; not yet;
He will not come so soon." Then much disturbed
King Desiderio asked: "What shall we do,
If he approach with a still greater army?"
And Olger answered: "When he shall appear,
You will behold what manner of man he is;
But what will then befall us I know not."

Then came the guard that never knew repose,
The Paladins of France; and at the sight

The Lombard King o'ercome with terror cried:
"This must be Charlemagne!" and as before
Did Olger answer: "No; not yet, not yet."

And then appeared in panoply complete
The Bishops and the Abbots and the Priests
Of the imperial chapel, and the Counts;
And Desiderio could no more endure
The light of day, nor yet encounter death,
But sobbed aloud and said: "Let us go down
And hide us in the bosom of the earth,
Far from the sight and anger of a foe
So terrible as this!" And Olger said:
"When you behold the harvests in the fields
Shaking with fear, the Po and the Ticino
Lashing the city walls with iron waves,
Then may you know that Charlemagne is come."
And even as he spake, in the northwest,
Lo! there uprose a black and threatening cloud,
Out of whose bosom flashed the light of arms
Upon the people pent up in the city;
A light more terrible than any darkness,
And Charlemagne appeared;—a Man of Iron!

His helmet was of iron, and his gloves
Of iron, and his breastplate and his greaves
And tassets were of iron, and his shield.
In his left hand he held an iron spear,
In his right hand his sword invincible.
The horse he rode on had the strength of iron,
And color of iron. All who went before him,
Beside him and behind him, his whole host,
Were armed with iron, and their hearts within them
Were stronger than the armor that they wore.
The fields and all the roads were filled with iron,
And points of iron glistened in the sun
And shed a terror through the city streets.

This at a single glance Olger the Dane
Saw from the tower, and turning to the King
Exclaimed in haste: "Behold! this is the man
You looked for with such eagerness!" and then
Fell as one dead at Desiderio's feet.

# HAWTHORNE

### *May 23, 1864*

How beautiful it was, that one bright day
    In the long week of rain!
Though all its splendor could not chase away
    The omnipresent pain.

The lovely town was white with apple-blooms,
    And the great elms o'erhead
Dark shadows wove on their aerial looms
    Shot through with golden thread.

Across the meadows, by the gray old manse,
    The historic river flowed:
I was as one who wanders in a trance,
    Unconscious of his road.

The faces of familiar friends seemed strange;
    Their voices I could hear,
And yet the words they uttered seemed to change
    Their meaning to my ear.

For the one face I looked for was not there,
    The one low voice was mute;
Only an unseen presence filled the air,
    And baffled my pursuit.

Now I look back, and meadow, manse, and stream
    Dimly my thought defines;
I only see—a dream within a dream—
    The hill-top hearsed with pines.

I only hear above his place of rest
    Their tender undertone,
The infinite longings of a troubled breast,
    The voice so like his own.

There in seclusion and remote from men
    The wizard hand lies cold,

Which at its topmost speed let fall the pen,
  And left the tale half-told.

Ah! who shall lift that wand of magic power,
  And the lost clew regain?
The unfinished window in Aladdin's tower
  Unfinished must remain!


## THE CROSS OF SNOW

In the long, sleepless watches of the night
  A gentle face—the face of one long dead—
  Looks at me from the wall, where round its head
  The night-lamp casts a halo of pale light.
Here in this room she died; and soul more white
  Never through martydrom of fire was led
  To its repose; nor can in books be read
  The legend of a life more benedight.
There is a mountain in the distant West
  That, sun-defying, in its deep ravines
  Displays a cross of snow upon its side.
Such is the cross I wear upon my breast
  These eighteen years, through all the changing scenes
  And seasons, changeless since the day she died.


## AMALFI

Sweet the memory is to me
Of a land beyond the sea,
Where the waves and mountains meet,
Where amid her mulberry-trees
Sits Amalfi in the heat,
Bathing ever her white feet
In the tideless summer seas.

In the middle of the town,
From its fountains in the hills,
Tumbling through the narrow gorge,
The Canneto rushes down,
Turns the great wheels of the mills,
Lifts the hammers of the forge.

'T is a stairway, not a street,
That ascends the deep ravine,
Where the torrent leaps between
Rocky walls that almost meet.
Toiling up from stair to stair
Peasant girls their burdens bear;
Sunburnt daughters of the soil,
Stately figures tall and straight,
What inexorable fate
Dooms them to this life of toil?

Lord of vineyards and of lands,
Far above the convent stands.
On its terraced walk aloof
Leans a monk with folded hands.
Placid, satisfied, serene,
Looking down upon the scene
Over wall and red-tiled roof;
Wondering unto what good end
All this toil and traffic tend,
And why all men cannot be
Free from care and free from pain,
And the sordid love of gain,
And as indolent as he.

Where are now the freighted barks
From the marts of east and west?
Where the knights in iron sarks
Journeying to the Holy Land,
Glove of steel upon the hand,
Cross of crimson on the breast?
Where the pomp of camp and court?
Where the pilgrims with their prayers?
Where the merchants with their wares,
And their gallant brigantines
Sailing safely into port
Chased by corsair Algerines?

Vanished like a fleet of cloud,
Like a passing trumpet-blast,
Are those splendors of the past,
And the commerce and the crowd!
Fathoms deep beneath the seas
Lie the ancient wharves and quays,

Swallowed by the engulfing waves;
Silent streets and vacant halls,
Ruined roofs and towers and walls;
Hidden from all mortal eyes
Deep the sunken city lies:
Even cities have their graves!

This is an enchanted land!
Round the headlands far away
Sweeps the blue Salernian bay
With its sickle of white sand:
Further still and furthermost
On the dim discovered coast
Pæstum with its ruins lies,
And its roses all in bloom
Seem to tinge the fatal skies
Of that lonely land of doom.

On his terrace, high in air,
Nothing doth the good monk care
For such worldly themes as these.
From the garden just below
Little puffs of perfume blow,
And a sound is in his ears
Of the murmur of the bees
In the shining chestnut trees;
Nothing else he heeds or hears.
All the landscape seems to swoon
In the happy afternoon;
Slowly o'er his senses creep
The encroaching waves of sleep,
And he sinks as sank the town,
Unresisting, fathoms down,
Into caverns cool and deep!

Walled about with drifts of snow,
Hearing the fierce north-wind blow,
Seeing all the landscape white
And the river cased in ice,
Comes this memory of delight,
Comes this vision unto me
Of a long-lost Paradise
In the land beyond the sea.

## A DUTCH PICTURE

Simon Danz has come home again,
 From cruising about with his buccaneers;
He has singed the beard of the King of Spain,
And carried away the Dean of Jaen
 And sold him in Algiers.

In his house by the Maese, with its roof of tiles,
 And weathercocks flying aloft in air,
There are silver tankards of antique styles,
Plunder of convent and castle, and piles
 Of carpets rich and rare.

In his tulip-garden there by the town,
 Overlooking the sluggish stream,
With his Moorish cap and dressing-gown,
The old sea-captain, hale and brown,
 Walks in a waking dream.

A smile in his gray mustachio lurks
 Whenever he thinks of the King of Spain,
And the listed tulips look like Turks,
And the silent gardener as he works
 Is changed to the Dean of Jaen.

The windmills on the outermost
 Verge of the landscape in the haze,
To him are towers on the Spanish coast,
With whiskered sentinels at their post,
 Though this is the river Maese.

But when the winter rains begin,
 He sits and smokes by the blazing brands,
And old seafaring men come in,
Goat-bearded, gray, and with double chin,
 And rings upon their hands.

They sit there in the shadow and shine
 Of the flickering fire of the winter night;
Figures in color and design

Like those by Rembrandt of the Rhine,
    Half darkness and half light.

And they talk of ventures lost or won,
    And their talk is ever and ever the same,
While they drink the red wine of Tarragon,
From the cellars of some Spanish Don,
    Or convent set on flame.

Restless at times with heavy strides
    He paces his parlor to and fro;
He is like a ship that at anchor rides,
And swings with the rising and falling tides,
    And tugs at her anchor-tow.

Voices mysterious far and near,
    Sound of the wind and sound of the sea,
Are calling and whispering in his ear,
"Simon Danz! Why stayest thou here?
    Come forth and follow me!"

So he thinks he shall take to the sea again
    For one more cruise with his buccaneers,
To singe the beard of the King of Spain,
And capture another Dean of Jaen
    And sell him in Algiers.


## THE WHITE CZAR

Dost thou see on the rampart's height
That wreath of mist, in the light
Of the midnight moon? Oh, hist!
It is not a wreath of mist;
It is the Czar, the White Czar,
    Batyushka! Gosudar!

He has heard, among the dead,
The artillery roll o'erhead;
The drums and the tramp of feet
Of his soldiery in the street;
He is awake! the White Czar,
    Batyushka! Gosudar!

He has heard in the grave the cries
Of his people: "Awake! arise!"
He has rent the gold brocade
Whereof his shroud was made;
He is risen! the White Czar,
    Batyushka! Gosudar!

From the Volga and the Don
He has led his armies on,
Over river and morass,
Over desert and mountain pass;
The Czar, the Orthodox Czar,
    Batyushka! Gosudar!

He looks from the mountain-chain
Toward the seas, that cleave in twain
The continents; his hand
Points southward o'er the land
Of Roumili! O Czar,
    Batyushka! Gosudar!

And the words break from his lips:
"I am the builder of ships,
And my ships shall sail these seas
To the Pillars of Hercules!
I say it; the White Czar,
    Batyushka! Gosudar!

"The Bosphorus shall be free;
It shall make room for me;
And the gates of its water-streets
Be unbarred before my fleets.
I say it; the White Czar,
    Batyushka! Gosudar!

"And the Christian shall no more
Be crushed, as heretofore,
Beneath thine iron rule,
O Sultan of Istamboul!
I swear it! I the Czar,
    Batyushka! Gosudar!"

## JUGURTHA

How cold are thy baths, Apollo!
 Cried the African monarch, the splendid,
As down to his death in the hollow
 Dark dungeons of Rome he descended,
 Uncrowned, unthroned, unattended;
How cold are thy baths, Apollo!

How cold are thy baths, Apollo!
 Cried the Poet, unknown, unbefriended,
As the vision, that lured him to follow,
 With the mist and the darkness blended,
 And the dream of his life was ended;
How cold are thy baths, Apollo!


## THE BELLS OF SAN BLAS

What say the Bells of San Blas
To the ships that southward pass
 From the harbor of Mazatlan?
To them it is nothing more
Than the sound of surf on the shore,—
 Nothing more to master or man.

But to me, a dreamer of dreams,
To whom what is and what seems
 Are often one and the same,—
The Bells of San Blas to me
Have a strange, wild melody,
 And are something more than a name.

For bells are the voice of the church;
They have tones that touch and search
 The hearts of young and old;
One sound to all, yet each
Lends a meaning to their speech,
 And the meaning is manifold.

They are a voice of the Past,
Of an age that is fading fast,
        Of a power austere and grand;
When the flag of Spain unfurled
Its folds o'er this western world,
        And the Priest was lord of the land.

The chapel that once looked down
On the little seaport town
        Has crumbled into the dust;
And on oaken beams below
The bells swing to and fro,
        And are green with mold and rust.

"Is, then, the old faith dead,"
They say, "and in its stead
        Is some new faith proclaimed,
That we are forced to remain
Naked to sun and rain,
        Unsheltered and ashamed?

"Once in our tower aloof
We rang over wall and roof
        Our warnings and our complaints;
And round about us there
The white doves filled the air,
        Like the white souls of the saints.

"The saints! Ah, have they grown
Forgetful of their own?
        Are they asleep, or dead,
That open to the sky
Their ruined Missions lie,
        No longer tenanted?

"Oh, bring us back once more
The vanished days of yore,
        When the world with faith was filled;
Bring back the fervid zeal,
The hearts of fire and steel,
        The hands that believe and build.

"Then from our tower again
We will send over land and main

Our voices of command,
Like exiled kings who return
To their thrones, and the people learn
That the Priest is lord of the land!"

O Bells of San Blas, in vain
Ye call back the Past again!
The Past is deaf to your prayer;
Out of the shadows of night
The world rolls into light;
It is daybreak everywhere.

## TOMORROW

### (Mañana)

#### BY LOPE DE VEGA

Lord, what am I, that, with unceasing care,
Thou didst seek after me, that thou didst wait,
Wet with unhealthy dews, before my gate,
And pass the gloomy nights of winter there?
Oh, strange delusion, that I did not greet
Thy blest approach! and oh, to Heaven how lost,
If my ingratitude's unkindly frost
Has chilled the bleeding wounds upon thy feet!
How oft my guardian angel gently cried,
"Soul, from thy casement look, and thou shalt see
How he persists to knock and wait for thee!"
And, oh! how often to that voice of sorrow,
"To-morrow we will open," I replied,
And when the morrow came I answered still,
"To-morrow."

## SANTA TERESA'S BOOK-MARK

*(Letrilla que llevaba por Registro en su Breviario)*

BY SANTA TERESA DE AVILA

> Let nothing disturb thee,
> Nothing affright thee;
> All things are passing;
> God never changeth;
> Patient endurance
> Attaineth to all things;
> Who God possesseth
> In nothing is wanting;
> Alone God sufficeth.


## THE RETURN OF SPRING

*(Renouveau)*

BY CHARLES D'ORLEANS

Now Time throws off his cloak again
Of ermined frost, and wind, and rain,
And clothes him in the embroidery
Of glittering sun and clear blue sky.
With beast and bird the forest rings,
Each in his jargon cries or sings;
And Time throws off his cloak again
Of ermined frost, and wind, and rain.

River, and fount, and tinkling brook
Wear in their dainty livery
Drops of silver jewelry;
In new-made suit they merry look;
And Time throws off his cloak again
Of ermined frost, and wind, and rain.

## THE COURTSHIP OF MILES STANDISH

### I

#### MILES STANDISH

In the Old Colony days, in Plymouth the land of the
Pilgrims,
To and fro in a room of his simple and primitive dwelling,
Clad in doublet and hose, and boots of Cordovan leather,
Strode, with a martial air, Miles Standish the Puritan
Captain.
Buried in thought he seemed, with his hands behind him,
and pausing
Ever and anon to behold his glittering weapons of war-
fare,
Hanging in shining array along the walls of the chamber,—
Cutlass and corselet of steel, and his trusty sword of Da-
mascus,
Curved at the point and inscribed with its mystical Ara-
bic sentence,
While underneath, in a corner, were fowling-piece, musket,
and matchlock.
Short of stature he was, but strongly built and athletic,
Broad in the shoulders, deep-chested, with muscles and
sinews of iron;
Brown as a nut was his face, but his russet beard was
already
Flaked with patches of snow, as hedges sometimes in
November.
Near him was seated John Alden, his friend and house-
hold companion,
Writing with diligent speed at a table of pine by the
window;
Fair-haired, azure-eyed, with delicate Saxon complexion,
Having the dew of his youth, and the beauty thereof, as
the captives
Whom Saint Gregory saw, and exclaimed, "Not Angles,
but Angels."
Youngest of all was he of the men who came in the May-
flower.

Suddenly breaking the silence, the diligent scribe interrupting,

Spake, in the pride of his heart, Miles Standish the Captain of Plymouth.

"Look at these arms," he said, "the war-like weapons that hang here

Burnished and bright and clean, as if for parade or inspection!

This is the sword of Damascus I fought with in Flanders; this breastplate,

Well I remember the day! Once saved my life in a skirmish;

Here in front you can see the very dint of the bullet

Fired point-blank at my heart by a Spanish arcabucero.

Had it not been of sheer steel, the forgotten bones of Miles Standish

Would at this moment be mold, in their grave in the Flemish morasses."

Thereupon answered John Alden, but looked not up from his writing:

"Truly the breath of the Lord hath slackened the speed of the bullet;

He in his mercy preserved you, to be our shield and our weapon!"

Still the Captain continued, unheeding the words of the stripling:

"See, how bright they are burnished, as if in an arsenal hanging;

That is because I have done it myself, and not left it to others.

Serve yourself, would you be well served, is an excellent adage;

So I take care of my arms, as you of your pens and your inkhorn.

Then, too, there are my soldiers, my great, invincible army,

Twelve men, all equipped, having each his rest and his matchlock,

Eighteen shillings a month, together with diet and pillage,

And, like Caesar, I know the name of each of my soldiers!"

This he said with a smile, that danced in his eyes, as the sunbeams

Dance on the waves of the sea, and vanish again in a
    moment.
Alden laughed as he wrote, and still the Captain con-
    tinued:
"Look! you can see from this window my brazen howitzer
    planted
High on the roof of the church, a preacher who speaks
    to the purpose,
Steady, straightforward, and strong, with irresistible logic,
Orthodox, flashing conviction right into the hearts of the
    heathen.
Now we are ready, I think, for any assault of the Indians;
Let them come, if they like, and the sooner they try it the
    better,—
Let them come, if they like, be it sagamore, sachem, or
    pow-wow,
Aspinet, Samoset, Corbitant, Squanto, or Tokamahamon!"

Long at the window he stood, and wistfully gazed on
    the landscape,
Washed with a cold gray mist, the vapory breath of the
    east-wind,
Forest and meadow and hill, and the steel-blue rim of
    the ocean,
Lying silent and sad, in the afternoon shadows and sun-
    shine.
Over his countenance flitted a shadow like those on the
    landscape,
Gloom intermingled with light; and his voice was subdued
    with emotion,
Tenderness, pity, regret, as after a pause he proceeded:
"Yonder there, on the hill by the sea, lies buried Rose
    Standish;
Beautiful rose of love, that bloomed for me by the way-
    side!
She was the first to die of all who came in the Mayflower!
Green above her is growing the field of wheat we have
    sown there,
Better to hide from the Indian scouts the graves of our
    people,
Lest they should count them and see how many already
    have perished!"

Sadly his face he averted, and strode up and down, and
    was thoughtful.

  Fixed to the opposite wall was a shelf of books, and
    among them
Prominent three, distinguished alike for bulk and for
    binding;
Bariffe's Artillery Guide, and the Commentaries of Cæsar
Out of the Latin translated by Arthur Goldinge of London,
And, as if guarded by these, between them was standing
    the Bible.
Musing a moment before them, Miles Standish paused,
    as if doubtful
Which of the three he should choose for his consolation
    and comfort,
Whether the wars of the Hebrews, the famous campaigns
    of the Romans,
Or the Artillery practice, designed for belligerent Chris-
    tians.
Finally down from its shelf he dragged the ponderous
    Roman,
Seated himself at the window, and opened the book, and
    in silence
Turned o'er the well-worn leaves, where thumb-marks
    thick on the margin,
Like the trample of feet, proclaimed the battle was hottest.
Nothing was heard in the room but the hurrying pen of the
    stripling,
Busily writing epistles important, to go by the Mayflower,
Ready to sail on the morrow, or next day at latest, God
    willing!
Homeward bound with the tidings of all that terrible
    winter,
Letters written by Alden, and full of the name of Priscilla!
Full of the name and the fame of the Puritan maiden
    Priscilla!

## II

### LOVE AND FRIENDSHIP

Nothing was heard in the room but the hurrying pen
    of the stripling,

Or an occasional sigh from the laboring heart of the
    Captain,
Reading the marvellous words and achievements of Julius
    Cæsar.
After a while he exclaimed, as he smote with his hand,
    palm downwards,
Heavily on the page: "A wonderful man was this Cæsar!
You are a writer, and I am a fighter, but here is a fellow
Who could both write and fight, and in both was equally
    skilful!"
Straightway answered and spake John Alden, the comely,
    the youthful:
"Yes, he was equally skilled, as you say, with his pen
    and his weapons.
Somewhere have I read, but where I forget, he could
    dictate
Seven letters at once, at the same time writing his
    memoirs."
"Truly," continued the Captain, not heeding or hearing
    the other,
"Truly a wonderful man was Caius Julius Cæsar!
Better be first, he said, in a little Iberian village,
Than be second in Rome, and I think he was right when
    he said it.
Twice was he married before he was twenty, and many
    times after;
Battles five hundred he fought, and a thousand cities he
    conquered;
He, too, fought in Flanders, as he himself has recorded;
Finally he was stabbed by his friend, the orator Brutus!
Now, do you know what he did on a certain occasion in
    Flanders,
When the rear-guard of his army retreated, the front giving
    way too,
And the immortal Twelfth Legion was crowded so closely
    together
There was no room for their swords? Why, he seized a
    shield from a soldier,
Put himself straight at the head of his troops, and com-
    manded the captains,
Calling on each by his name, to order forward the en-
    signs;

Then to widen the ranks, and give more room for their
    weapons;
So he won the day, the battle of something-or-other.
That's what I always say; if you wish a thing to be well
    done,
You must do it yourself, you must not leave it to others!"

All was silent again; the Captain continued his reading.
Nothing was heard in the room but the hurrying pen of
    the stripling
Writing epistles important to go next day by the May-
    flower,
Filled with the name and the fame of the Puritan maiden
    Priscilla;
Every sentence began or closed with the name of Priscilla,
Till the treacherous pen, to which he confided the secret,
Strove to betray it by singing and shouting the name of
    Priscilla!
Finally closing his book, with a bang of the ponderous
    cover,
Sudden and loud as the sound of a soldier grounding his
    musket,
Thus to the young man spake Miles Standish the Captain
    of Plymouth:
"When you have finished your work, I have something
    important to tell you.
Be not however in haste; I can wait; I shall not be im-
    patient!"
Straightway Alden replied, as he folded the last of his
    letters,
Pushing his papers aside, and giving respectful attention:
"Speak; for whenever you speak, I am always ready to
    listen,
Always ready to hear whatever pertains to Miles Stand-
    ish."
Thereupon answered the Captain, embarrassed, and
    culling his phrases:
" 'Tis not good for a man to be alone, say the Scriptures.
This I have said before, and again and again I repeat it;
Every hour in the day, I think it, and feel it, and say it.
Since Rose Standish died, my life has been weary and
    dreary;

Sick at heart have I been, beyond the healing of friend-
  ship;
Oft in my lonely hours have I thought of the maiden
  Priscilla.
She is alone in the world; her father and mother and
  brother
Died in the winter together; I saw her going and coming,
Now to the grave of the dead, and now to the bed of the
  dying,
Patient, courageous, and strong, and said to myself, that if
  ever
There were angels on earth, as there are angels in heaven,
Two have I seen and known; and the angel whose name
  is Priscilla
Holds in my desolate life the place which the other
  abandoned.
Long have I cherished the thought, but never have dared
  to reveal it,
Being a coward in this though valiant enough for the
  most part.
Go to the damsel Priscilla, the loveliest maiden of Ply-
  mouth,
Say that a blunt old Captain, a man not of words but
  of actions,
Offers his hand and his heart, the hand and heart of a
  soldier.
Not in these words, you know, but this in short is my
  meaning;
I am a maker of war, and not a maker of phrases.
You, who are bred as a scholar, can say it in elegant
  language,
Such as you read in your books of the pleadings and
  wooings of lovers,
Such as you think best adapted to win the heart of a
  maiden."

  When he had spoken, John Alden, the fair-haired, taci-
  turn stripling,
All aghast at his words, surprised, embarrassed, bewild-
  ered,
Trying to mask his dismay by treating the subject with
  lightness,

Trying to smile, and yet feeling his heart stand still in his
    bosom,
Just as a timepiece stops in a house that is stricken by
    lightning,
Thus made answer and spake, or rather stammered than
    answered:
"Such a message as that, I am sure I should mangle and
    mar it;
If you would have it well done,—I am only repeating your
    maxim,—
You must do it yourself, you must not leave it to others!"
But with the air of a man whom nothing can turn from his
    purpose,
Gravely shaking his head, made answer the Captain of
    Plymouth:
"Truly the maxim is good, and I do not mean to gain-
    say it;
But we must use it discreetly, and not waste powder for
    nothing.
Now, as I said before, I was never a maker of phrases.
I can march up to a fortress and summon the place to
    surrender,
But march up to a woman with such a proposal, I dare
    not.
I'm not afraid of bullets, nor shot from the mouth of a
    cannon,
But of a thundering 'No!' point-blank from the mouth
    of a woman,
That I confess I'm afraid of, nor am I ashamed to confess
    it!
So you must grant my request, for you are an elegant
    scholar,
Having the graces of speech, and skill in the turning of
    phrases."
Taking the hand of his friend, who still was reluctant and
    doubtful,
Holding it long in his own, and pressing it kindly, he
    added:
"Though I have spoken thus lightly, yet deep is the
    feeling that prompts me;
Surely you cannot refuse what I ask in the name of our
    friendship!"

Then made answer John Alden: "The name of friendship
    is sacred;
What you demand in that name, I have not the power to
    deny you!"
So the strong will prevailed, subduing and molding the
    gentler,
Friendship prevailed over love, and Alden went on his
    errand.


# III

## THE LOVER'S ERRAND


So the strong will prevailed, and Alden went on his
    errand,
Out of the street of the village, and into the paths of the
    forest,
Into the tranquil woods, where bluebirds and robins were
    building
Towns in the populous trees, with hanging gardens of
    verdure,
Peaceful, aerial cities of joy and affection and freedom.
All around him was calm, but within him commotion
    and conflict,
Love contending with friendship, and self with each gen-
    erous impulse.
To and fro in his breast his thoughts were heaving and
    dashing,
As in a foundering ship, with every roll of the vessel,
Washes the bitter sea, the merciless surge of the ocean!
"Must I relinquish it all," he cried with a wild lamenta-
    tion,—
"Must I relinquish it all, the joy, the hope, the illusion?
Was it for this I have loved, and waited, and worshipped
    in silence?
Was it for this I have followed the flying feet and the
    shadow
Over the wintry sea, to the desolate shores of New Eng-
    land?

Truly the heart is deceitful, and out of its depths of cor-
ruption
Rise, like an exhalation, the misty phantoms of passion;
Angels of light they seem, but are only delusions of
Satan.
All is clear to me now; I feel it, I see it distinctly!
This is the hand of the Lord; it is laid upon me in anger,
For I have followed too much the heart's desires and
devices,
Worshipping Astaroth blindly, and impious idols of Baal.
This is the cross I must bear; the sin and the swift
retribution."

So through the Plymouth woods John Alden went on
his errand;
Crossing the brook at the ford, where it brawled over
pebble and shallow,
Gathering still, as he went, the Mayflowers blooming
around him,
Fragrant, filling the air with a strange and wonderful
sweetness,
Children lost in the woods, and covered with leaves
in their slumber.
"Puritan flowers," he said, "and the type of Puritan
maidens,
Modest and simple and sweet, the very type of Priscilla!
So I will take them to her; to Priscilla the Mayflower of
Plymouth,
Modest and simple and sweet, as a parting gift will I
take them;
Breathing their silent farewells, as they fade and wither
and perish,
Soon to be thrown away as is the heart of the giver."
So through the Plymouth woods John Alden went on his
errand;
Came to an open space, and saw the disk of the ocean,
Sailless, sombre and cold with the comfortless breath of
the east-wind;
Saw the new-built house, and people at work in a meadow;
Heard, as he drew near the door, the musical voice of
Priscilla
Singing the hundredth Psalm, the grand old Puritan
anthem,

Music that Luther sang to the sacred words of the Psalmist,
Full of the breath of the Lord, consoling and comforting
many.
Then, as he opened the door, he beheld the form of the
maiden
Seated beside her wheel, and the carded wool like a snow-
drift
Piled at her knee, her white hands feeding the ravenous
spindle,
While with her foot on the treadle she guided the wheel
in its motion.
Open wide on her lap lay the well-worn psalm-book of
Ainsworth,
Printed in Amsterdam, the words and the music together,
Rough-hewn, angular notes, like stones in the wall of a
churchyard,
Darkened and overhung by the running vine of the verses.
Such was the book from whose pages she sang the old
Puritan anthem,
She, the Puritan girl, in the solitude of the forest,
Making the humble house and the modest apparel of
homespun
Beautiful with her beauty, and rich with the wealth of her
being!
Over him rushed, like a wind that is keen and cold and
relentless,
Thoughts of what might have been, and the weight and
woe of his errand;
All the dreams that had faded, and all the hopes that had
vanished,
All his life henceforth a dreary and tenantless mansion,
Haunted by vain regrets, and pallid, sorrowful faces.
Still he said to himself, and almost fiercely he said it,
"Let not him that putteth his hand to the plough look
backwards;
Though the ploughshare cut through the flowers of life
to its fountains,
Though it pass o'er the graves of the dead and the
hearts of the living,
It is the will of the Lord; and his mercy endureth forever!"

So he entered the house: and the hum of the wheel
and the singing

Suddenly ceased; for Priscilla, aroused by his step on the
    threshold,
Rose as he entered, and gave him her hand in signal of
    welcome,
Saying, "I knew it was you, when I heard your step in the
    passage;
For I was thinking of you, as I sat there singing and
    spinning."
Awkward and dumb with delight, that a thought of him
    had been mingled
Thus in the sacred psalm, that came from the heart of
    the maiden,
Silent before her he stood, and gave her the flowers for
    an answer,
Finding no words for his thought. He remembered that
    day in the winter,
After the first great snow, when he broke a path from the
    village,
Reeling and plunging along through the drifts that en-
    cumbered the doorway,
Stamping the snow from his feet as he entered the house,
    and Priscilla
Laughed at his snowy locks, and gave him a seat by the
    fireside,
Grateful and pleased to know he had thought of her in
    the snow-storm.
Had he but spoken then! perhaps not in vain had he
    spoken;
Now it was all too late; the golden moment had vanished!
So he stood there abashed, and gave her the flowers for
    an answer.

    Then they sat down and talked of the birds and the
    beautiful Spring-time,
Talked of their friends at home, and the Mayflower that
    sailed on the morrow.
"I have been thinking all day," said gently the Puritan
    maiden,
"Dreaming all night, and thinking all day, of the hedge-
    rows of England,—
They are in blossom now, and the country is all like a
    garden:

Thinking of lanes and fields, and the song of the lark and
  the linnet,
Seeing the village street, and familiar faces of neighbors
Going about as of old, and stopping to gossip together,
And, at the end of the street, the village church, with the
  ivy
Climbing the old gray tower, and the quiet graves in the
  churchyard.
Kind are the people I live with, and dear to me my
  religion;
Still my heart is so sad, that I wish myself back in Old
  England.
You will say it is wrong, but I cannot help it: I almost
Wish myself back in Old England, I feel so lonely and
  wretched."

   Thereupon answered the youth: "Indeed I do not con-
  demn you;
Stouter hearts than a woman's have quailed in this terrible
  winter.
Yours is tender and trusting, and needs a stronger to
  lean on;
So I have come to you now, with an offer and proffer of
  marriage
Made by a good man and true, Miles Standish the Captain
  of Plymouth!"

   Thus he delivered his message, the dexterous writer of
  letters,—
Did not embellish the theme, nor array it in beautiful
  phrases,
But came straight to the point, and blurted it out like a
  school-boy;
Even the Captain himself could hardly have said it more
  bluntly.
Mute with amazement and sorrow, Priscilla the Puritan
  maiden
Looked into Alden's face, her eyes dilated with wonder,
Feeling his words like a blow, that stunned her and
  rendered her speechless;
Till at length she exclaimed, interrupting the ominous
  silence:

"If the great Captain of Plymouth is so very eager to wed
    me,
Why does he not come himself, and take the trouble to
    woo me?
If I am not worth the wooing, I surely am not worth the
    winning!"
Then John Alden began explaining and smoothing the
    matter,
Making it worse as he went, by saying the Captain was
    busy,—
Had no time for such things—such things! the words grat-
    ing harshly
Fell on the ear of Priscilla; and swift as a flash she made
    answer:
"Has he no time for such things, as you call it, before
    he is married,
Would he be likely to find it, or make it, after the wed-
    ding?
That is the way with you men; you don't understand us,
    you cannot.
When you have made up your minds, after thinking of
    this one and that one,
Choosing, selecting, rejecting, comparing one with an-
    other,
Then you make known your desire, with abrupt and sud-
    den avowal,
And are offended and hurt, and indignant perhaps, that a
    woman
Does not respond at once to a love that she never sus-
    pected,
Does not attain at a bound the height to which you have
    been climbing.
This is not right nor just: for surely a woman's affection
Is not a thing to be asked for, and had for only the asking.
When one is truly in love, one not only says it, but
    shows it.
Had he but waited awhile, had he only showed that he
    loved me,
Even this Captain of yours—who knows?—at last might
    have won me,
Old and rough as he is; but now it never can happen."

Still John Alden went on, unheeding the words of Pris-
cilla,
Urging the suit of his friend, explaining, persuading, ex-
panding;
Spoke of his courage and skill, and of all his battles in
Flanders,
How with the people of God he had chosen to suffer
affliction;
How, in return for his zeal, they had made him Captain
of Plymouth;
He was a gentleman born, could trace his pedigree plainly
Back to Hugh Standish of Duxbury Hall, in Lancashire,
England,
Who was the son of Ralph, and the grandson of Thurs-
ton de Standish;
Heir unto vast estates, of which he was basely defrauded,
Still bore the family arms, and had for his crest a cock
argent,
Combed and wattled gules, and all the rest of the blazon.
He was a man of honor, of noble and generous nature;
Though he was rough, he was kindly; she knew how dur-
ing the winter
He had attended the sick, with a hand as gentle as
woman's;
Somewhat hasty and hot, he could not deny it, and head-
strong,
Stern as a soldier might be, but hearty, and placable
always,
Not to be laughed at and scorned, because he was little of
stature;
For he was great of heart, magnanimous, courtly, coura-
geous;
Any woman in Plymouth, nay, any woman in England,
Might be happy and proud to be called the wife of Miles
Standish!

But as he warmed and glowed, in his simple and elo-
quent language,
Quite forgetful of self, and full of the praise of his rival,
Archly the maiden smiled, and, with eyes overrunning
with laughter,
Said, in a tremulous voice, "Why don't you speak for
yourself, John?"

## IV

### JOHN ALDEN

Into the open air John Alden, perplexed and bewildered,
Rushed like a man insane, and wandered alone by the
    sea-side;
Paced up and down the sands, and bared his head to the
    east-wind,
Cooling his heated brow, and the fire and fever within
    him.
Slowly as out of the heavens, with apocalyptical splendors,
Sank the City of God, in the vision of John the Apostle,
So, with its cloudy walls of chrysolite, jasper, and sap-
    phire,
Sank the broad red sun, and over its turrets uplifted
Glimmered the golden reed of the angel who measured
    the city.

"Welcome, O wind of the East!" he exclaimed in his
    wild exultation,
"Welcome, O wind of the East. from the caves of the
    misty Atlantic!
Blowing o'er fields of dulse, and measureless meadows
    of sea-grass,
Blowing o'er rocky wastes, and the grottoes and gardens
    of ocean!
Lay thy cold, moist hand on my burning forehead, and
    wrap me
Close in thy garments of mist, to allay the fever within
    me!"

Like an awakened conscience, the sea was moaning
    and tossing,
Beating remorseful and loud the mutable sands of the
    sea-shore.
Fierce in his soul was the struggle and tumult of pas-
    sions contending;

Love triumphant and crowned, and friendship wounded
    and bleeding,
Passionate cries of desire, and importunate pleadings of
    duty!
"Is it my fault," he said, "that the maiden has chosen
    between us?
Is it my fault that he failed,—my fault that I am the
    victor?"
Then within him there thundered a voice, like the voice of
    the Prophet:
"It hath displeased the Lord!"—and he thought of David's
    transgression,
Bathsheba's beautiful face, and his friend in the front
    of the battle!
Shame and confusion of guilt, and abasement and self-
    condemnation,
Overwhelmed him at once; and he cried in the deepest
    contrition:
"It hath displeased the Lord! It is the temptation of
    Satan!"

    Then, uplifting his head, he looked at the sea, and
    beheld there
Dimly the shadowy form of the Mayflower riding at
    anchor,
Rocked on the rising tide, and ready to sail on the
    morrow;
Heard the voices of men through the mist, the rattle
    of cordage
Thrown on the deck, the shouts of the mate, and the
    sailors' "Ay, ay, Sir!"
Clear and distinct, but not loud, in the dripping air
    of the twilight.
Still for a moment he stood and listened, and stared at
    the vessel,
Then went hurriedly on, as one who, seeing a phantom,
Stops, then quickens his pace, and follows the beckoning
    shadow.
"Yes, it is plain to me now," he murmured; "the hand of
    the Lord is
Leading me out of the land of darkness, the bondage of
    error,

Through the sea, that shall lift the walls of its waters
    around me,
Hiding me, cutting me off, from the cruel thoughts that
    pursue me.
Back will I go o'er the ocean, this dreary land will
    abandon,
Her whom I may not love, and him whom my heart has
    offended.
Better to be in my grave in the green old churchyard
    in England,
Close by my mother's side, and among the dust of my
    kindred;
Better be dead and forgotten, than living in shame and
    dishonor;
Sacred and safe and unseen, in the dark of the narrow
    chamber
With me my secret shall lie, like a buried jewel that
    glimmers
Bright on the hand that is dust, in the chambers of
    silence and darkness,—
Yes, as the marriage ring of the great espousal here-
    after!"

  Thus as he spake, he turned, in the strength of his
    strong resolution,
Leaving behind him the shore, and hurried along in the
    twilight,
Through the congenial gloom of the forest silent and
    sombre,
Till he beheld the lights in the seven houses of Plymouth,
Shining like seven stars in the dusk and mist of the
    evening.
Soon he entered his door, and found the redoubtable
    Captain
Sitting alone, and absorbed in the martial pages of
    Cæsar,
Fighting some great campaign in Hainault or Brabant
    or Flanders.
"Long have you been on your errand," he said with a
    cheery demeanor,
Even as one who is waiting an answer, and fears not
    the issue.

"Not far off is the house, although the woods are be-
tween us;
But you have lingered so long, that while you were go-
ing and coming
I have fought ten battles and sacked and demolished
a city.
Come, sit down, and in order relate to me all that has
happened."

Then John Alden spake, and related the wondrous
adventure,
From beginning to end, minutely, just as it happened;
How he had seen Priscilla, and how he had sped in his
courtship,
Only smoothing a little, and softening down her refusal.
But when he came at length to the words Priscilla had
spoken,
Words so tender and cruel: "Why don't you speak for
yourself, John?"
Up leaped the Captain of Plymouth, and stamped on the
floor, till his armor
Clanged on the wall, where it hung, with a sound of
sinister omen.
All his pent-up wrath burst forth in a sudden explosion,
E'en as a hand-grenade, that scatters destruction around
it.
Wildly he shouted, and loud: "John Alden! you have
betrayed me!
Me, Miles Standish, your friend! have supplanted, de-
frauded, betrayed me!
One of my ancestors ran his sword through the heart of
Wat Tyler;
Who shall prevent me from running my own through the
heart of a traitor?
Yours is the greater treason, for yours is a treason to
friendship!
You, who lived under my roof, whom I cherished and
loved as a brother;
You, who have fed at my board, and drunk at my cup,
to whose keeping
I have intrusted my honor, my thoughts the most sacred
and secret,—

You too, Brutus! ah woe to the name of friendship here-
　　after!
Brutus was Cæsar's friend, and you were mine, but
　　henceforward
Let there be nothing between us save war, and implacable
　　hatred!"


So spake the Captain of Plymouth, and strode about
　　in the chamber,
Chafing and choking with rage; like cords were the veins
　　on his temples.
But in the midst of his anger a man appeared at the
　　doorway,
Bringing in uttermost haste a message of urgent impor-
　　tance,
Rumors of danger and war and hostile incursions of
　　Indians!
Straightway the Captain paused, and, without further
　　question or parley,
Took from the nail on the wall his sword with its scab-
　　bard of iron,
Buckled the belt round his waist, and, frowning fiercely,
　　departed.
Alden was left alone. He heard the clank of the scab-
　　bard
Growing fainter and fainter, and dying away in the
　　distance.
Then he arose from his seat, and looked forth into the
　　darkness,
Felt the cool air blow on his cheek, that was hot with
　　the insult,
Lifted his eyes to the heavens, and, folding his hands as
　　in childhood,
Prayed in the silence of night to the Father who seeth
　　in secret.


Meanwhile the choleric Captain strode wrathful away to
　　the council,
Found it already assembled, impatiently waiting his com-
　　ing;
Men in the middle of life, austere and grave in deport-
　　ment,
Only one of them old, the hill that was nearest to heaven,

Covered with snow, but erect, the excellent Elder of
    Plymouth.
God had sifted three kingdoms to find the wheat for
    this planting,
Then had sifted the wheat, as the living seed of a
    nation;
So say the chronicles old, and such is the faith of the
    people!
Near them was standing an Indian, in attitude stern and
    defiant,
Naked down to the waist, and grim and ferocious in
    aspect;
While on the table before them was lying unopened a
    Bible,
Ponderous, bound in leather, brass-studded, printed in
    Holland,
And beside it outstretched the skin of a rattlesnake
    glittered,
Filled, like a quiver, with arrows; a signal and challenge
    of warfare,
Brought by the Indian, and speaking with arrowy tongues
    of defiance.
This Miles Standish beheld, as he entered, and heard
    them debating
What were an answer befitting the hostile message and
    menace,
Talking of this and of that, contriving, suggesting, ob-
    jecting;
One voice only for peace, and that the voice of the Elder,
Judging it wise and well that some at least were converted,
Rather than any were slain, for this was but Christian
    behavior!
Then out spake Miles Standish, the stalwart Captain of
    Plymouth,
Muttering deep in his throat, for his voice was husky with
    anger,
"What! do you mean to make war with milk and the water
    of roses?
Is it to shoot red squirrels you have your howitzer planted
There on the roof of the church, or is it to shoot red
    devils?
Truly the only tongue that is understood by a savage

Must be the tongue of fire that speaks from the mouth
    of the cannon!"
Thereupon answered and said the excellent Elder of
    Plymouth,
Somewhat amazed and alarmed at this irreverent lan-
    guage;
"Not so thought St. Paul, nor yet the other Apostles;
Not from the cannon's mouth were the tongues of fire
    they spake with!"
But unheeded fell this mild rebuke on the Captain,
Who had advanced to the table, and thus continued dis-
    coursing:
"Leave this matter to me, for to me by right it pertaineth.
War is a terrible trade; but in the cause that is righteous,
Sweet is the smell of powder; and thus I answer the chal-
    lenge!"

   Then from the rattlesnake's skin, with a sudden, con-
    temptuous gesture,
Jerking the Indian arrows, he filled it with powder and
    bullets
Full to the very jaws, and handed it back to the savage,
Saying, in thundering tones: "Here, take it! this is your
    answer!"
Silently out of the room then glided the glistening savage,
Bearing the serpent's skin, and seeming himself like a
    serpent,
Winding his sinuous way in the dark to the depths of the
    forest.

V

THE SAILING OF THE MAYFLOWER

Just in the gray of the dawn, as the mists uprose from
    the meadows,
There was a stir and a sound in the slumbering village of
    Plymouth;

Clanging and clicking of arms, and the order imperative,
"Forward!"
Given in tone suppressed, a tramp of feet, and then silence.
Figures ten, in the mist, marched slowly out of the village.
Standish the stalwart it was, with eight of his valorous
army,
Led by their Indian guide, by Hobomok, friend of the
white men,
Northward marching to quell the sudden revolt of the
savage.
Giants they seemed in the mist, or the mighty men of King
David;
Giants in heart they were, who believed in God and the
Bible,—
Ay, who believed in the smiting of Midianites and Philis-
tines.
Over them gleamed far off the crimson banners of morn-
ing;
Under them loud on the sands, the serried billows, ad-
vancing,
Fired along the line, and in regular order retreated.

Many a mile had they marched, when at length the
village of Plymouth
Woke from its sleep, and arose, intent on its manifold
labors.
Sweet was the air and soft; and slowly the smoke from the
chimneys
Rose over roofs of thatch, and pointed steadily eastward;
Men came forth from the doors, and paused and talked
of the weather,
Said that the wind had changed, and was blowing fair for
the Mayflower;
Talked of their Captain's departure, and all the dangers
that menaced,
He being gone, the town, and what should be done in his
absence.
Merrily sang the birds, and the tender voices of women
Consecrated with hymns the common cares of the house-
hold.
Out of the sea rose the sun, and the billows rejoiced at his
coming;

Beautiful were his feet on the purple tops of the moun-
tains;
Beautiful on the sails of the Mayflower riding at anchor,
Battered and blackened and worn by all the storms of the
winter.
Loosely against her masts was hanging and flapping her
canvas,
Rent by so many gales, and patched by the hands of the
sailors.
Suddenly from her side, as the sun rose over the ocean,
Darted a puff of smoke, and floated seaward; anon rang
Loud over field and forest the cannon's roar, and the
echoes
Heard and repeated the sound, the signal gun of departure!
Ah! but with louder echoes replied the hearts of the people!
Meekly, in voices subdued, the chapter was read from
the Bible,
Meekly the prayer was begun, but ended in fervent en-
treaty!
Then from their houses in haste came forth the Pilgrims
of Plymouth,
Men and women and children, all hurrying down to the
sea-shore,
Eager, with tearful eyes, to say farewell to the Mayflower,
Homeward bound o'er the sea, and leaving them here in
the desert.

Foremost among them was Alden. All night he had lain
without slumber,
Turning and tossing about in the heat and unrest of his
fever.
He had beheld Miles Standish, who came back late from
the council,
Stalking into the room, and heard him mutter and mur-
mur;
Sometimes it seemed a prayer, and sometimes it sounded
like swearing.
Once he had come to the bed, and stood there a moment
in silence;
Then he had turned away, and said: "I will not awake
him;
Let him sleep on, it is best; for what is the use of more
talking!"

Then he extinguished the light, and threw himself down
    on his pallet,
Dressed as he was, and ready to start at the break of the
    morning,—
Covered himself with the cloak he had worn in his cam-
    paigns in Flanders,—
Slept as a soldier sleeps in his bivouac, ready for action.
But with the dawn he arose; in the twilight Alden beheld
    him
Put on his corselet of steel, and all the rest of his armor,
Buckle about his waist his trusty blade of Damascus,
Take from the corner his musket, and so stride out of the
    chamber.
Often the heart of the youth had burned and yearned to
    embrace him,
Often his lips had essayed to speak, imploring for pardon;
All the old friendship came back, with its tender and grate-
    ful emotions;
But his pride overmastered the nobler nature within
    him,—
Pride, and the sense of his wrong, and the burning fire of
    the insult.
So he beheld his friend departing in anger, but spake not,
Saw him go forth to danger, perhaps to death, and he
    spake not!
Then he arose from his bed, and heard what the people
    were saying,
Joined in the talk at the door, with Stephen and Richard
    and Gilbert,
Joined in the morning prayer, and in the reading of Scrip-
    ture,
And, with the others, in haste went hurrying down to the
    sea-shore,
Down to the Plymouth Rock, that had been to their feet as
    a doorstep
Into a world unknown,—the corner-stone of a nation!

There with his boat was the Master, already a little
    impatient
Lest he should lose the tide, or the wind might shift to the
    eastward,
Square-built, hearty, and strong, with an odor of ocean
    about him,

Speaking with this one and that, and cramming letters and
 parcels
Into his pockets capacious, and messages mingled to-
 gether
Into his narrow brain, till at last he was wholly bewildered.
Nearer the boat stood Alden, with one foot placed on the
 gunwale,
One still firm on the rock, and talking at times with the
 sailors,
Seated erect on the thwarts, all ready and eager for start-
 ing.
He too was eager to go, and thus put an end to his anguish,
Thinking to fly from despair, that swifter than keel is or
 canvas,
Thinking to drown in the sea the ghost that would rise and
 pursue him.
But as he gazed on the crowd, he beheld the form of Pris-
 cilla
Standing dejected among them, unconscious of all that was
 passing.
Fixed were her eyes upon his, as if she divined his inten-
 tion,
Fixed with a look so sad, so reproachful, imploring, and
 patient,
That with a sudden revulsion his heart recoiled from its
 purpose
As from the verge of a crag, where one step more is de-
 struction.
Strange is the heart of man, with its quick, mysterious
 instincts!
Strange is the life of man, and fatal or fated are moments,
Whereupon turn, as on hinges, the gates of the wall ada-
 mantine!
"Here I remain!" he exclaimed, as he looked at the heav-
 ens above him,
Thanking the Lord whose breath had scattered the mist
 and the madness,
Wherein, blind and lost, to death he was staggering head-
 long.
"Yonder snow-white cloud, that floats in the ether above
 me,
Seems like a hand that is pointing and beckoning over
 the ocean.

There is another hand, that is not so spectral and ghost-
    like,
Holding me, drawing me back, and clasping mine for pro-
    tection.
Float, O hand of cloud, and vanish away in the ether!
Roll thyself up like a fist, to threaten and daunt me; I
    heed not
Either your warning or menace, or any omen of evil!
There is no land so sacred, no air so pure and so whole-
    some,
As is the air she breathes, and the soil that is pressed by
    her footsteps.
Here for her sake will I stay, and like an invisible presence
Hover around her forever, protecting, supporting her
    weakness;
Yes! as my foot was the first that stepped on this rock
    at the landing,
So, with the blessing of God, shall it be the last of the
    leaving!"

  Meanwhile the Master alert, but with dignified air and
    important,
Scanning with watchful eye the tide and the wind and the
    weather,
Walked about on the sands, and the people crowded
    around him
Saying a few last words, and enforcing his careful remem-
    brance.
Then, taking each by the hand, as if he were grasping a
    tiller,
Into the boat he sprang, and in haste shoved off to his
    vessel,
Glad in his heart to get rid of all this worry and flurry,
Glad to be gone from a land of sand and sickness and
    sorrow,
Short allowance of victual, and plenty of nothing but
    Gospel!
Lost in the sound of the oars was the last farewell of the
    Pilgrims.
O strong hearts and true! not one went back in the May-
    flower!
No, not one looked back, who had set his hand to this
    ploughing!

Soon were heard on board the shouts and songs of the
    sailors
Heaving the windlass round, and hoisting the ponderous
    anchor.
Then the yards were braced, and all sails set to the west-
    wind,
Blowing steady and strong; and the Mayflower sailed from
    the harbor,
Rounded the point of the Gurnet, and leaving far to the
    southward
Island and cape of sand, and the Field of the First
    Encounter,
Took the wind on her quarter, and stood for the open
    Atlantic,
Borne on the send of the sea, and the swelling hearts of
    the Pilgrims.

Long in silence they watched the receding sail of the
    vessel,
Much endeared to them all, as something living and
    human;
Then, as if filled with the spirit, and wrapt in a vision
    prophetic,
Baring his hoary head, the excellent Elder of Plymouth
Said, "Let us pray!" and they prayed, and thanked the
    Lord and took courage.
Mournfully sobbed the waves at the base of the rock, and
    above them
Bowed and whispered the wheat on the hill of death, and
    their kindred
Seemed to awake in their graves, and to join in the prayer
    that they uttered.
Sun-illumined and white, on the eastern verge of the
    ocean
Gleamed the departing sail, like a marble slab in a
    graveyard;
Buried beneath it lay forever all hope of escaping.
Lo! as they turned to depart, they saw the form of an
    Indian,
Watching them from the hill; but while they spake with
    each other,
Pointing with outstretched hands, and saying, "Look!" he
    had vanished.

So they returned to their homes; but Alden lingered a
    little,
Musing alone on the shore, and watching the wash of the
    billows
Round the base of the rock, and the sparkle and flash of
    the sunshine,
Like the spirit of God, moving visibly over the waters.


## VI

### PRISCILLA

Thus for a while he stood, and mused by the shore of
    the ocean,
Thinking of many things, and most of all of Priscilla;
And as if thought had the power to draw to itself, like the
    loadstone,
Whatsoever it touches, by subtile laws of its nature,
Lo! as he turned to depart, Priscilla was standing beside
    him.

"Are you so much offended, you will not speak to me?"
    said she.
"Am I so much to blame, that yesterday, when you were
    pleading
Warmly the cause of another, my heart, impulsive and
    wayward,
Pleaded your own, and spake out, forgetful perhaps of
    decorum?
Certainly you can forgive me for speaking so frankly, for
    saying
What I ought not to have said, yet now I can never
    unsay it;
For there are moments in life, when the heart is so full
    of emotion,
That if by chance it be shaken, or into its depths like a
    pebble
Drops some careless word, it overflows, and its secret,
Spilt on the ground like water, can never be gathered
    together.

Yesterday I was shocked, when I heard you speak of Miles
    Standish,
Praising his virtues, transforming his very defects into
    virtues,
Praising his courage and strength, and even his fighting
    in Flanders,
As if by fighting alone you could win the heart of a
    woman,
Quite overlooking yourself and the rest, in exalting your
    hero.
Therefore I spake as I did, by an irresistible impulse.
You will forgive me, I hope, for the sake of the friendship
    between us,
Which is too true and too sacred to be so easily broken!"
Thereupon answered John Alden, the scholar, the friend
    of Miles Standish:
"I was not angry with you, with myself alone I was
    angry,
Seeing how badly I managed the matter I had in my
    keeping."
"No!" interrupted the maiden, with answer prompt and
    decisive;
"No; you were angry with me, for speaking so frankly
    and freely.
It was wrong, I acknowledge; for it is the rate of a
    woman
Long to be patient and silent, to wait like a ghost that is
    speechless,
Till some questioning voice dissolves the spell of its
    silence.
Hence is the inner life of so many suffering women
Sunless and silent and deep, like subterranean rivers
Running through caverns of darkness, unheard, unseen,
    and unfruitful,
Chafing their channels of stone, with endless and profitless
    murmurs."
Thereupon answered John Alden, the young man, the
    lover of women:
"Heaven forbid it, Priscilla; and truly they seem to me
    always
More like the beautiful rivers that watered the garden of
    Eden,

More like the river Euphrates, through deserts of Havilah
    flowing,
Filling the land with delight, and memories sweet of the
    garden!"
"Ah, by these words, I can see," again interrupted the
    maiden,
"How very little you prize me, or care for what I am
    saying.
When from the depths of my heart, in pain and with secret
    misgiving,
Frankly I speak to you, asking for sympathy only and
    kindness,
Straightway you take up my words, that are plain and
    direct and in earnest,
Turn them away from their meaning, and answer with
    flattering phrases.
This is not right, is not just, is not true to the best that is
    in you;
For I know and esteem you, and feel that your nature is
    noble,
Lifting mine up to a higher, a more ethereal level.
Therefore I value your friendship, and feel it perhaps the
    more keenly
If you say aught that implies I am only as one among
    many,
If you make use of those common and complimentary
    phrases
Most men think so fine, in dealing and speaking with
    women,
But which women reject as insipid, if not as insulting."

    Mute and amazed was Alden; and listened and looked
    at Priscilla,
Thinking he never had seen her more fair, more divine in
    her beauty.
He who but yesterday pleaded so glibly the cause of
    another,
Stood there embarrassed and silent, and seeking in vain
    for an answer.
So the maiden went on, and little divined or imagined
What was at work in his heart, that made him so awkward
    and speechless.

"Let us, then, be what we are, and speak what we think,
    and in all things
Keep ourselves loyal to truth, and the sacred professions of
    friendship.
It is no secret I tell you, nor am I ashamed to declare it:
I have liked to be with you, to see you, to speak with
    you always.
So I was hurt at your words, and a little affronted to
    hear you
Urge me to marry your friend, though he were the Captain
    Miles Standish.
For I must tell you the truth: much more to me is your
    friendship
Than all the love he could give, were he twice the hero
    you think him."
Then she extended her hand, and Alden, who eagerly
    grasped it,
Felt all the wounds in his heart, that were aching and
    bleeding so sorely,
Healed by the touch of that hand, and he said, with a
    voice full of feeling:
"Yes, we must ever be friends; and of all who offer you
    friendship
Let me be ever the first, the truest, the nearest and
    dearest!"

    Casting a farewell look at the glimmering sail of the
    Mayflower,
Distant, but still in sight, and sinking below the horizon,
Homeward together they walked, with a strange, indefinite
    feeling,
That all the rest had departed and left them alone in the
    desert.
But, as they went through the fields in the blessing and
    smile of the sunshine,
Lighter grew their hearts, and Priscilla said very archly:
"Now that our terrible Captain has gone in pursuit of the
    Indians,
Where he is happier far than he would be commanding a
    household,
You may speak boldly, and tell me of all that happened
    between you,

When you returned last night, and said how ungrateful
    you found me."
Thereupon answered John Alden, and told her the whole
    of the story,—
Told her his own despair, and the direful wrath of Miles
    Standish.
Whereat the maiden smiled, and said between laughing
    and earnest,
"He is a little chimney, and heated hot in a moment!"
But as he gently rebuked her, and told her how he had
    suffered,—
How he had even determined to sail that day in the
    Mayflower,
And had remained for her sake, on hearing the dangers
    that threatened,—
All her manner was changed, and she said with a faltering
    accent,
"Truly I thank you for this: how good you have been to
    me always!"

  Thus, as a pilgrim devout, who toward Jerusalem
    journeys,
Taking three steps in advance, and one reluctantly back-
    ward,
Urged by importunate zeal, and withheld by pangs of
    contrition;
Slowly but steadily onward, receding yet ever advancing,
Journeyed this Puritan youth to the Holy Land of his
    longings,
Urged by the fervor of love, and withheld by remorseful
    misgivings.

# VII

## THE MARCH OF MILES STANDISH

Meanwhile the stalwart Miles Standish was marching
    steadily northward,
Winding through forest and swamp, and along the trend
    of the sea-shore,

All day long, with hardly a halt, the fire of his anger
Burning and crackling within, and the sulphurous odor of
    powder
Seeming more sweet to his nostrils than all the scents of
    the forest.
Silent and moody he went, and much he revolved his
    discomfort;
He who was used to success, and to easy victories always,
Thus to be flouted, rejected, and laughed to scorn by a
    maiden,
Thus to be mocked and betrayed by the friend whom most
    he had trusted!
Ah! 'twas too much to be borne, and he fretted and chafed
    in his armor!

   "I alone am to blame," he muttered, "for mine was the
    folly.
What has a rough old soldier, grown grim and gray in the
    harness,
Used to the camp and its ways, to do with the wooing of
    maidens?
'Twas but a dream,—let it pass,—let it vanish like so
    many others!
What I thought was a flower, is only a weed, and is
    worthless;
Out of my heart will I pluck it, and throw it away, and
    henceforward
Be but a fighter of battles, a lover and wooer of dangers!"
Thus he revolved in his mind his sorry defeat and dis-
    comfort,
While he was marching by day or lying at night in the
    forest,
Looking up at the trees, and the constellations beyond
    them.

   After three days' march he came to an Indian encamp-
    ment
Pitched on the edge of a meadow, between the sea and the
    forest;
Women at work by the tents, and warriors, horrid with
    war-paint,
Seated about a fire, and smoking and talking together;
Who, when they saw from afar the sudden approach of the
    white men,

Saw the flash of the sun on breastplate and sabre and
 musket,
Straightway leaped to their feet, and two, from among
 them advancing,
Came to parley with Standish, and offer him furs as a
 present;
Friendship was in their looks, but in their hearts there was
 hatred.
Braves of the tribe were these, and brothers, gigantic in
 stature,
Huge as Goliath of Gath, or the terrible Og, king of
 Bashan;
One was Pecksuot named, and the other was called
 Wattawamat.
Round their necks were suspended their knives in scab-
 bards of wampum,
Two-edged, trenchant knives, with points as sharp as a
 needle.
Other arms had they none, for they were cunning and
 crafty.
"Welcome, English!" they said,—these words they had
 learned from the traders
Touching at times on the coast, to barter and chaffer for
 peltries.
Then in their native tongue they began to parley with
 Standish,
Through his guide and interpreter, Hobomok, friend of the
 white man,
Begging for blankets and knives, but mostly for muskets
 and powder,
Kept by the white man, they said, concealed, with the
 plague, in his cellars,
Ready to be let loose, and destroy his brother the red
 man!
But when Standish refused, and said he would give them
 the Bible,
Suddenly changing their tone, they began to boast and to
 bluster.
Then Wattamat advanced with a stride in front of the
 other,
And, with a lofty demeanor, thus vauntingly spake to the
 Captain:

"Now Wattawamat can see, by the fiery eyes of the
    Captain,
Angry is he in his heart; but the heart of the brave
    Wattawamat
Is not afraid at the sight. He was not born of a woman,
But on a mountain at night, from an oak-tree riven by
    lightning,
Forth he sprang at a bound, with all his weapons about
    him,
Shouting, 'Who is there here to fight with the brave
    Wattawamat?' "
Then he unsheathed his knife, and, whetting the blade
    on his left hand,
Held it aloft and displayed a woman's face on the handle;
Saying, with bitter expression and look of sinister meaning:
"I have another at home, with the face of a man on the
    handle;
By and by they shall marry; and there will be plenty of
    children!"

   Then stood Pecksuot forth, self-vaunting, insulting
    Miles Standish:
While with his fingers he patted the knife that hung at
    his bosom,
Drawing it half from its sheath, and plunging it back, as
    he muttered,
"By and by it shall see; it shall eat; ah, ha! but shall
    speak not!
This is the mighty Captain the white men have sent to
    destroy us!
He is a little man; let him go and work with the women!"

   Meanwhile Standish had noted the faces and figures of
    Indians
Peeping and creeping about from bush to tree in the
    forest,
Feigning to look for game, with arrows set on their bow-
    strings,
Drawing about him still closer and closer the net of their
    ambush.
But undaunted he stood, and dissembled and treated them
    smoothly;
So the old chronicles say, that were writ in the days of
    the fathers.

But when he heard their defiance, the boast, the taunt,
and the insult,
All the hot blood of his race, of Sir Hugh and of Thurston
de Standish,
Boiled and beat in his heart, and swelled in the veins of
his temples.
Headlong he leaped on the boaster, and, snatching his
knife from its scabbard,
Plunged it into his heart, and, reeling backward, the
savage
Fell with his face to the sky, and a fiendlike fierceness
upon it.
Straight there arose from the forest the awful sound of the
war-whoop.
And, like a flurry of snow on the whistling wind of De-
cember,
Swift and sudden and keen came a flight of feathery
arrows.
Then came a cloud of smoke, and out of the cloud came
the lightning,
Out of the lightning thunder; and death unseen ran before
it.
Frightened the savages fled for shelter in swamp and in
thicket,
Hotly pursued and beset; but their sachem, the brave
Wattawamat,
Fled not; he was dead. Unswerving and swift had a bullet
Passed through his brain, and he fell with both hands
clutching the greensward,
Seeming in death to hold back from his foe the land of
his fathers.

There on the flowers of the meadow the warriors lay,
and above them,
Silent, with folded arms, stood Hobomok, friend of the
white man.
Smiling at length he exclaimed to the stalwart Captain
of Plymouth:—
"Pecksuot bragged very loud, of his courage, his strength,
and his stature,—
Mocked the great Captain, and called him a little man; but
I see now

Big enough have you been to lay him speechless before
    you!"

  Thus the first battle was fought and won by the stalwart
    Miles Standish.
When the tidings thereof were brought to the village of
    Plymouth,
And as a trophy of war the head of the brave Wattawa-
    mat
Scowled from the roof of the fort, which at once was a
    church and a fortress,
All who beheld it rejoiced, and praised the Lord, and took
    courage.
Only Priscilla averted her face from this spectre of terror,
Thanking God in her heart that she had not married
    Miles Standish;
Shrinking, fearing almost, lest, coming home from his
    battles,
He should lay claim to her hand, as the prize and reward
    of his valor.


## VIII

### THE SPINNING WHEEL

Month after month passed away, and in Autumn the
    ships of the merchants
Came with kindred and friends, with cattle and corn for
    the Pilgrims.
All in the village was peace; the men were intent on their
    labors,
Busy with hewing and building, with garden-plot and with
    merestead,
Busy with breaking the glebe, and mowing the grass in
    the meadows,
Searching the sea for its fish, and hunting the deer in the
    forest.
All in the village was peace; but at times the rumor of
    warfare
Filled the air with alarm, and the apprehension of danger.

Bravely the stalwart Standish was scouring the land with
    his forces,
Waxing valiant in fight and defeating the alien armies,
Till his name had become a sound of fear to the nations.
Anger was still in his heart, but at times the remorse and
    contrition
Which in all noble natures succeed the passionate out-
    break,
Came like a rising tide, that encounters the rush of a
    river,
Staying its current awhile, but making it bitter and brack-
    ish.

    Meanwhile Alden at home had built him a new habi-
    tation,
Solid, substantial, of timber rough-hewn from the firs of
    the forest.
Wooden-barred was the door, and the roof was covered
    with rushes;
Latticed the windows were, and the window-panes were
    of paper,
Oiled to admit the light, while wind and rain were ex-
    cluded.
There too he dug a well, and around it planted an
    orchard:
Still may be seen to this day some trace of the well and
    the orchard.
Close to the house was the stall, where, safe and secure
    from annoyance,
Raghorn, the snow-white bull, that had fallen to Alden's
    allotment
In the division of cattle, might ruminate in the night-
    time
Over the pastures he cropped, made fragrant by sweet
    pennyroyal.

    Oft when his labor was finished, with eager feet would
    the dreamer
Follow the pathway that ran through the woods to the
    house of Priscilla,
Led by illusions romantic and subtile deceptions of fancy,
Pleasure disguised as duty, and love in the semblance of
    friendship.

Ever of her he thought, when he fashioned the walls of
  his dwelling;
Ever of her he thought, when he delved in the soil of his
  garden;
Ever of her he thought, when he read in his Bible on
  Sunday
Praise of the virtuous woman, as she is described in the
  Proverbs,—
How the heart of her husband doth safely trust in her
  always,
How all the days of her life she will do him good, and
  not evil,
How she seeketh the wool and the flax and worketh with
  gladness,
How she layeth her hand to the spindle and holdeth the
  distaff,
How she is not afraid of the snow for herself or her
  household,
Knowing her household are clothed with the scarlet cloth
  of her weaving!

So as she sat at her wheel one afternoon in the Autumn,
Alden, who opposite sat, and was watching her dexterous
  fingers,
As if the thread she was spinning were that of his life and
  his fortune,
After a pause in their talk, thus spake to the sound of the
  spindle.
"Truly, Priscilla," he said, "when I see you spinning and
  spinning,
Never idle a moment, but thrifty and thoughtful of others,
Suddenly you are transformed, are visibly changed in a
  moment;
You are no longer Priscilla, but Bertha the Beautiful
  Spinner."
Here the light foot on the treadle grew swifter and swifter;
  the spindle
Uttered an angry snarl, and the thread snapped short
  in her fingers;
While the impetuous speaker, not heeding the mischief,
  continued:
"You are the beautiful Bertha, the spinner, the queen of
  Helvetia;

She whose story I read at a stall in the streets of South-
ampton,
Who, as she rode on her palfrey, o'er valley and meadow
and mountain,
Ever was spinning her thread from a distaff fixed to her
saddle.
She was so thrify and good, that her name passed into a
proverb.
So shall it be with your own, when the spinning-wheel shall
no longer
Hum in the house of the farmer, and fill its chambers with
music.
Then shall the mothers, reproving, relate how it was in
their childhood,
Praising the good old times, and the days of Priscilla the
spinner!"
Straight uprose from her wheel the beautiful Puritan
maiden,
Pleased with the praise of her thrift from him whose praise
was the sweetest,
Drew from the reel on the table a snowy skein of her
spinning,
Thus making answer, meanwhile, to the flattering phrases
of Alden:
"Come, you must not be idle; if I am a pattern for house-
wives,
Show yourself equally worthy of being the model of
husbands.
Hold this skein on your hands, while I wind it, ready for
knitting;
Then who knows but hereafter, when fashions have
changed and the manners,
Fathers may talk to their sons of the good old times of
John Alden!"
Thus, with a jest and a laugh, the skein on his hands she
adjusted,
He sitting awkwardly there, with his arms extended
before him,
She standing graceful, erect, and winding the thread from
his fingers,
Sometimes chiding a little his clumsy manner of holding,
Sometimes touching his hands, as she disentangled ex-
pertly

Twist or knot in the yarn, unawares—for how could she
    help it?—
Sending electrical thrills through every nerve in his body.

  Lo! in the midst of this scene, a breathless messenger
    entered,
Bringing in hurry and heat the terrible news from the
    village.
Yes; Miles Standish was dead!—an Indian had brought
    them the tidings,—
Slain by a poisoned arrow, shot down in the front of the
    battle,
Into an ambush beguiled, cut off with the whole of his
    forces;
All the town would be burned, and all the people be
    murdered!
Such were the tidings of evil that burst on the hearts of
    the hearers.
Silent and statue-like stood Priscilla, her face looking
    backward
Still at the face of the speaker, her arms uplifted in
    horror;
But John Alden, upstarting, as if the barb of the arrow
Piercing the heart of his friend had struck his own, and
    had sundered
Once and forever the bonds that held him bound as a
    captive,
Wild with excess of sensation, the awful delight of his
    freedom,
Mingled with pain and regret, unconscious of what he was
    doing,
Clasped, almost with a groan, the motionless form of
    Priscilla,
Pressing her close to his heart, as forever his own, and
    exclaiming:
"Those whom the Lord hath united, let no man put them
    asunder!"

  Even as rivulets twain, from distant and separate
    sources,
Seeing each other afar, as they leap from the rocks, and
    pursuing

Each one its devious path, but drawing nearer and
    nearer,
Rush together at last, at their trysting-place in the forest;
So these lives that had run thus far in separate channels,
Coming in sight of each other, then swerving and flowing
    asunder,
Parted by barriers strong, but drawing nearer and nearer,
Rushed together at last, and one was lost in the other.


# IX

## THE WEDDING-DAY

Forth from the curtain of clouds, from the tent of purple
    and scarlet,
Issued the sun, the great High-Priest, in his garments re-
    splendent,
Holiness unto the Lord, in letters of light, on his fore-
    head,
Round the hem of his robe the golden bells and pome-
    granates.
Blessing the world he came, and the bars of vapor beneath
    him
Gleamed like a grate of brass, and the sea at his feet was
    a laver!

   This was the wedding morn of Priscilla the Puritan
    maiden.
Friends were assembled together; the Elder and Magistrate
    also
Graced the scene with their presence, and stood like the
    Law and the Gospel,
One with the sanction of earth and one with the blessing
    of heaven.
Simple and brief was the wedding, as that of Ruth and of
    Boaz.
Softly the youth and the maiden repeated the words of
    betrothal,

Taking each other for husband and wife in the Magistrate's
presence,
After the Puritan way, and the laudable custom of
Holland.
Fervently then, and devoutly, the excellent Elder of
Plymouth
Prayed for the hearth and the home, that were founded
that day in affection,
Speaking of life and of death, and imploring Divine bene-
dictions.

Lo! when the service was ended, a form appeared on the
threshold,
Clad in armor of steel, a sombre and sorrowful figure!
Why does the bridegroom start and stare at the strange
apparition?
Why does the bride turn pale, and hide her face on his
shoulder?
Is it a phantom of air,—a bodiless, spectral illusion?
Is it a ghost from the grave, that has come to forbid the
betrothal?
Long had it stood there unseen, a guest uninvited, un-
welcomed;
Over its clouded eyes there had passed at times an ex-
pression
Softening the gloom and revealing the warm heart hidden
beneath them,
As when across the sky the driving rack of the rain-cloud
Grows for a moment thin, and betrays the sun by its
brightness.
Once it had lifted its hand, and moved its lips, but was
silent,
As if an iron will had mastered the fleeting intention.
But when were ended the troth and the prayer and the
last benediction,
Into the room it strode, and the people beheld with
amazement
Bodily there in his armor Miles Standish, the Captain of
Plymouth!
Grasping the bridegroom's hand, he said with emotion,
"Forgive me!
I have been angry and hurt,—too long have I cherished
the feeling;

I have been cruel and hard, but now, thank God! it is
ended.
Mine is the same hot blood that leaped in the veins of
Hugh Standish,
Sensitive, swift to resent, but as swift in atoning for
error.
Never so much as now was Miles Standish the friend of
John Alden.'
Thereupon answered the bridegroom: "Let all be forgotten
between us,—
All save the dear old friendship, and that shall grow older
and dearer!"
Then the Captain advanced, and, bowing, saluted Priscilla,
Gravely, and after the manner of old-fashioned gentry in
England,
Something of camp and of court, of town and of country,
commingled,
Wishing her joy of her wedding, and loudly lauding her
husband.
Then he said with a smile: "I should have remembered
the adage,—
If you would be well served, you must serve yourself; and
moreover,
No man can gather cherries in Kent at the season of
Christmas!"

Great was the people's amazement, and greater yet
their rejoicing,
Thus to behold once more the sunburnt face of their
Captain,
Whom they had mourned as dead; and they gathered
and crowded about him,
Eager to see him and hear him, forgetful of bride and of
bridegroom,
Questioning, answering, laughing, and each interrupting
the other,
Till the good Captain declared, being quite overpowered
and bewildered,
He had rather by far break into an Indian encampment,
Than come again to a wedding to which he had not been
invited.

Meanwhile the bridegroom went forth and stood with
the bride at the doorway,

Breathing the perfumed air of that warm and beautiful
morning.
Touched with autumnal tints, but lonely and sad in the
sunshine,
Lay extended before them the land of toil and privation;
There were the graves of the dead, and the barren waste
of the sea-shore,
There the familiar fields, the groves of pine, and the
meadows;
But to their eyes transfigured, it seemed as the Garden of
Eden,
Filled with the presence of God, whose voice was the
sound of the ocean.

Soon was their vision disturbed by the noise and stir of
departure,
Friends coming forth from the house, and impatient of
longer delaying,
Each with his plan for the day, and the work that was left
uncompleted.
Then from a stall near at hand, amid exclamations of
wonder,
Alden the thoughtful, the careful, so happy, so proud of
Priscilla,
Brought out his snow-white bull, obeying the hand of its
master,
Led by a cord that was tied to an iron ring in its nostrils,
Covered with crimson cloth, and a cushion placed for a
saddle.
She should not walk, he said, through the dust and heat of
the noonday;
Nay, she should ride like a queen, not plod along like a
peasant.
Somewhat alarmed at first, but reassured by the others,
Placing her hand on the cushion, her foot in the hand of
her husband,
Gaily, with joyous laugh, Priscilla mounted her palfrey.
"Nothing is wanting now," he said with a smile, "but the
distaff;
Then you would be in truth my queen, my beautiful
Bertha!"

Onward the bridal procession now moved to their new
habitation,

Happy husband and wife, and friends conversing together.
Pleasantly murmured the brook, as they crossed the ford
    in the forest,
Pleased with the image that passed, like a dream of love,
    through its bosom,
Tremulous, floating in air, o'er the depths of the azure
    abysses.
Down through the golden leaves the sun was pouring his
    splendors,
Gleaming on purple grapes, that, from branches above
    them suspended,
Mingled their odorous breath with the balm of the pine
    and the fir tree,
Wild and sweet as the clusters that grew in the valley of
    Eshcol.
Like a picture it seemed of the primitive, pastoral ages,
Fresh with the youth of the world, and recalling Rebecca
    and Isaac,
Old and yet ever new, and simple and beautiful always,
Love immortal and young in the endless succession of
    lovers.
So through the Plymouth woods passed onward the bridal
    procession.

# APPENDIX

## MARTIN FRANC AND THE MONK OF SAINT ANTHONY

*Seignor, oiez une merveille,*
*C'onques n'oïstes sa pareille,*
*Que je vos vueil dire et conter;*
*Or metez cuer a l'escouter.*
FABLIAU DU BOUCHIER D'ABBEVILLE

*Lystyn Lordyngs to my tale,*
*And ye shall here of one story,*
*Is better than any wyne or ale,*
*That ever was made in this country.*
ANCIENT METRICAL ROMANCE

IN times of old there lived in the city of Rouen a trades-man named Martin Franc, who by a series of misfortunes had been reduced from opulence to poverty. But poverty, which generally makes men humble and laborious, only served to make him proud and lazy; and in proportion as he grew poorer and poorer, he grew also prouder and lazier. He contrived, however, to live along from day to day, by now and then pawning a silken robe of his wife, or selling a silver spoon or some other trifle, saved from the wreck of his better fortunes; and passed his time pleas-antly enough in loitering about the marketplace, and walk-ing up and down on the sunny side of the street.

The fair Marguerite, his wife, was celebrated through the whole city for her beauty, her wit, and her virtue. She was a brunette, with the blackest eye, the whitest teeth, and the ripest nut-brown cheek in all Normandy; her figure was tall and stately, her hands and feet most delicately moulded, and her swimming gait like the motion of a swan. In happier days she had been the delight of the richest tradesmen in the city, and the envy of the fairest dames.

The friends of Martin Franc, like the friends of many a ruined man before and since, deserted him in the day of adversity. Of all that had eaten his dinners, and drunk his

242

wine, and flattered his wife, none sought the narrow alley and humble dwelling of the broken tradesman save one, and that one was Friar Gui, the sacristant of the abbey of St. Anthony. He was a little, jolly, red-faced friar, with a leer in his eye and rather a doubtful reputation; but as he was a kind of travelling gazette, and always brought the latest news and gossip of the city, and besides was the only person that condescended to visit the house of Martin Franc—in fine, for the want of a better, he was considered in the light of a friend.

In these constant assiduities, Friar Gui had his secret motives, of which the single heart of Martin Franc was entirely unsuspicious. The keener eye of his wife, however, soon discovered two faces under the hood; but she persevered in misconstruing the friar's intentions, and in dexterously turning aside any expressions of gallantry that fell from his lips. In this way Friar Gui was for a long time kept at bay; and Martin Franc preserved in the day of poverty and distress that consolation of all this world's afflictions—a friend. But, finally, things came to such a pass, that the honest tradesman opened his eyes and wondered he had been asleep so long. Whereupon he was irreverent enough to thrust Friar Gui into the street by the shoulders.

Meanwhile the times grew worse and worse. One family relic followed another—the last silken robe was pawned, the last silver spoon sold; until at length poor Martin Franc was forced to "drag the devil by the tail"; in other words, beggary stared him full in the face. But the fair Marguerite did not even then despair. In those days, a belief in the immediate guardianship of the saints was much more strong and prevalent than in these lewd and degenerate times; and as there seemed no great probability of improving their condition by any lucky change which could be brought about by mere human agency, she determined to try what could be done by intercession with the patron saint of her husband. Accordingly she repaired one evening to the abbey of St. Anthony, to place a votive candle, and offer her prayer at the altar which stood in the little chapel dedicated to St. Martin.

It was already sunset when she reached the church, and the evening service of the Virgin had commenced. A cloud of incense floated before the altar of the Madonna, and the organ rolled its deep melody along the dim arches of the church. Marguerite mingled with the kneeling crowd, and repeated the responses in Latin with as much devotion as the most learned clerk of the convent. When the service was over, she repaired to the chapel of St. Martin, and, lighting her votive taper at the silver lamp which burned before his altar, knelt down in a retired part of the chapel, and, with tears in her eyes, besought the saint for aid and protection. While she was thus engaged, the church became gradually deserted till she was left, as she thought, alone. But in this she was mistaken; for, when she arose to depart, the portly figure of Friar Gui was standing close at her elbow!

"Good evening, fair Marguerite," said he. "St. Martin has heard your prayer and sent me to relieve your poverty."

"Then," replied she, "the good saint is not very fastidious in the choice of his messengers."

"Nay, goodwife," answered the friar, not at all abashed by this ungracious reply, "if the tidings are good, what matters it who the messenger may be? And how does Martin Franc these days?"

"He is well," replied Marguerite; "and were he present, I doubt not would thank you heartily for the interest you still take in him and his poor wife."

"He has done me wrong," continued the friar. "But it is our duty to forgive our enemies, and so let the past be forgotten. I know that he is in want. Here, take this to him, and tell him I am still his friend."

So saying, he drew a small purse from the sleeve of his habit and proffered it to his companion. I know not whether it were a suggestion of St. Martin, but true it is that the fair wife of Martin Franc seemed to lend a more willing ear to the earnest whispers of the friar. At length she said—

"Put up your purse; today I can neither deliver your gift nor your message. Martin Franc has gone from home."

"Then keep it for yourself."

"Nay," replied Marguerite, casting down her eyes; "I can take no bribes here in the church, and in the very chapel of my husband's patron saint. You shall bring it to me at my house, if you will."

The friar put up the purse, and the conversation which followed was in a low and indistinct undertone, audible only to the ears for which it was intended. At length the interview ceased; and—O woman!—the last words that the virtuous Marguerite uttered, as she glided from the church, were—

"Tonight—when the abbey-clock strikes twelve—remember!"

It would be useless to relate how impatiently the friar counted the hours and the quarters as they chimed from the ancient tower of the abbey, while he paced to and fro along the gloomy cloister. At length the appointed hour approached; and just before the convent bell sent forth its summons to call the friars of St. Anthony to their midnight devotions, a figure with a cowl stole out of a postern gate, and, passing silently along the deserted streets, soon turned into the little alley which led to the dwelling of Martin Franc. It was none other than Friar Gui. He rapped softly at the tradesman's door, and casting a look up and down the street, as if to assure himself that his motions were unobserved, slipped into the house.

"Has Martin Franc returned?" inquired he in a whisper.

"No," answered the sweet voice of his wife; "he will not be back tonight."

"Then all good angels befriend us!" continued the monk, endeavoring to take her hand.

"Not so, good monk," said she, disengaging herself. "You forget the conditions of our meeting."

The friar paused a moment; and then, drawing a heavy leathern purse from his girdle, he threw it upon the table; at the same moment a footstep was heard behind him, and a heavy blow from a club threw him prostrate upon the floor. It came from the strong arm of Martin Franc himself!

It is hardly necessary to say that his absence was feigned. His wife had invented the story to decoy the monk, and thereby to keep her husband from beggary and to relieve herself, once for all, from the importunities of a false friend. At first Martin Franc would not listen to the proposition, but at length he yielded to the urgent entreaties of his wife; and the plan finally agreed upon was that Friar Gui, after leaving his purse behind him, should be sent back to the convent with a severer discipline than his shoulders had ever received from any penitence of his own.

The affair, however, took a more serious turn than was intended; for, when they tried to raise the friar from the ground—he was dead. The blow aimed at his shoulders fell upon his shaven crown; and, in the excitement of the moment, Martin Franc had dealt a heavier stroke than he intended. Amid the grief and consternation which followed this discovery, the quick imagination of his wife suggested an expedient of safety. A bunch of keys at the friar's girdle caught her eye. Hastily unfastening the ring, she gave the keys to her husband, exclaiming—

"For the holy Virgin's sake, be quick! One of these keys doubtless unlocks the gate of the convent garden. Carry the body thither and leave it among the trees!"

Martin Franc threw the dead body of the monk across his shoulders, and with a heavy heart took the way to the abbey. It was a clear, starry night; and though the moon had not yet risen, her light was in the sky and came reflected down in a soft twilight upon earth. Not a sound was heard through all the long and solitary streets, save at intervals the distant crowing of a cock, or the melancholy hoot of an owl from the lofty tower of the abbey. The silence weighed like an accusing spirit upon the guilty conscience of Martin Franc. He started at the sound of his own breathing, as he panted under the heavy burden of the monk's body; and if, perchance, a bat flitted near him on drowsy wings, he paused and his heart beat audibly with terror. At length he reached the garden wall of the abbey, opened the postern gate with the key, and bearing the monk into the garden, seated him upon a stone bench by the edge of the fountain, with his head resting against a column, upon which was sculptured an image of the Madonna. He then replaced the bunch of keys at the monk's girdle and returned home with hasty steps.

When the prior of the convent, to whom the repeated delinquencies of Friar Gui were but too well known, observed that he was again absent from his post at midnight prayers, he waxed exceedingly angry; and no sooner were the duties of the chapel finished than he sent a monk in pursuit of the truant sacristan, summoning him to appear immediately at his cell. By chance it happened that the monk chosen for this duty was an enemy of Friar Gui; and very shrewdly supposing that the sacristan had stolen out of the garden gate on some midnight adventure, he took that direction in pursuit. The moon was just climbing the convent wall, and threw its silvery light through the trees of the garden, and on the sparkling waters of the fountain that fell with a soft lulling sound into the deep basin below. As the monk passed on his way, he stopped to quench his thirst with a draught of cool water, and was turning to depart, when his eye caught the motionless form of the sacristan, sitting erect in the shadow of the stone column.

"How is this, Friar Gui?" quoth the monk. "Is this a place to be sleeping at midnight, when the brotherhood are all at their prayers?"

Friar Gui made no answer.

"Up, up! thou eternal sleeper, and do penance for thy negligence. The prior calls for thee at his cell!" continued the monk, growing angry, and shaking the sacristan by the shoulder.

But still no answer.

"Then, by Saint Anthony, I'll wake thee!"

And saying this, he dealt the sacristan a heavy box on the ear. The body bent slowly forward from its erect position, and, giving a headlong plunge, sank with a heavy splash into the basin of the fountain. The monk waited a few moments in expectation of seeing Friar Gui rise dripping from his cold bath; but he waited in vain; for he lay motionless at the bottom of the basin—his eyes open, and his ghastly face distorted by the ripples of the water. With a beating heart the monk stooped down, and, grasping the skirt of the sacristan's habit, at length succeeded in drawing him from the water. All efforts, however, to resuscitate him were unavailing. The monk was filled with terror, not doubting that the friar had died untimely by his hand; and as the animosity between them was no secret in the convent, he feared that when the deed was known he should be accused of murder. He therefore looked round for an expedient to relieve himself from the dead body; and the well-known character of the sacristan soon suggested one. He determined to carry the body to the house of the most noted beauty of Rouen, and leave it on the doorstep; so that all suspicion of the murder might fall upon the shoulders of some jealous husband. The beauty of Martin Franc's wife had penetrated even the thick walls of the convent, and there was not a friar in the whole abbey of Saint Anthony who had not done penance for his truant imagination. Accordingly, the dead body of Friar Gui was laid upon the monk's brawny shoulders, carried back to the house of Martin Franc, and placed in an erect position against the door. The monk knocked loud and long; and then, gliding through a by-lane, stole back to the convent.

A troubled conscience would not suffer Martin Franc and his wife to close their eyes; but they lay awake, lamenting the doleful events of the night. The knock at the door sounded like a death knell in their ears. It still continued at intervals, rap—rap—rap!—with a dull, low sound, as if something heavy were swinging against the panel; for the wind had risen during the night, and every angry gust that swept down the alley swung the arms of the lifeless sacristan against the door. At length Martin Franc mustered courage enough to dress himself and go down, while his wife followed him with a lamp in her hand: but no sooner had he lifted the latch, than the ponderous body of Friar Gui fell stark and heavy into his arms.

"Jesu Maria!" exclaimed Marguerite, crossing herself; "here is the monk again!"

"Yes, and dripping wet, as if he had just been dragged out of the river!"

"Oh, we are betrayed!" exclaimed Marguerite in agony.

"Then the Devil himself has betrayed us," replied Martin Franc, disengaging himself from the embrace of the sacristan; "for I met not a living being; the whole city was as silent as the grave."

"Saint Martin defend us!" continued his terrified wife. "Here, take this scapulary to guard you from the Evil One; and lose no time. You must throw the body into the river, or we are lost! Holy Virgin! How bright the moon shines!"

Saying this, she threw round his neck a scapulary, with the figure of a cross on one end and an image of the Virgin on the other; and Martin Franc again took the dead friar upon his shoulders, and with fearful misgivings departed on his dismal errand. He kept as much as possible in the shadow of the houses, and had nearly reached the quay, when suddenly he thought he heard footsteps behind him. He stopped to listen; it was no vain imagination; they came along the pavement, tramp, tramp! and every step grew louder and nearer. Martin Franc tried to quicken his pace —but in vain: his knees smote together, and he staggered against the wall. His hand relaxed its grasp, and the monk slid from his back and stood ghastly and straight beside him, supported by chance against the shoulder of his bearer. At that moment a man came round the corner, tottering beneath the weight of a huge sack. As his head was bent downwards, he did not perceive Martin Franc till he was close upon him; and when, on looking up, he saw two figures standing motionless in the shadow of the wall, he thought himself waylaid, and, without waiting to be assaulted, dropped the sack from his shoulders and ran off at full speed. The sack fell heavily on the pavement, and directly at the feet of Martin Franc. In the fall the string was broken; and out came the bloody head, not of a dead monk, as it first seemed to the excited imagination of Martin Franc, but of a dead hog! When the terror and surprise caused by this singular event had a little subsided, an idea came into the mind of Martin Franc, very similar to what would have come into the mind of almost any person in similar circumstances. He took the hog out of the sack, and putting the body of the monk into its place, secured it well with the remnants of the broken string, and then hurried homeward with the animal upon his shoulders.

He was hardly out of sight when the man with the sack returned, accompanied by two others. They were surprised to find the sack still lying on the ground, with no one near it, and began to jeer the former bearer, telling him he had been frightened at his own shadow on the wall. Then one of them took the sack upon his shoulders without the least suspicion of the change that had been made in its contents, and all three disappeared.

Now it happened that the city of Rouen was at that time infested by three street robbers, who walked in darkness like the pestilence, and always carried the plunder of their midnight marauding to the Tête-de-Bœuf, a little tavern in one of the darkest and narrowest lanes of the city. The host of the Tête-de-Bœuf was privy to all their schemes, and had an equal share in the profits of their nightly excursions. He gave a helping hand, too, by the length of his bills, and by plundering the pockets of any chance traveller that was luckless enough to sleep under his roof.

On the night of the disastrous adventure of Friar Gui, this little marauding party had been prowling about the city until a late hour, without finding anything to reward their labors. At length, however, they chanced to spy a

hog hanging under a shed in a butcher's yard, in readiness
for the next day's market; and as they were not very fas-
tidious in selecting their plunder, but, on the contrary,
rather addicted to taking whatever they could lay their
hands on, the hog was straightway purloined, thrust into a
large sack, and sent to the Tête-de-Bœuf on the shoulders
of one of the party, while the other two continued their
nocturnal excursion. It was this person who had been so
terrified at the appearance of Martin Franc and the dead
monk; and as this encounter had interrupted any further
operations of the party, the dawn of day being now near
at hand, they all repaired to their gloomy den in the Tête-
de-Bœuf. The host was impatiently waiting their return
and, asking what plunder they had brought with them, pro-
ceeded without delay to remove it from the sack. The first
thing that presented itself, on untying the string, was the
monk's hood.

"The devil take the devil!" cried the host, as he opened
the neck of the sack; "what's this? Your hog wears a
cowl!"

"The poor devil has become disgusted with the world,
and turned monk!" said he who held the light, a little sur-
prised at seeing the head covered with a coarse gray cloth.

"Sure enough he has," exclaimed another, starting back
in dismay, as the shaven crown and ghastly face of the friar
appeared. "Holy St. Benedict be with us! It is a monk
stark dead!"

"A dead monk, indeed!" said a third, with an incredu-
lous shake of the head; "how could a dead monk get into
this sack? No, no; there is some sorcery in this. I have
heard it said that Satan can take any shape he pleases; and
you may rely upon it this is Satan himself, who has taken
the shape of a monk to get us all hanged."

"Then we had better kill the devil than have the devil
kill us!" replied the host, crossing himself; "and the sooner
we do it the better; for it is now daylight, and the people
will soon be passing in the street."

"So say I," rejoiced the man of magic; "and my advice
is, to take him to the butcher's yard, and hang him up in
the place where we found the hog."

This proposition so pleased the others that it was exe-
cuted without delay. They carried the friar to the butcher's
house, and, passing a strong cord round his neck, sus-

pended him to a beam in the shed, and there left him.

When the night was at length past, and daylight began
to peep into the eastern windows of the city, the butcher
arose and prepared himself for market. He was casting up
in his mind what the hog would bring at his stall, when,
looking upward, lo! in its place he recognized the dead
body of Friar Gui.

"By St. Denis!" quoth the butcher. "I always feared
that this friar would not die quietly in his cell; but I never
thought I should find him hanging under my own roof.
This must not be; it will be said that I murdered him, and
I shall pay for it with my life. I must contrive some way
to get rid of him."

So saying, he called his man, and, showing him what had
been done, asked him how he should dispose of the body so
that he might not be accused of murder. The man, who was
of a ready wit, reflected a moment, and then answered—

"This is indeed a difficult matter, but there is no evil
without its remedy. We will place the friar on horse-
back"—

"What! a dead man on horseback?—impossible!" inter-
rupted the butcher. "Who ever heard of a dead man on
horseback!"

"Hear me out, and then judge. We must place the body
on horseback as well as we may and bind it fast with cords;
and then set the horse loose in the street, and pursue him,
crying out that the monk has stolen the horse. Thus all
who meet him will strike him with their staves as he
passes, and it will be thought that he came to his death
that way."

Though this seemed to the butcher rather a mad proj-
ect, yet, as no better one offered itself at the moment, and
there was no time for reflection, mad as the project was,
they determined to put it into execution. Accordingly the
butcher's horse was brought out, and the friar was bound
upon his back, and with much difficulty fixed in an up-
right position. The butcher then gave the horse a blow
upon the crupper with his staff, which set him into a smart
gallop down the street, and he and his man joined in pur-
suit, crying—

"Stop thief! Stop thief! The friar has stolen my horse!"

As it was now sunrise, the streets were full of people—
peasants driving their goods to market, citizens going to

their daily avocations. When they saw the friar dashing at full speed down the street, they joined in the cry of "Stop thief!—Stop thief!" and many who endeavored to seize the bridle, as the friar passed them at full speed, were thrown upon the pavement, and trampled under foot; others joined in the halloo and the pursuit; but this only served to quicken the gallop of the frightened steed, who dashed down one street and up another like the wind, with two or three mounted citizens clattering in full cry at his heels. At length they reached the market-place. The people scattered right and left in dismay; and the steed and rider dashed onward, overthrowing in their course men and women, and stalls, and piles of merchandise, and sweeping away like a whirlwind. Tramp—tramp—tramp! they clattered on; they had distanced all pursuit. They reached the quay; the wide pavement was cleared at a bound—one more wild leap—and splash!—both horse and rider sank into the rapid current of the river—swept down the stream —and were seen no more!

                                    HENRY WADSWORTH LONGFELLOW

# COMMENTARIES

### VAN WYCK BROOKS

*Longfellow at Cambridge*

The Craigie house in Cambridge had grown accustomed to distinguished lodgers when, in the summer of 1837, a young man of thirty, Henry Wadsworth Longfellow, the new professor of modern languages, applied at the door for chambers. Jared Sparks had lived there, Edward Everett had brought his bride there. Dr. Joseph Worcester, the lexicographer, was living there at present, working on his *American Dictionary.* Dr. Worcester had recently moved from Salem, where he had been a schoolmaster and had among his evening pupils the new professor's friend and Bowdoin class-mate, the young Nathaniel Hawthorne. The dictionary on which he was working now was a counterblast to Webster, his fellow Yale-man, who had removed from the language, in the interest of American independence, so many of its ancestral elegances. In matters of quantity, numbers of words and the like, together with the excellence of his definitions, the utilitarian Webster had won the day, even against the English dictionaries. In matters of quality, he was much at fault. Dr. Worcester saw no reason why the speech of his countrymen should lose its inherited succulence and fullness. In the name of Massachusetts, he wished to protest against the Connecticut school, with its thin and calculated rigours.*

Early as one rose in Brattle Street, Dr. Worcester was up and out already. One saw him on his black horse, jogging along in the shadows of dawn. Then he vanished into his cave of notes. The new professor was equally unobtrusive. It was true that he had a rakish air. With his rosy cheeks and china-blue eyes, he wore his hair in curls.

* From *The Flowering of New England* by Van Wyck Brooks, Copyright, 1936, 1952, by Van Wyck Brooks. Renewal, ©, 1964, by Gladys Brooks. Reprinted by permission of E. P. Dutton & Co., Inc.

He was fond of colour in his raiment. His neckties and his waistcoats were open to question; so were his gloves and his cane. Mrs. Craigie, much as she loved Voltaire, regarded him with suspicion. But she had read the extravagant *Sorrows of Werther;* moreover, she had read a recent book, *Outre-Mer* by name, the work of the young professor, a sort of all-European continuation of Washington Irving's *Sketch Book.* She liked the book, she liked the young man. It was plainly another case, like Bancroft's, of having studied abroad, and the new professor, unlike Bancroft, was willing to live it down. He got his own tea and toast for breakfast, quietly went about his college duties and buried himself in his rooms. And he soon exchanged the garments of his heart for a broad-brimmed black hat, a black frock-coat and a black cane.

Change his skin as he might, the young professor could not change his spots. He was a romantic soul. He was a born poet whose every fancy clothed itself in images and rhymes as naturally as an apple-tree in May clothes itself with blossoms. He was a poet like those Troubadours, those early-morning "finders" of poetry, who found it on every bush and sang as the vireo sings in summer, about whom he was lecturing to his classes. For he was also a scholar, the man in all America best fitted to fill Professor Ticknor's vacant chair. Ticknor, who wished to resign in order to visit Europe again and write his history of Spanish literature, had virtually appointed his successor. He had seen some of the young man's translations; and eleven years before, when Longfellow had set out for Europe to fit himself to teach at Bowdoin College, he had given him letters to Southey and Washington Irving, advising him to study at Göttingen. Longfellow had spent three years wandering over the continent, taught at Bowdoin six years more and gone back to Europe for another year, in Germany and Scandinavia, in preparation for his new position. He had shown the practical sense that makes the professor, worthy of the son of a Portland lawyer who had been Dr. Channing's Harvard class-mate. He had

Dutton and Company, Inc. Reprinted by permission of the publishers.
*Worcester remained for a generation the dictionary of the best New England writers. See Holmes, *The Poet at the Breakfast Table:* "Mr. Worcester's Dictionary, on which, as is well known, the literary men of this metropolis are by special statute allowed to be sworn in place of the Bible."

formed an acquaintance with various eminent men in
every corner of Europe, Lafayette in Paris, who remem-
bered his family pleasantly in Portland, the Swedish poet
Nicander, whom he met at Naples, Thomas Carlyle in
London, Grillparzer at Salzburg, Bryant, who was already
known as the "father of American poetry," with whom he
shared long walks at Heidelberg. He had taken a leaf from
Sir William Jones's letters and learned not only the usual
languages, all that Ticknor knew, but also Finnish and
Swedish, and had published several text-books, French
and Italian grammars, and a Spanish reader. But he was
a poet all the time. As a boy, he had written ballads of
the Revolution, songs of the Maine woods, elegiac verses
about Indian hunters whose race was falling like the
withered leaves when autumn strips the forest. He had
planned a series of poetic sketches dealing with aspects
of New England life, the taverns, the village customs, the
parson, the squire, the husking-frolics and the Indian
dances, the French-Canadian peasants. And in Europe,
where others were to be so conscious of all that America
lacked,—the castles and cathedrals and ivied ruins,—he
had recalled the corn-fields of New England, garnished
with yellow pumpkins, the green trees and orchards by the
roadside, the bursting barns, the fences and the well-poles,
the piles of winter firewood, the fresh, cheerful, breezy
scenes of home. Everywhere, the Europe that he witnessed,
—the Europe of the "Romantic Reaction,"— had gone
back to its national origins, and the poet had become the
skald again, the bard, the singer and the story-teller, the
moulder and hierophant of the national life, the people's
aspirations. Longfellow had felt this world-impulse.

Settled now in Cambridge, in the gracious mansion, so
like an Italian villa, the young professor, who was always
ready to draw forth some scrop of song or story to enter-
tain some fair Angélique, found willing ears also in his
classes. Beside the round mahogany table in University
Hall, he sat among his pupils, discoursing with a silvery
courtesy,—how different from the harsh, monastic fash-
ion of most of the older professors,—in a style that was
far too flowery, the older professors thought, but with a
feeling for the romance of letters that was much more
intimate than Ticknor's. In Ticknor one felt the glow of
a marble surface. This lecturer was a painter and a poet.

All the tones of his voice were soft and warm. He was a master of the pastel shades, whose mind was suffused with the light of Claude Lorrain. The facts, the details, the philology he left to his large corps of young instructors,— for the university, having abandoned itself to these degenerate modern languages, wished to do it handsomely. His task was to provide the general outlines, to give the aroma, the bouquet; and in what corner of the house of song was there a chamber where he had not lived? From the mouldering walls of the Anglo-Saxon bards, weather-stained and ruined, he passèd to the courts and gardens of the French Trouvères, *en route* for the Minnesingers and the Mastersingers. (One had to use these French words now and then, silly as they seemed in Cambridge ears.) He told again the ancient Frankish legends, the Chansons de Geste, the story of Reynard the Fox, souvenirs of far-off springs and summers that seemed to have a sort of occult relation to these early-morning days of the young republic. One heard the New England birds in the old French gardens, the songs like cherry-blossoms, drifting through an air of dawn, notes of expectation. Were some of the ballads rather grim and ghostly for a bright May morning in the college yard? The lecturer knew how to win his pupils . . . How joyously this ballad opens! It is the Feast of Pentecost. The crimson banners wave on the castle walls. You see how well-arranged the contrast is. The knight appears in his black mail, the mighty shadow trembles in the dance, the faded flowers drop. However, this ballad tells its own story. It needs no explanation. Here is something in a different vein, *The Castle by the Sea.* A somewhat sombre piece. Would you like me to read it? . . . Grim as the poem might be, it was inviting beside the Paley, the Locke or the mathematics one heard in the other class-rooms.

Warmly, too, with what a gift for colour, the young professor spoke of his life in Europe. This was not the cold, old classical Europe that everybody knew or had read about, the Europe that one crossed in a travelling-carriage, on grand tours, with letters of introduction. It was a garden of memories, songs and tears, softly bright as a spring bouquet, tinted with rose and apple-green, palè canary-yellow and the palest blue. One followed the professor on his travels, whether one had read his book or

not, shared his pipe in homely Flemish inns, floated with
him in a Dutch canal-boat, through meadows laden with
tulips, played on his flute, like Goldsmith, on the Loire,
among the peasants busy in the fields. One stopped for a
month or two in a Spanish village, ambled through Tyr-
olese valleys, over the blossoming carpet, lay beside him
on a flowery ledge, drenched with a summer silence that
was broken only by the sound of evening bells. One
walked through the still Swedish forests, heard the hem-
locks murmuring, watched the sunlight on the waterfalls;
one saw the yellow leaves drifting over Denmark. One
called upon old Dannecker, Goethe's friend, the great
Canova's pupil, the sculptor of the charming "Ariadne,"
and shared the young man's thoughts on his homeward
stroll,—whether he too might not accomplish something,
bring something permanent out of this fleeting life, and
then, serenely old, seat himself in his garden, like the
artist, wrapped in a flowered morning-gown, and fold his
hands in silence.

The young professor often spoke of Goethe. Once he
dreamed that Goethe came to Cambridge. The professor
gave him a dinner at Willard's Tavern and told him he
thought Clärchen's song in *Egmont* was one of his best
lyrics. The god smiled. He liked to speak of Heidelberg,
where, to the music of the nightingales that flooded the
castle garden, he had filled his heart with the old German
lore. His friends there dwelt in a land of fancy where
brooklets gushed and hemlock-trees were faithful, where
maidens' bosoms were not always faithless, where graves
were the footprints of angels and all things that lived sang
together, the roses, the tulips, the birds, the storms, the
fountains. The flowers melodiously kissed one another,
keeping time with the music of the moonbeams. Many
were the talks the young men had about fame and the
lives of authors. Where should the poet and the scholar
live, in solitude or in society, in the green stillness of the
country or in the grey town?—urgent problems to be
passed along to the young men at Harvard. There were
admirable examples at Heidelberg, students with their six-
teen hours a day and men of letters with retired habits:
Thibaut, poring over his Pandects, and that wild mystic
who spent his nights reading Schubert's *History of the
Soul*, while his own soul dwelt in the Middle Ages. There

with his German Minna, lived the French poet, Edgar
Quinet, who, having helped to revive the long-forgotten
Chansons de Geste, had written his fantastic *Ahasvérus*,
with its Holy Roods and Galilee-steeples, its arabesques
and roses, hoping to do in words what Strasbourg Cathe-
dral had done in stone. Lives of great men to remind one
... toiling upward in the night. One had to learn patience,
especially in the world that surrounded Harvard, where
the pulse of life beat with such feverish throbs. At Heidel-
berg, one heard tales of Richter, of Goethe, Hoffmann,
Schiller, who loved to write by candle-light, with the
Rhine-wine always on his table. What more could a pro-
fessor do, for his aspiring pupils,—and who was not as-
piring at Harvard?—than to picture all these French and
German scholars, toiling, in want, in pain, sickness, sor-
row, familiar with the weeping walls of dungeons, to
carry out their noble purposes? But for them, who would
have kept alight the undying lamp of thought? But for
them, the flapping of some conqueror's banner would have
blown it out forever.

Thus the professor discoursed, beside the mahogany
table, while the shadows of the elm-trees in the Yard
danced on the white pilasters of the class-room. His mind
was like a music-box, charged with all the poetry of the
world.* Ballads that rippled with the River Neckar. Bal-
lads of summer mornings and golden corn, blossoms,
red and blue, leafy lanes and hedge-rows. Spanish, Swed-
ish, Danish ballads. Epics and fragments of epics, like
*Frithiof's Saga*, by the mad Scandinavian bishop, Esaias
Tegnér, half pagan Viking, half Lutheran priest, who had
revived the chants of the ancient skalds in the pastoral
setting of a Swedish Wakefield. Sagas of ships and sea-
craft and laughing Saxons, dashing their beards with
wine. Songs of Norwegian chieftains, proud of their flow-
ing locks, night-songs, songs of childhood, Christmas
carols, stately Italian sonnets. The music-box unrolled
its coloured stream; but the lecturer was not an antiquary.
He was a poet and teacher of poets who spoke with a
mildly apostolic fervour. He had published an essay de-
fending his vocation. Poetry did not enervate the mind
or unfit the mind for the practical duties of life. He hoped

*For the range of Longfellow's knowledge of poetry, see his pro-
digious collection, *The Poets and Poetry of Europe*, 1845.

that poets would rise to convince the nation that, properly understood, "utility" embraces whatever contributes to make men happy. What had retarded American poetry? What but the want of exclusive cultivation? American poetry had been a pastime, beguiling the idle moments of merchants and lawyers. American scholarship had existed solely to serve the interests of theology. Neither had been a self-sufficient cause for lofty self-devotion. Henceforth, let it be understood that he who, in the solitude of his chamber, quickened the inner life of his countrymen, lived not for himself or lived in vain. The hour had struck for poets. Let them be more national and more natural, but only national as they were natural. Eschew the sky-lark and the nightingale, birds that Audubon had never found. A national literature ought to be built, as the robin builds its nest, out of the twigs and straws of one's native meadows. But seek not the great in the gigantic! Leave Niagara to its own voices! Let the American poets go back to the olden time, studying not the individual bard but the whole body of the world's song. They could only escape from their colonial heritage in this all-human testament of beauty. . . .

For softly, without effort, as he sat in the vast shadow at his open windows, the poems rose in his mind, like exhalations,—*Voices of the Night*. The black hulks of the trees rode at their moorings on the billowy sea of grass. The stars glistened through the heaving branches, the silver Charles gleamed across the meadow. Stanza by stanza, the poems came, sometimes all at once, songs, reveries, echoes of German verses, mingling with the whispers of the summer wind,—youthful regrets, youthful aspirations, psalms of a life which, on such an evening, might well appear a dream, though far from empty: *Footsteps of Angels, The Light of Stars, The Reaper and the Flowers, Hymn to the Night*. On these very evenings, at their open windows, thousands of young men in Hollis Hall, at Bowdoin, Yale, Princeton, in Cincinnati, up and down the Hudson and the Mississippi, in England, Scotland, Holland, in far-off Russia, beside the Neva as beside the Danube, heard the trailing garments of the night, shared these reveries of the New England springtime that Longfellow was putting into words, with such a lucid,

natural, velvety sweetness,—verses drifting through the
poet's mind as the yellow leaves drift from the trees in
autumn and silently fall to the ground.

In later days, when other fashions came, when the great
wheel of time had passed beyond them, one saw these
poems in another light. They seemed to lack finality and
distinction, whether in thought or phrase. But no one
could quite forget their dreamy music, their shadowy
languor, their melodious charm, their burden of youthful
nostalgia; and the world of the Age of Revolutions, which
knew the Romantic poets, shared this poet's mood of ex-
altation. A day was to come when a Chinese mandarin
transcribed *The Psalm of Life* on an ivory fan, and a
dying soldier at Sebastopol repeated the stirring lines.
When *Excelsior* appeared in a German version, the stu-
dents of Innsbrück, meeting the translator, thronged about
him and embraced and kissed him, with such joy and
transport, as he said, that he always looked upon that
moment as the happiest of his life. These were the days
when to be "up and doing, with a heart for any fate,"
seemed, after the drought of Calvinism, the drought of
monarchism and reaction, in the continental Europe of
'48, when people had thought they were powerless, a
miracle and a sudden inspiration; and Longfellow spoke
for the youth of all the world. He spoke for the young in
his verses, even in his prose *Hyperion,* the romance of the
American student who looked like Harold the Fair-hair
and bore the name of an old German poet. This was his
own romance, more or less, in the high-flown style of
Richter. Many and many a reader, as the years went by,
readers in English, Swedish, Dutch and French, followed
in the footsteps of the hero, sought out the inns where
Paul had slept, the Star at Salzig, the White Horse at
Bingen, turned aside for a Sunday at St. Gilgen, lingered,
book in hand, under the lindens and wept over the night at
Heidelberg when the lovely star, Elizabeth, fell from
heaven.

Such were the "voices of the night." The voices of the
day were firmer and clearer. On these summer mornings
at Craigie House, when the birds were carolling in the
trees, when insects chirped in the grass and the sunlight
and the perfume of the flowers poured through his open

windows, Longfellow's mind went back to Sweden, to the
still Scandinavian woodlands, carpeted with blossoms at
this balmy season, where, in a simple, primeval world,
like that of his own Maine, the leaves and ribbons
streamed from the lofty May-poles, and the old pagan
gods awoke once more, and one heard the hammers of
the Vikings, so like the hammers that one heard in Port-
land, building their oak-ribbed ships. That was his great
discovery, after all, that was the brightest feather in his
cap: other American writers and scholars were rediscov-
ering Italy and Spain, recapturing France and Germany.
He was the first who had visited, amply, at least, with a
living imagination, the lands of the skalds and the sagas,
where one found traces of one's forbears, in the days of
the Danish invasions, forests like one's own New Eng-
land forests, builders of boats with masts of the lordly
pine, the Baltic dashing on the northern strand, desolate
as one's own North Shore, village ways like the New
England ways, houses of hewn timber, white-painted
churches, maidens with flaxen hair, brown ale worthy of
King Olaf, apples such as a village blacksmith loved, poets,
too, like the mad Esaias, scarcely concealing under his
bishop's gown the robe of the chanting gleeman, chant-
ing now not the deeds of blood but the wild freedom of
the days of old. There, in those northern lands, the ballad,
like the ancient yeoman's life,—the life that was fit for
free men and simple, fishermen, farmers, sailors, fit for
Nantucket men and Portland men, as for the men of Gott-
land and Malmö,—there the epic and the story-poem still
played living parts in human lives, not as mere survivals
and revivals, as they were in the rest of Europe. One of
the best of Longfellow's translations,—perhaps, like that
of the Spanish funeral hymn, it could not have been better,
—was *The Children of the Lord's Supper,* in which Teg-
nér had revived for Swedish ears, as Goethe had revived
it for German ears, in *Hermann und Dorothea,* the metre
that Homer had used and Longfellow was to use in *Evan-
geline.* He had passed into this northern mind by such
a line of sympathy that the old poet-bishop found his
versions of *Frithiof's Saga* the only ones that fully satisfied
him.

In Sweden, or in Scandinavia,—for he found in the

Finnish *Kalevala* the form he was to use in *Hiawatha*,—
he had gone to school to better purpose than elsewhere
in his multi-coloured Europe. Before his eyes waved, and
were to wave, the mingled shapes and figures of the past,
the myths and scenes of European legend, "like a faded
tapestry," faded then, how much more faded later. The
Scandinavian world had given him something far more
vital, rhythms that signified a secret kinship, deeper than a
student's acquisitions, between the pastoral children of
the Vikings and the child of Maine for whom the sea and
the forest possessed an unfailing magic. The Scandinavians
had given him a feeling for the value of the forms,—the
ballad, the folk-poem, the epic fragment, vehicles of the
national sentiment that had come to life in America, as it
had come to a second life in the North,—through which
his mind was to flow with its greatest vigour. All his evoca-
tions of feudal Europe, of the mediæval world that haunted
him, of the biblical world and the world of the Renais-
sance, what were they ever to mean,—these incidents of
an endless panorama, which the patient and facile show-
man unrolled for a generation before the eyes of his en-
raptured public, a Panorama of Athens, such as they had
set up in Cambridge, extended over the history of the
world's culture,—beside a handful of ballads and two or
three narrative poems, redolent of the vast American
woodlands, the prairies, the prodigious Mississippi, the
sylvan solitudes of Canada, the gusty New England sea-
coast, poems fragrant still with hemlock, fir and balsam,
the salt breeze of the rocky shore, the wild-brier, the
rose and the syringa, breathing a tonic piety, as of pater-
nal altars and forest gods?

Such were the voices of the day, which the poet heard,
with a soft excitement, as he took his morning walk at
sunrise, or, when evening came, lighted the long candles
on his upright desk.

❖    ❖    ❖

In Cambridge, as in Concord, where the "little women"
and the "little men" were about to appear in books, chil-
dren filled the scene. All the New England writers under-
stood them and wrote about them, sometimes with ex-

quisite feeling.* *Uncle Tom's Cabin* was composed, under the lamp, on a table surrounded by children conning their lessons, in a hum of earnest voices asking questions. Hawthorne's stories were as full of children as ever the summer woods were filled with birds; and Whittier's shy affections and Holmes's salty humours were addressed as often as not to boys and girls. Lowell, so self-conscious in most of his letters, only showed how deep his feelings were in these domestic relations. Perhaps they were deep only in these relations, like the feelings of Henry James. In later times, when boys and girls were "problems," and most of their fathers and mothers were also problems, more problematic than the children, when the old cultural forms had broken down, and literature was produced by childless rebels,—or largely so produced,—against the abuses of the older culture in the hour of its rigidity and decay, when the nation had lost much of its faith and even so much of its will-to-live that "race-suicide" was a pressing question, one found it difficult to return in fancy to Longfellow's "children's hour," when life flowed so freely between the generations. This ever-present consciousness of children, in minds so unconscious of themselves, spoke for a culture at its highest tide, a community that believed in itself, serenely sure of itself and sure of its future, eager to perpetuate its forms.

Longfellow had bought an orange-tree, with a hundred buds and blossoms. It flourished in his window beside the lemon-tree, which, for the last ten years, had kept the summer blooming through the winter in his white-panelled study. A springtime fragrance of Italy filled the room. On his table stood Coleridge's ink-stand, the gift of an English admirer. A Tintoretto hung near by. One saw an agate cup of Cellini. The folding doors opened into the spacious library, with its two Corinthian columns. There was something large, bland and sweet, something

---

* "Pliable as she was to all outward appearance, the child had her own still, interior world, where all her little notions and opinions stood up crisp and fresh, like flowers that grow in cool, shady places. If anybody too rudely assailed a thought or suggestion she put forth, she drew it back again into this quiet inner chamber and went on.... There is no independence and pertinacity like that of these seemingly soft, quiet creatures, whom it is so easy to silence, and so difficult to convince."— Harriet Beecher Stowe, *The Pearl of Orr's Island*.

See also Emerson's remarks on children, in the opening paragraphs of his essay, *Domestic Life*.

fresh and sunny in the atmosphere of the house that re-
flected the soul of the generous poet, he whom neither
fame nor the praise of kings could ever spoil or alter.
A fathomless calm of innocent goodness brooded in the
air that spread with Longfellow's poems over the world.*
Nothing disturbed the poet's magnanimous mildness,
neither the vanity that he never knew nor the fools whom
he suffered gladly. By no effort of any man could any
malicious phrase be drawn from his lips. Were you pulling
some rhymester to pieces, Longfellow had culled and was
ready to quote, in the poor bard's favour, the only good
line he had ever written. Did you beg him not to waste his
time on the cranks who were always besetting him. "Who
would be kind to him if I were not?" was Longfellow's
only possible answer. As his fame spread like the morning
sun over the English-speaking peoples, with its notes of
domestic affection and the love of the sea, of landscape
and legend, till twenty-four English publishing-houses
brought out his work in competition and ten thousand
copies of *The Courtship of Miles Standish* were sold in
London in a single day, as the royalties of his poems rose
till they rivalled those of Byron and even those which, in
ancient Rome, Tiberius lavished on his poetasters,—four
hundred thousand sesterces for a dialogue,—the flood of
interruptions became so great that he longed for a snow-
storm to block the door. A stranger who came to see
Washington's rooms asked him if Shakespeare did not live
near by. Some of his visitors thought he was greater than
Shakespeare. An Englishman stopped to see him because
there were no American ruins to visit. Longfellow smiled
when a Frenchman asked him for *révélations intimes* re-
garding his domestic life, to appear in a Paris newspaper;
but he gave a loaf of bread to every beggar, even when
the beggars, disappointed, left the loaves upright on his
gate-post. Now and then a great man came of whom Long-
fellow had never heard but who had heard of Longfellow,
perhaps in Russia. One day, in 1861, Bakunin arrived at
noon. He had escaped from Siberia. Longfellow asked him
to stay to lunch. "Yiss, and I will dine with you, too,"

*"I had many things to say about the sense I have of the good you
might do this old world by staying with us a little, and giving the peace-
ful glow of your fancy to our cold, troubled, unpeaceful spirit. Strange,
that both you and Norton come as such *calm* influences to me and
others." —Ruskin to Longfellow.

Bakunin replied, and he stayed till almost midnight. There was another Cambridge tableau.

Walking in his garden, among the birds, to the trilling of the frogs in his pond, like the chorus of a Grecian tragedy, Longfellow revolved in his mind the stories he was telling his children, passing them on to a larger world that was an extension of his household. He told them with a childlike air of trust, as if he knew in advance that the listening earth shared his faith in true love and homeland, his hatred of cruelty and his joy in nature,—the humble sweetness of a courteous heart. He ranged, in the *Tales of a Wayside Inn,*—the old Sudbury tavern, on the postroad to New York, where he assembled, in fancy, in imitation of Chaucer, some of his friends, the poet, Dr. Parsons, the Sicilian, Luigi Monti, the landlord, Mr. Howe, —over New England, Norway, Italy, Spain. Most of these tales were of the pretty kind in which the romantic poets abounded. Longfellow, who liked to say, "To stay at home is best," who had nothing of the adventurous in him and did not like extremes or excess, the extreme of heat, the extreme of cold, treated the tragic in the tales with the guileless impassivity of a Florentine monk picturing the miseries of the damned. He, whose eye had never missed an old stone church or a winding lane, an unusual tree, a wall, a crumbling house, in his own American country, by which to endow the scene with associations, paused at every page of the storybook of history and read it again aloud with a smile of his own. But in the New England stories, *Paul Revere's Ride, The Courtship of Miles Standish,*—"full of the name and the fame of the Puritan maiden Priscilla,"—another tone appeared in his voice. He spoke with a spirit or a tender conviction that sprang from the blood within him. One heard this note in *My Lost Youth;* one heard it in the sea-poems, the ballad of *The Cumberland, The Warden of the Cinque Ports.* One heard it in *The Saga of King Olaf,* the songs of the Norsemen. In these runes and rhymes one heard

> the ocean's dirges,
> When the old harper heaves and rocks,
> His hoary locks
> Flowing and flashing in the surges!

Longfellow's soul was not an ocean. It was a lake,

clear, calm and cool. The great storms of the sea never reached it. And yet this lake had its depths. Buried cities lay under its surface. One saw the towers and domes through the quiet water; one even seemed to catch the sound of church-bells ringing like the bells of the city of Is. Transparent as this mind was, there were profundities of moral feeling beneath the forms through which it found expression, the fruits of an old tradition of Puritan culture, and, behind this culture, all that was noble in the Northern races. If Longfellow's poetic feeling had had the depth of his moral feeling, he would have been one of the major poets, instead of the "chief minor poet of the English language,"—a phrase of Arnold Bennett's that strikes one as happy, if "minor" is understood as "popular," popular in the high sense, not the machine-made popular of later times. Longfellow's flaccidity debarred him from the front rank; but his work possessed a quality, a unity of feeling and tone, that gave him a place apart among popular poets. Of all the sons of the New England morning, save only the lonely men of Concord, he was the largest in his golden sweetness.

## VAN WYCK BROOKS

### Schoolcraft on the Hiawatha Myth

.... Still earlier, Henry Rowe Schoolcraft, the Indian agent at Mackinaw, who was working on his *Algic Researches,* soon to be published, had stirred New York with his large and splendid collection of minerals, Indian relics and drawings of the West. This was in 1821, before Schoolcraft had taken up ethnology, when he had surveyed the mineral wealth of the Mississippi valley and revealed its resources for trade as well as for science. His New York

From *The World of Washington Irving* by Van Wyck Brooks. New York: E. P. Dutton and Company, Inc., 1950, pp. 382-83; 411-14. London: J. M. Dent. Copyright 1944, 1950 by Van Wyck Brooks. Reprinted by permission of the publishers.

rooms were thronged with merchants, scientists and writers who came to examine this collection, and De Witt Clinton offered Schoolcraft the use of his own library in order that he might prepare his journal for the press. Natural science, at that time, was largely in the hands of physicians, and Dr. Mitchill vied with Dr. Hosack in forwarding Schoolcraft's work, while Benjamin Silliman also profited by School-craft's discoveries and the painter Henry Inman redrew some of his views. . . .

\*　　\*　　\*

. . . Henry Rowe Schoolcraft explored and described their inner and spiritual existence. Not how they lived, dressed and amused themselves but how they thought and felt was Schoolcraft's chief preoccupation, for he had set out to search the dark cave of the Indian mind, its poetry, philosophy, dogmas, beliefs and opinions, when the Indians were seen as warriors mainly. It had scarcely occurred to anyone that the Indians had a mind, indeed, aside from one or two writers like Fenimore Cooper, and illiterate interpreters and dishonest traders had stood be-tween them and the enquiring whites. Since they were always flitting and fighting, it was far from easy to study them, and Schoolcraft's were the first attempts to fathom the nature of their thinking and the first to record and pub-lish their legends and myths. The son of a glass-manufac-turer who had grown up near Albany, Schoolcraft had built glass-works in New York and Vermont, and, studying at Union and Middlebury College, he had learned Hebrew and German, although at first mineralogy was his principal interest. After the War of 1812, the soldiers who returned from the West had brought back marvellous tales of the prairie-country, and a new wave of emigrants moved out to the Wabash and Illinois to plough the Mississippi valley from its head to its foot. But little was known about those regions. What were their resources? Was not this just the time to explore and describe them? Schoolcraft went West himself on a mineralogical ramble, in 1817, by way of Pittsburgh, and he drew up the first report on the mines and the mineralogy of the country beyond the Alleghanies. Returning to New York, he exhibited the specimens that first revealed the wealth of the Mississippi valley, and President Monroe appointed him agent for Indian affairs

on the northwest frontier at Mackinac island. His house
on the island stood on a bluff, with a garden that sloped to
the lake, and the beach along the shore of the crescent bay
was studded with the wigwams of the friendly Algonquins.
Chippewa was the lingua franca of most of the Algonquin
tribes, the Ottawas, Pottawottamies and Winnebagos, and
Schoolcraft married the cultivated half-Chippewa daugh-
ter of the local Irish magnate John Johnston. He found it
intolerable to talk with the traders who used the native
language without any knowledge of mood, person or
tense; and, thrown as he was with the Indians all day
long, he had soon written a Chippewa lexicon and gram-
mar. He found the Indians peaceable and sociable, open-
hearted, affectionate, responsive and festive. In their
winter wigwams, safe for the season, they gave them-
selves over to music, poetry and songs. Like the Arabs,
they had professional story-tellers who went from lodge
to lodge, sure of the best seat and the choicest food,
amusing the inmates with traditional tales and histories of
their ancestors, exploits and inventions. Schoolcraft was
astonished by their parables and allegories. Who had ever
known they possessed this resource? What had all the ob-
servers been about, from the days of Cabot and Raleigh
down, never to have drawn this curtain from the Indian
mind?

The Mackinac winters were long and cold, and School-
craft spent his evenings collecting these tales and allegories
for seventeen years; and he never knew an Indian to break
a promise. Not once did the Indians violate a treaty
in all his constant dealing with them. He studied their
Manito-worship and translated their stories, and Mrs.
Schoolcraft helped him in this, while others, at his instiga-
tion, gathered similar tales from neighbouring tribes.* The
governor of Michigan, Lewis Cass, was deeply interested
in his work, as De Witt Clinton had formerly been in New

---

*Mrs. Jameson, the Anglo-Irish writer, visited the Schoolcrafts in
1838. She became a friend of Mrs. Schoolcraft and her sister and their
remarkable mother at Sault Ste.-Marie. Mrs. Schoolcraft had been
educated in Europe with her father's relations. Mrs. Jameson published
some of the Schoolcraft translations in her *Winter Studies and Summer
Rambles in Canada,* and most of the second volume of this book con-
sists of a description of her visit with the Schoolcrafts. It is the best
account of their life and work.

York, and Schoolcraft had correspondents all over the country. He published the legends and tales in his *Algic Researches*† and his voluminous *History of the Indian Tribes,* preserving as much as he could of the Indian style and the Indian thought-work, moods and metaphors. Regarding the stories as "wild vines," he tried to keep their wildness, with a little dressing and pruning that could scarcely be avoided, for the Indians were extremely prolix and he was obliged to lop away a measure of their redundant verbiage. These tales of the woods, the canoe and the wigwam revealed the Indian views of life, of death and the after-life, metamorphosis, religion, and they showed the Indians in every relation, as hunter, warrior, singer, magician, as husband, father, stranger, foe and friend. Some of them inculcated domestic union and brotherly love, perseverance, courage, filial obedience and cunning, while others dealt with fairies and dwarfs, the conflict of Manito with Manito, giants, enchanters, monsters, demons. Some were prophetic, some were animistic, many of them personified inanimate objects, and they were full of talking animals, hares and squirrels, lynxes, raccoons, while all the phenomena of nature were included in them, thunder, lightning, the Milky Way, the morning and the evening stars, meteors, the aurora borealis and the rainbow. As a rule, they came down from the age of flint and earthen pots and skins, and they never mentioned guns, knives or blankets; the father of the winds made battle with a flagroot and the king of the reptiles was shot with a dart. Most of the heroes rose from lowly circumstances and always by the help of Manitos. Here, among these Indian tales of the charmed arrow, the summer-maker, the red swan and the origin of Indian corn, first appeared Mudgekewis and the south wind Shawondasse and the story of Hiawatha, the hero and sage. It was in Schoolcraft that Longfellow found this foremost of the Indian myths, which hallowed the lakes and streams of the northern frontier, and Schoolcraft's writings were the gate through which all of the lore of the Indians passed gradually into American literature.

†Schoolcraft invented the word "Algic," deriving it from Alleghany and Atlantic. In his conception, the Algic nations were those that originally occupied all the lands east of the Mississippi.

# NORMAN HOLMES PEARSON

## Both Longfellows

THE now blunted anecdote of Emerson's lapse of memory at the grave of Longfellow has lost both its original gentle tribute and the sardonics of its later use. "I cannot recall the name of our friend," Emerson said, "but he was a good man." Our present difficulty is that we know the name of Henry Wadsworth Longfellow only too well; it is his poetry, and perhaps actually his "goodness," that we have forgotten. Longfellow stands as a symbol of all that is derivative and all that is *kitsch* in nineteenth-century American letters. His name is enough.

What is left is the privilege of beginning again. What is required is, if not absolutely a fresh trail, at least a willingness to avoid "footprints on the sands of time." Taken by and large Longfellow is what he is said to have been: derivative, sentimental, and minor. But there is no reason why we should continue to take him "by and large," if he can appear to better advantage. The remembered quality of a poet's work frequently is no more than a residuum. Reputations have been maintained on the evidence of a handful of poetic craft. It is questionable whether any of even the most moderately critical sensibilities of Longfellow's own age regarded him as a major poet in terms of the achievements of poetry. Yet they recognized, what we are not always presently willing to admit, that to be a good minor poet is an excellence.

Longfellow himself may have desired greater stature, but there are few poets who do not. Catholic in his talents he was equally catholic in his ambitions. Writing in *Outre-Mer* of the literature of the past, he observed:

From *The University of Kansas City Review*, XVI, No. 4. (Summer, 1950). Reprinted by permission of *The University of Kansas City Review*.

The same remark is true of the Middle Ages as of our own and of every age. If the state of society is shadowed forth in its literature, then this literature must necessarily represent two distinct and strongly marked characters: one, of the castle and the court; another, of the middle classes and the populace;—the former, elegant, harmonious, and delicate; the latter, rude, grotesque, and vulgar. Each of these classes has its own peculiar merits; but our manuscripts, by presenting them to us united, sometimes in the same volume, and always upon the same shelves of our libraries, have led us insensibly into the habit of confounding the manners of the court with those of the city.

Longfellow's ambition included equivalents of both audiences, and the consequent poetry seems at times to have been confounded not only by historians but by himself. There were in fact two Longfellows, whose careers were in conflict. There was the "better maker" who, like an Ezra Pound *de ses jours,* wished to bring to the craft of American poetry and to the resources of the court of Cambridge and of the Harvard Yard all that was dextrous and ennobling from the resources of the past; and there was the familiar bard, he who for the middle classes and the populace could now through periodicals and collected-editions sing to the people by their firesides, in strains as uplifted from crudity as their new government was from old cruelty, of the valor and the virtue of the race.

To both circles he tried to maintain a benign loyalty. "Longfellow kept his friendships in excellent repair," as Charles Eliot Norton was to remark after his death, "even those which might seem to an outsider to cost more than they were worth. He was true to what had been; remembrance maintained life in the ashes of the old affection, and he never made his own fame or his many occupations an excuse for disregarding the claims of a dull acquaintance, or of one fallen in the world." To the quickening of the court he remained alert, but to the plaintive cry of "Who'll pluck me the verities?" he could never be deaf. "One day," said Norton, "when I ventured to remonstrate with him for permitting the devastation of his hours by one of the most pertinacious and undeserving of habitual visitors, he listened with a humorous smile, and then rebuked me by saying, 'Why, Charles, who will be kind to him if I

am not?' " What was true of his personal life was also
true of his artistic.

## II

That the public was grateful for his kindness finds its
evidence in the love which they maintained for so many of
his popular ballads and lyrics, and for the tales which he
spun from the thinnest threads. They gave him their
highest tribute, that of memory. His poems they recited
until Longfellow became *a per se* the poet laureate of the
common man, though his "hoarded household words"
seem so often the utterance of the laureate of the com-
monplace. Yet different as the manner of the Yard may
be from that of the more ubiquitous and domestic yard,
measurable elements of quality are to be found in the
poetry addressed to each. What must be avoided is the
confusion of which Longfellow spoke in *Outre-Mer*. Each
audience has its genre, and each poetry its measure.

Poems so commonly popular as certain of Longfellow's
take on the characteristics of old saws. It should be within
the critic's powers to achieve something of the resharpen-
ing which the situation demands. Given this facility one
can recognize, for example, Longfellow's great mythopoeic
powers. This was an element of the literary imagination
which he possessed perhaps beyond the capacities of any
other American poet of his time or later. Though Walt
Whitman, the American master, can be said to have
created a *mystique* of the body, such a *mystique* was
operative chiefly in terms of emotional thrust. Far greater
in absolute value and significance as Whitman's poetical
powers were, there is nothing in his poems quite like the
firm outlines with which Longfellow endowed such figures
as Paul Revere, John Alden and Priscilla, or even the
village blacksmith. Their appearance was not an accident.
One of Longfellow's expressed objectives as a poet was
to supply his country with the mythical figures lacking
to its psyche. His success was immense. Its achievement
lay beyond any mnemonic gifts which verse or rhyme
alone could have brought. These enriching characters were
his own creations; they exist in and because of his poems.

"Paul Revere's Ride" can only be regarded as a dis-
tinguished artistic success within its genre. It is by intent

not a reflective piece, nor is its purpose to present the imponderables of ambiguity. No definition of poetry as the precise presentation of the imprecise will obtain in its case. Its purpose is to create a figure from the past whose virtues of immediate decision and action will coincide with and catch up the virtues of what had been America's chief moral action as a nation. Its operation was within the realm of race memory. "You know the rest," Longfellow says. He said it because he knew that he could depend upon his audience to bring the history of fact and emotion to bear upon the poem as an extra dimension to its moral intensity as well as to the dramatic urgency of the ride itself. The Revolution endowed it with enforcing color and warmth. The spread of the alarm was the symbolic rising of the nation to arms and to action. This was Paul Revere. His definition is abrupt. "He said to his friends" gives the simple introduction, once the *moment et milieu,* which are the cue, have been established. With it we have not only the concise economy of the true beginning of a ballad but also a sense of implied character which is essential to the poem and especially to the validity of "a cry of defiance and not of fear" which occurs in summation. Nothing is accidental. Revere acts; he does not talk except precisely and decisively to give directions. Even his orders have poetic efficiency, for with artistic economy we are so discreetly given an outline of the scene and scope of action that we are hardly aware of how much may later be omitted which might otherwise have hobbled the hurry of hoofs along the country lanes.

The enforcing merit of Longfellow's metrics should be as obvious as the swift pace of the ride. Longfellow is blanketed with the accusation of sentimentality, but only critical predisposition can detect sentimentality in the actual tone of the poem. Nor is it derivative in any ascertainable degree. "John Gilpin's Ride" has lately come into critical favor, and its irony applauded. There is only irony in "Paul Revere's Ride." Irony is hardly a requisite for a national hero, unless one desires a Don Quixote. Paul Revere is, as he was intended to be, a national hero. The poem is, as it was intended to be, a popular ballad. It effects, as Longfellow hoped it to do, a successful restoration of a past function of poetry.

"The Children's Hour" is another popular poem that
deserves to be rescued from predisposition and parody.
The occasion of the poem differs from that of "Paul Re-
vere's Ride." Here the circumstance and the mood are
meditative. There is leisure for speculative fancy and for
affection. The time is set in a twilight of reality in which
the demands of pure reason have been softened by con-
ventional attitude. What is desired is not the magnified
hero but the common denominator. The nature of senti-
mentality has been described as "emotional response in
excess of the occasion." But that a father should love his
daughters is not so much a matter of excess emotion as of
natural affection, and Longfellow has given us its presen-
tation in terms of organic suitability. For if the home is not
a cultural stronghold, and the father is not its center, and
the children in seizing upon their support should not make
their onslaught in a burst of love, it is permissible for a
father to fancy it so. Such a fancy is at least consistently
presented, and the achieved tone is such that few parents
cannot honestly share it. "The Children's Hour" is a
domestic conceit. The intent of the poem is modest, but
English poetry has few poems of similar modesty, as it
has but few successful domestic poems. Among adult
poems about children, one can think perhaps of Coventry
Patmore's "The Toys," but for a poem of the particular
nature of "The Children's Hour" one can remember no
equivalent.

### III

In moving from the homespun, which is Longfellow's
mellowed substitution for the "rude, grotesque, and vul-
gar," to examples of what he called the "elegant, har-
monious, and delicate" in verse, we have not left the
realm of achieved merit. Though there are in his poems
for the court perhaps fewer successes in relation to the
type, and those of a minor quality, there is, all the same,
much to admire. We cannot picture Longfellow as one
brought up in a court, but only as one who had visited
there, as he had travelled first in books and then by car-
riage through Spain and Italy, Sweden and Denmark, Ger-
many and France in a similar search to that which was to
impel the elder James to seek for his sons the rich sen-

suous education which America lacked. Longfellow's effort was to transplant the selected *données* and to help create a new court. His attempts to bring, both in translation and facsimile, the poets and poetry of Europe to his own less cultivated land were occasioned both by an honest admission of restricted attainment and by a determined effort that America should not in having given up its colonial status replace it with the hardly more commendable role of provincialism. If others moved towards an exploitation of what was native, Longfellow was to balance their exploits by a reminder that the craft of poetry like the dignity of man can be universal.

Given simply as situation, Longfellow's admiration for Tegnér was not much different from what T. S. Eliot's was to be for Laforgue. Eliot continued the search for resources beyond the indigenous, longing for deeper roots. Given in terms of result, Eliot was to escape from any bondage into a distinguished idiom of his own and into a philosophy beyond the limits of mere learning. But it is at least useful to suggest that his further step beyond Longfellow's achievement may have been rendered easier because he wrote, though unwittingly, with the advantages of Longfellow's tradition in his bones. One may profit from that whose limitations one escapes.

A line between the two can, I think, be traced. Longfellow's career as Smith Professor of Modern Languages at Harvard, with all the resources which his travels and translations brought to it, was to lay the foundation there for a more than perfunctory respect for what *The Poets and Poetry of Europe* represented. Not only the subject of Longfellow's collegiate lectures and the title of his influential anthology—a book, incidentally, all too widely ignored in the history of American literary culture—it was a significant basis for a continued program of humanistic cultivation. The book was the three-quarter-morocco-bound equivalent of what the Fenway Court palace of Mrs. Jack Gardner was to represent in the importation of *objets d'art*. Charles Eliot Norton was a hyphen between the two: sitting first with the Dante group at the feet of Longfellow at Craigie House, and moving later to a place of honor in the salon at Fenway Court where he could conduct his meticulous tuition of its jewelled mistress.

Even Berenson, who was to edge him out and take over Mrs. Gardner and so many others in a widening circle, was as much Norton's and Harvard's product as he was that of his native Lithuania. There were many students and many missionaries. Eliot the increasingly literary student of philosophy had both studied in the Harvard Yard and taken tea at Fenway Court. The impacts never disappeared of a world larger than New England. What has been lost sight of is the sense of Longfellow's sustained nerve. There had to be the chance to meet an Apollinax.

Despite, however, the immediate and potential enrichment which such importations could bring to Longfellow, they carried in their wake, for him and for the succeeding generation of men around Trumbull Stickney, a suggested limitation. Once imported into the consciousness, they led to the development of a tragedy of connoisseurship. It was as though the importation itself was enough, and the mere possession of these things had brought their virtues with them. In regarding them, one tended to be content with the external glaze; in learning from them, if one wished himself to create, one worked from the outside. Thus Longfellow, who wished not only to import but also to create, sought constantly for an analogous spot where the foreign metrics and manner could be placed onto the American scene. It was a habit of decoration based on assumed relevance of bases, and his poetic imagination was by this, as otherwise, developed in terms of the simile. The simile is a modest figure; it does not claim identification with anything, but only discernible similarity. It displays taste more than emotional conviction. It has its values but lacks boldness. Longfellow was discerning but seldom valiant in his poetry, and one is struck, in reading his poems, with how little he used the resources of the metaphor as a device. One can contrast his poetry, ultimately unfavorably, with the sometimes crabbed but potentially richer poetical method of Emerson and Thoreau. Such a reliance on simple similitude as Longfellow pursued tended to give a kind of flatness to his poetry, a deft but not multidimensionally suggestive relation between things or situations which was based on externals. Longfellow chiefly concerned himself with craftsmanship.

## IV

It was his concept of the poet as craftsman, rather than as divinely endowed seer that makes Longfellow closer in spirit to the poets of the late eighteenth century than to such American contemporaries as Emerson and Whitman who in their importations took over Romantic philosophy rather than manners. Longfellow's desire was to develop not so much a personal style as one correct in conformity. Though his method allowed for a wealth of formal variety, this was cosmopolitanism rather than individual idiom. Longfellow was on the humanistic road to the position where Eliot was later to place Irving Babbitt, and himself to pause, as one who "knows too much" and loses the power to feel. Longfellow's theory of poetic composition was based on something not unlike what W. H. Auden has described as

... the results of the co-operation of three mental faculties, Memory, Judgment and Fancy. Memory provides the raw material, Judgment arranges all this into a coherent pattern from which Fancy can select whatever she need for the task at hand. The first and last of these are private to the individual. Judgment is public and social; Judgment is to art what Public Spirit is to politics. or the laws of nature to astronomy

Longfellow's was on the whole a secular mind. His mode of communication therefore was not so much through the resources of the imagination as through those of reason. For such purposes it is the simile which serves the poet better than the metaphor does. The results, however, are as relatively limited as is the secular mind itself.

But despite this despite, Longfellow had both an ear and an eye for the poetic. They could carry him in the art of translation to such creditable achievements as his version of the Danish song "Kong Christian stod ved hoien mast"; the ancient hymn which begins "O gladsome light"; and the excerpts from the ornate *Frithiofs Saga*. That the sentimental mode of Tegnér has passed does not detract from Longfellow's accomplishment of translation. From the Spanish, on the other hand, as though to contrast with the highly figurative Tegnér, is the simplicity of his trans-

lation from Santa Teresa de Avila in her "Letrilla que
llevaba por Registro en su Breviario," which is fortunately
brief enough so that we may place the original and Long-
fellow's version in juxtaposition. There is no embarrass-
ment.

> Nada te turbe,
> Nada te espante,
> Todo se pasa;
> Dios no se muda,
> La paciencia
> Todo lo alcanza;
> Quien a Dios tiene
> Nada le falta:
> Sólo Dios basta.

> Let nothing disturb thee,
> Nothing affright thee;
> All things are passing;
> God never changeth;
> Patient endurance
> Attaineth to all things;
> Who God possesseth
> In nothing is wanting;
> Alone God sufficeth.

Longfellow's eye and ear could carry him as well into
his own poetic perceptions which are worth the effort of
our eyes and ears to recognize:

> Leafless are the trees;
>     their purple branches
> Spread themselves abroad,
>     like reefs of coral, Rising silent
> In the Red Sea of the winter sunset.

or the faceted sensitivities of the description of his old
Danish songbook:

> Yellow are thy time-worn pages,
> As the russet, rain-molested
> Leaves of autumn.

or the delicately played metrics and the suggestion of in-
substantiality in:

> White phantom city, whose
>      untrodden streets
> Are rivers, and whose pavements
>      are the shifting
> Shadows of palaces and strips
>      of sky;

or the symbolic reinforcement of mood by color, in:

> A moment only, and the
>      light and glory
> Faded away, and the
>      disconsolate shore
>      Stood lonely as before;
> And the wild-roses of
>      the promontory
> Around me shuddered in the
>      wind, and shed
>      Their petals of pale red.

or the manipulation of qualitative hexameters in the much-
belabored *Evangeline:*

> Thus ere another noon they
>      emerged from the shades,
>      and before them
> Lay, in the golden sun, the lakes
>      of the Atchafalaya.
> Water-lilies in myriads rocked on
>      the slight undulations
> Made by the passing oars, and,
>      resplendent in beauty, the lotus
> Lifted her golden crown above the
>      heads of the boatmen.
> Faint was the air with the odorous
>      breath of magnolia blossoms,
> And with the heat of noon; and
>      numberless sylvan islands,
> Fragrant and thickly embowered
>      with blossoming hedges of roses,
> Near to whose shores they glided
>      along, invited to slumber,
> Soon by the fairest of these their
>      weary oars were suspended.

These are fragments to be considered with respect, but
what so frequently trips Longfellow in the achievement

of maintained distinction through poems as a whole is perhaps to be found in a combination of his habit of the simile with the conflict between the two Longfellows. The poetic presentation of a situation in and for itself was not enough. Having presented it he must determine an analogy, point out and all too frequently spell out its implication. The principle of such relationship is that of the simile extended into gross structure. What was true for him in terms of unexpected likenesses between otherwise disparate objects was also true in terms of the relevance of a physical situation to a moral one. This was a possible way of gaining extra dimension for his poems, but one limited to the resources of Fancy. For one of Longfellow's particular personality it held a special danger. What might have been in its presentation suited to the court often was in its moral analogy cut down and fitted to the middle-class and the people.

In a poem like "Seaweed" whose four opening stanzas present a deftly contrived picture of some vivid immediacy, these lines are balanced by four concluding stanzas of bourgeois moral analogy linked by the poetically frightening word *So*. If he omits *so* or *like* from the concluding stanzas of his otherwise not unsuccessful poem "The Golden Mile-Stone," the invisible ink of intent still comes to the surface. Bryant's failures might have taught him otherwise, but Longfellow had his generosity also to blame. What is chiefly disturbing in Longfellow's poems is his confusion of audiences, the frequency with which a poem for the court is turned by simile into a poem for the people. To serve both at once is a democratic concept, but it makes for awkward poetical relationships.

But the moments when Longfellow did not achieve success are not so important for us as those when he did, nor should the failures cast too enveloping a shadow. If the shadow has fallen it can be lifted in the case of poems like "Snow-Flakes," which if not a major is at least a fine minor achievement:

> Out of the bosom of the Air,
>   Out of the cloud-folds of her
>     garments shaken,
> Over the woodlands brown and bare,
>   Over the harvest-fields forsaken,

Silent, and soft, and slow
Descends the snow.

Even as our cloudy fancies take
   Suddenly shape in some divine
      expression,
Even as the troubled heart
   doth make
   In the white countenance
      confession,
         The troubled sky reveals
         The grief it feels.

This is the poem of the air,
   Slowly in silent syllables recorded;
This is the secret of despair,
   Long in its cloudy bosom hoarded,
         Now whispered and revealed
         To wood and field.

What may be done with the simile can be observed in
the case of this poem, but the similitude which relates our
fancies and our heart to the heavens is not insisted on and
is itself actually enveloped in a congeries of metaphors
by which man, physical nature, the atmosphere, and God
become inextricably interwoven. Meanwhile the arrange-
ment of sound which falls like compassionate snow be-
comes the poem not only of Longfellow's craft and sensi-
bility but of the air itself which is represented. The clouded
sky is mingled with the clouded face of man. Snow-drift
and cloud-drift merge in what Hawthorne would have
called "the sympathy of nature." By implication the wood-
lands and field, now bare of the harvest, now cold, are like
man in his desolation. But land and man will be warmed
and comforted, for the troubled sky sympathizes with
the troubled, and its tears of God bring no flood of anger
but instead a blanket of shared compassion. Gently the
distinctions take on significant irrelevance. What is a
chief virtue of the poem is the impossibility of definitive
explication. The poem is, as a poem should be, what it is.
The poem is, so to speak, a secret whose significance we
can feel without subjecting it to rational surgery; we can
see the kinship of the aspects, and we can, as Longfellow
especially in the final stanza has given the poem to us,
hear the envelopment of a tenderness which comes as a
natural concomitant to grief and gives to despair another
definition.

## V

It seems reasonably obvious that the greatest service to be rendered to Longfellow's confused reputation would be to pare down the body of his poems to a core, or two cores, which can be regarded without undue condescension. Such, I am afraid, is not the present situation as represented either in anthologies or in criticism. If the necessary paring seems too ruthless in its excisions, when subsequent additions are made the acts will bring a sense of increased and perhaps unexpected profit. The important attitude is neither to be seduced by popular fame nor to shy away from a poem because of it. Mr. I. A. Richards, in this case as in so many others, has given us a significant lesson both in criticism in general and with reference to Longfellow in particular. In *Practical Criticism*, his example XIII is Longfellow's "In the Churchyard at Cambridge." The responses indicated it to be "by far the most disliked of all the poems." Mr. Richard's finger pointed in admonition is worth remembering:

As has been remarked before, a very wary eye is needed with any poetry that tends to implicate our stock responses. And this for two opposite reasons. If the easiest way to popularity is to exploit some stock response, some poem already existent, fully prepared, in the reader's mind, an appearance of appealing to such stock responses, should the reader happen to have discarded them, is a very certain way of courting failure. So that a poet who writes on what appears to be a familiar theme, in a way which, superficially, is only slightly unusual, runs a double risk. On the one hand, very many readers will not really read him at all. They will respond with the poem they suppose him to have written and then, if emancipated, recoil in horror to heap abuse on the poet's head. On the other hand, less emancipated readers, itching to release their own stock responses, may be pulled up by something in the poem which prevents them. The result will be more abuse for the hapless author.

For his subsequent reflections on the animadversions called forth by the reading of the poem, one can only refer to *Practical Criticism* itself. But his conclusion that another than a stock reading is possible is worth repetition for its relevance to any revaluation of Longfellow:

But another reading is possible, one by which the poem becomes a very unusual kind of thing that it would be a pity to miss. That so few read it in this way is not surprising, for if there is any character in poetry that modern readers—who derive their ideas of it rather from the best known poems of Wordsworth, Shelley and Keats or from our contemporaries, than from Dryden, Poe or Cowper—are unprepared to encounter, it is this social, urbane, highly cultivated, self-confident, temperate and easy kind of humour.

The lesson to be learned, perhaps, both by the critic and the general reader, is that it is easier to find virtue when one wishes to find it.

# LEWIS CARROLL

## Hiawatha's Photographing

*Hiawatha's Photographing* was finished on November 13th 1857 and first appeared in *The Train*, December 1857. It was republished in *Phantasmagoria and Other Poems* (1869) and in *Rhyme? and Reason?* (1883) with six illustrations by A. B. Frost.

In Lewis Carroll's opinion, Longfellow was "the greatest living master of language," and in this parody of *The Song of Hiawatha* he describes the worries and troubles of a photographer, no doubt drawing to a large extent upon his own experience. He introduces his parody with a note written in the same metre but printed as prose.

(IN AN age of imitation, I can claim no special merit for this slight attempt at doing what is known to be so easy. Any fairly practised writer, with the slightest ear for rhythm, could compose, for hours together, in the easy running metre of *The Song of Hiawatha*. Having, then, distinctly stated that I challenge no attention in the following little poem to its merely verbal jingle, I must beg the candid reader to confine his criticism to its treatment of the subject.)

From his shoulder Hiawatha
Took the camera of rosewood,

From *Lewis Carroll, Photographer* by Helmut Gernsheim. New York: Chanticleer Press, Inc., 1949.

Made of sliding, folding rosewood;
Neatly put it all together.
In its case it lay compactly,
Folded into nearly nothing;
But he opened out the hinges,
Pushed and pulled the joints and hinges,
Till it looked all squares and oblongs,
Like a complicated figure
In the Second Book of Euclid.

This he perched upon a tripod—
Crouched beneath its dusky cover—
Stretched his hand, enforcing silence—
Said, "Be motionless, I beg you!"
Mystic, awful was the process.

All the family in order
Sat before him for their pictures:
Each in turn as he was taken,
Volunteered his own suggestions,
His ingenious suggestions,
First the Governor, the Father:
He suggested velvet curtains
Looped about a massy pillar;
And the corner of a table,
Of a rosewood dining-table.
He would hold a scroll of something.
Hold it firmly in his left-hand;
He would keep his right-hand buried
(Like Napoleon) in his waistcoat;
He would contemplate the distance
With a look of pensive meaning,
As of ducks that die in tempests.

Grand, heroic was the notion:
Yet the picture failed entirely:
Failed, because he moved a little,
Moved, because he couldn't help it.

Next, his better half took courage;
*She* would have her picture taken.
She came dressed beyond description,
Dressed in jewels and in satin
Far too gorgeous for an empress.
Gracefully she sat down sideways,
With a simper scarcely human,
Holding in her hand a bouquet
Rather larger than a cabbage.
All the while that she was sitting,
Still the lady chattered, chattered,
Like a monkey in the forest.

"Am I sitting still?" she asked him.
"Is my face enough in profile?
Shall I hold the bouquet higher?
Will it come into the picture?"
And the picture failed completely.

Next the Son, the Stunning-Cantab:
He suggested curves of beauty,
Curves pervading all his figure,
Which the eye might follow onward,
Till they centred in the breast-pin,
Centred in the golden breast-pin.
He had learnt it all from Ruskin
(Author of "The Stones of Venice",
"Seven Lamps of Architecture",
"Modern Painters", and some others);
And perhaps he had not fully
Understood his author's meaning;
But, whatever was the reason,
All was fruitless, as the picture
Ended in an utter failure.

Next to him the eldest daughter:
She suggested very little,
Only asked if he would take her
With her look of "passive beauty".

Her idea of passive beauty
Was a squinting of the left-eye,
Was a drooping of the right-eye,
Was a smile that went up sideways
To the corner of the nostrils.

Hiawatha, when she asked him,
Took no notice of the question,
Looked as if he hadn't heard it;
But, when pointedly appealed to,
Smiled in his peculiar manner,
Coughed and said it "didn't matter",
Bit his lip and changed the subject.

Nor in this was he mistaken,
As the picture failed completely.

So in turn the other sisters.

Last, the youngest son was taken:
Very rough and thick his hair was,
Very round and red his face was,
Very dusty was his jacket,
Very fidgety his manner.
And his overbearing sisters
Called him names he disapproved of:
Called him Johnny, "Daddy's Darling",

Called him Jacky, "Scrubby School-boy",
And, so awful was the picture,
In comparison the others
Seemed, to one's bewildered fancy,
To have partially succeeded.
Finally my Hiawatha
Tumbled all the tribe together,
("Grouped" is not the right expression),
And, as happy chance would have it
Did at last obtain a picture
Where the faces all succeeded:
Each came out a perfect likeness.

Then they joined and all abused it,
Unrestrainedly abused it,
As the worst and ugliest picture
They could possibly have dreamed of.
"Giving one such strange expressions—
Sullen, stupid, pert expressions.
Really anyone would take us
(Anyone that did not know us)
For the most unpleasant people!"
(Hiawatha seemed to think so,
Seemed to think it not unlikely.)
All together rang their voices.
Angry, loud, discordant voices,
As of dogs that howl in concert,
As of cats that wail in chorus.

But my Hiawatha's patience,
His politeness and his patience,
Unaccountably had vanished,
And he left that happy party.
Neither did he leave them slowly,
With the calm deliberation
The intense deliberation
Of a photographic artist:
But he left them in a hurry,
Left them in a mighty hurry,
Stating that he would not stand it,
Stating in emphatic language
What he'd be before he'd stand it.
Hurriedly he packed his boxes:
Hurriedly the porter trundled
On a barrow all his boxes:
Hurriedly he took his ticket:
Hurriedly the train received him:
Thus departed Hiawatha.

# SIGNET CLASSICS for Your Library

☐ **EVELINA by Fanny Burney.** Introduction by Katherine M. Rogers.
(525604—$6.95)

☐ **EMMA by Jane Austen.** Afterword by Graham Hough.      (523067—$4.95)

☐ **MANSFIELD PARK by Jane Austen.** Afterword by Marvin Murdick.
(525019—$4.95)

☐ **PERSUASION by Jane Austen.** Afterword by Marvin Murdick.   (522893—$3.95)

☐ **SENSE AND SENSIBILITY by Jane Austen.** Afterword by Caroline G. Mercer.
(524195—$3.95)

☐ **JANE EYRE by Charlotte Brontë.** Afterword by Arthur Ziegler.   (523326—$4.95)

☐ **VILLETTE by Charlotte Brontë.** Afterword by Jerome Beaty.    (520831—$5.95)

☐ **WUTHERING HEIGHTS by Emily Brontë.** Foreword by Geoffrey Moore.
(523385—$4.95)

☐ **TESS OF THE D'URBERVILLES by Thomas Hardy.** Afterword by Donald Hall.
(525469—$4.95)

☐ **THE AWAKENING and SELECTED SHORT STORIES by Kate Chopin.** Edited by Barbara Solomon.
(524489—$4.95)

☐ **MIDDLEMARCH by George Eliot.** Afterword by Frank Kermode.   (517504—$5.95)

☐ **THE MILL ON THE FLOSS by George Eliot.** Afterword by Morton Berman.
(523962—$5.95)

☐ **SILAS MARNER by George Eliot.** Afterword by Walter Allen.   (524276—$3.95)

Prices slightly higher in Canada.

---

Buy them at your local bookstore or use this convenient coupon for ordering.

**PENGUIN USA**
P.O. Box 999 — Dept. #17109
Bergenfield, New Jersey 07621

Please send me the books I have checked above.
I am enclosing $_____ (please add $2.00 to cover postage and handling). Send check or money order (no cash or C.O.D.'s) or charge by Mastercard or VISA (with a $15.00 minimum). Prices and numbers are subject to change without notice.

Card #_____ Exp. Date _____
Signature_____
Name_____
Address_____
City _____ State _____ Zip Code _____

For faster service when ordering by credit card call **1-800-253-6476**

Allow a minimum of 4-6 weeks for delivery. This offer is subject to change without notice.